PRAISE FOR
A Leader's Guide to Unlocking Gen Z
AND HANNAH GRADY WILLIAMS

"*A Leader's Guide to Unlocking Gen Z* will become mandatory reading for all industry leaders looking to build their workforce in the coming years. Speaking for her generation, Hannah Grady Williams offers succinct insight and ideas for recruiting, retaining, and advancing the next generation of leaders."

—*Mark A. Bado, MCM, CCE, General Manager/COO, Houston Country Club, Past Chair, Club Management Association of America, Houston, TX*

"One of the most frequently asked questions I hear is, "How do you work with Gen Z?" Rather than offer my perspective, I can now offer a better response: read Hannah's book! Thanks for giving voice to your generation. I'm excited about the future you and your peers will create!"

—*Mark Miller, VP High Performance Leadership, Chick-fil-A, International Best-Selling Author of* Chess Not Checkers, *Atlanta, GA*

"Hannah Grady Williams provides insights on the importance of acting now to stay ahead and relevant to the next generation. Anyone looking to recruit top talent from Gen Z—talent that wants to learn, grow, and contribute within your company for the long haul—needs to read *A Leader's Guide to Unlocking Gen Z*."

—*Kevin Harry, Managing Partner, The BCJ Group, Former Sales Director, The Walt Disney Company, Orlando, FL*

"The entrepreneurial spirit, the drive, and the perspective that Gen Z brings to the workforce is unparalleled. As a Gen Z'r myself and an employer of other Z'rs, I can confidently say that without a culture and process that encourages these things, you'll lose Gen Z'rs just as quickly as you got them. Hannah brings a strong, experience-driven approach to leading Gen Z'rs in the workplace—an approach rooted in the incomparably valuable aspect of being Gen Z herself. A must-read for all thoughtful managers."

— *Andrew Roth, Founder, Gen Z Designs, Nashville, TN*

"Cross-generational coexistence in the workforce has never been so complicated. The most senior and junior talent have basically grown up on different planets, with different norms and different access to technology. Hannah goes under the hood in *A Leader's Guide to Unlocking Gen Z* to share exactly what it feels like to be a Gen Z employee getting ready to enter the workforce, and how we as leaders need to adapt to welcome this new generation to their professional home. This is a must-read for any hiring manager."

— *Tommy McNulty, Founder & CEO, Reps, Brooklyn, NY*

"Knowing Hannah for several years I am not surprised at all by the quality, timeliness, and relevance of her new book, *A Leader's Guide to Unlocking Gen Z*. What she shares will not only empower you with the tools you need to successfully "team up" with the wave of Gen Z'rs to come, but to do it in a way that will create the ultimate "win-win" for the individual and your organization. Hannah's succinct, witty, and incredibly useful work will, I believe, be a staple for future thinking organizations for years to come."

—*Dr. Bradford Butler, CEO, Oakland Spine & Physical Therapy, Oakland, NJ*

"*A Leader's Guide to Unlocking Gen Z* is a must-have resource for modern-day HR professionals. Written about Gen Z'rs, by a Gen Z'r, *A Leader's Guide* provides key insights into the motivations, preferences, and work styles of this growing, and highly capable, segment of our labor force. By utilizing some of the techniques outlined in this book, our company has hired some highly effective Gen Z'rs whose generational perspectives and expertise have helped us hire others like them, impact policy development, and positively influence our culture."

—*Scott Ledford, Director of Human Resources, General Shale, Inc., Johnson City, TN*

"Every now and then I run into someone who takes my breath away. Hannah Williams is one of those people. Smart, articulate, servant leader, who has the wisdom of someone two or three times her age. If you want to walk through the door to unlock the psyche of a Gen Z'r, you should read this book and engage in her community."

—*Mitchell Levy, Global Credibility Expert and Founder of Credibility Nation, Cupertino, CA*

"Hannah is a very talented leader, who cares deeply about helping individuals and organizations maximize their potential and achieve positive results. I have gotten to know her over the past few years and have been impressed by her knowledge, energy, and focus on innovation and leading change."

— *Mike Kelly, Founder of Right Path Enterprises, Cincinnati, OH*

"If you have just started to get your arms around the millennial generation, you may be surprised to know that the next big generational wave is upon us: Introducing Gen Z. Hannah Grady Williams has given us the gift to know how to embrace this generational shift through her beacon of a book—*A Leader's Guide to Unlocking Gen Z*. This is invaluable to anyone looking to get their arms around the newest entrant to our workforce and who wants to harness the power and potential of this driven, creative, original generation.

Hannah will inspire you to connect with Gen Z'rs and help them reach their full potential, all while keeping space for the needs and contributions of Gen X and Boomers. She lives out her philosophy of #RadicalEmpathy in the pages of *A Leader's Guide to Unlocking Gen Z* and you'll leave the book with the tools to create a workplace where everyone can thrive."

—*Deb Knupp, Managing Director, Growth Play, Chicago, IL*

"After 20 years of developing and branding top-performing Gen Z'rs, I know firsthand how magical a generation they are. However, to capitalize on that magic and retain it, you must understand how to unlock it while simultaneously empowering them to strengthen their weaknesses. THIS can be a struggle because their drive comes from a much different place than generations before them! Thankfully, Hannah has brilliantly created a blueprint in this book, with clear and concise tools on how to master the process."

—*Jonathan George, Human Hitmaker and Founder of Unleash Your Rockstar, Los Angeles, CA*

"*A Leader's Guide to Unlocking Gen Z* is a one-of-a-kind handbook for anyone looking at understanding Gen Z better. What makes this book unique is the fact that it is written by a Gen Z'r herself. Hannah has beautifully encapsulated her years of experience into a few hundred pages for us to learn from. I would definitely recommend this book to all CXOs, recruiting managers, and leaders; believe me, you won't be disappointed: this book provides clear, precise strategies along with a practical approach when it comes to employing, managing, and retaining the Gen Z workforce. As a Gen Z student, this book has given me a voice, which I would want all hiring managers and employers to listen to. Well done, Hannah!"

—*Twisha Soni, Founder and Host, Gen Z Chat; Content Writer and Creator, Mumbai, Maharashtra, India*

"We raised Hannah before the term *Gen Z* even existed. For her to become an adult OF this generation and IN this generation gives her incredible firsthand perspective. She grew up immersed in a variety of cultural and generational interactions and has always been highly inquisitive when learning about people, behaviors, and environmental influences that affect them. Hannah graduated with her bachelor's degree in business at age 18, and has not only a brilliant mind but is also a thorough thinker. Her insight as a business leader is profound and inarguably useful to any leader who desires to unlock and reach her generation."

—*Anjie and David Grady, Hannah's Parents, Asheville, NC*

"From the first time I met Hannah Grady Williams I knew she would leave her mark on the world. Hannah is wise beyond her years and her insights will stir your thinking and challenge your notions of Gen Z. What better way to gain insight into the generation that is entering our workplaces and leading us into the future than to see it through the lens of a rising Gen Z leader herself?"

—*Dave McAuley, Founder at Summit Leadership Foundation, Johnson City, TN*

A LEADER'S GUIDE TO
UNLOCKING GEN Z

INSIDER STRATEGIES
TO EMPOWER YOUR TEAM

A LEADER'S GUIDE TO UNLOCKING GEN Z

INSIDER STRATEGIES TO EMPOWER YOUR TEAM

By Gen Z'r

HANNAH GRADY WILLIAMS

The author and publisher have taken reasonable precautions in the preparation of this book and believe the facts presented within are accurate as of the date it was written. However, neither the author nor the publisher assumes any responsibility for any errors or omissions. The author and publisher specifically disclaim any liability resulting from the use or application of the information contained in this book, and the information is not intended to serve as legal, financial, psychological, or other professional advice related to individual situations.

© 2021 Hannah Grady Williams. All rights reserved.

No part of this book may be reproduced, stored in a retrieval system, or transmitted by any means, electronic, mechanical, photocopying, recording, or otherwise, without written permission from the publisher.

If you purchase this book without a cover, you should be aware that this book may have been stolen property and reported as "unsold and destroyed" to the publisher. In such case, neither the author nor the publisher has received any payment for this "stripped book."

Published by Black Balsam Press.

For ordering information or special discounts for bulk purchases as well as booking Hannah Grady Williams to speak or host an event:

www.hannahgwilliams.com

Cover and Interior design by Kim Baker (Orange Brain Studio)
Editing by Alyssa Rabins
Copyediting and proofreading by Anne Kelley Conklin
Composition by Accelerate Media Partners, LLC

ISBN-13: 978-1-7376165-1-1

BUSINESS & ECONOMICS / Human Resources & Personnel Management

DEDICATION

Oh, hi there! You must not be from Gen Z. Just a guess.

If you were from my generation, you'd probably have skipped straight over this part of the book (or heck, you probably didn't pick it up in the first place).

Yeah, I just called you old.

But that's a good thing—I'm glad you're not a Gen Z'r.

You see, if you are from Gen Y, Gen X, or the boomer Gen, this book is dedicated to you.

Before I get all serious, I want to say thanks on behalf of Gen Z. Thanks for putting up with our shenanigans. Thanks for calling us out when we're stupid. You're our heroes even if we don't treat you that way sometimes. You're the reason I wrote this book, so thanks for helping shape the future.

Alright, enough of that. Maybe I'll be more serious in the actual book… no promises, though.

TABLE OF CONTENTS

Foreword xiii

Introduction 1

Meet Gen Z 9

The Difference Between Gen Z and Millennials 17

Section I: Attract 25
   Chapter 1: Be a Part of Our NarcisStory 27
   Chapter 2: Create a Personal Brand 41
   Chapter 3: Watch Your Reviews 47
   Chapter 4: Understand the "Gen Z Trinity" 55
   Chapter 5: Appeal to Our Digital Lifestyle 69
   Chapter 6: Inspire Intrapreneurs 77
   Chapter 7: Enable Extreme Customization 87

Section II: Recruit 93
   Chapter 8: Use Culture-Centric Recruiting 95
   Chapter 9: Encourage Nontraditional Résumés 103
   Chapter 10: Meet Us Where We Are 111
   Chapter 11: Eliminate Hiring Nuisances 121
   Chapter 12: Focus on Skills Over Experience 133

Section III: Retain 139
   Chapter 13: Rethink Your Employee Journey, Part I: The Jungle Gym Model 141
   Chapter 14: Rethink Your Employee Journey, Part II: Consider the Video Game Model 151
   Chapter 15: Recognize the Importance of Day One 161

Chapter 16: Perfect the First Week 169
Chapter 17: Bridge the College-to-Workplace Gap 179
Chapter 18: Recognize Our Risk Aversion 193
Chapter 19: Retain Us Through Empowerment 205
Chapter 20: Focus on Individual Effort 213
Chapter 21: Understand the Shared Economy 223
Chapter 22: Engage Us Face-to-Face 233
Chapter 23: Support Us with Direct Feedback 241
Chapter 24: Rethink Compensation Packages 251

Section IV: Engage **263**
Chapter 25: Become a Mentor 269
Chapter 26: Be Open to Our Inexperience 277
Chapter 27: Give Us a Voice 283
Chapter 28: Support Our Mental Health 293
Chapter 29: Create Psychological Safety 303

Where Do We Go from Here? **313**

Acknowledgments **317**

Endnotes **319**

Recommended Resources **327**

About the Author **329**

FOREWORD

Warning: Stereotypes kill. Well, I suppose they don't literally kill people. But stereotypes have certainly killed many career opportunities. They've killed relationships. And they've killed understanding between the generations. In our current age, one of the most harmful things we can do to another human is to cast judgment without any real knowledge of their story. We all want people to listen and hear our story, to feel seen and valued—yet we often struggle to offer this same courtesy to others. Time and again, we jump to conclusions. There is a specific type of judgment that I believe is now harming businesses—and ultimately the economy—resulting in severe profitability, productivity, and creativity losses: the stereotyping of generations. It simplifies the world, creates easy-to-use categories, and doesn't spare many people. We often stereotype our senior employees as being unwilling to learn and out of fresh ideas. We stereotype younger employees as lacking a solid work ethic, entitled, and obsessed with technology. All of these stereotypes are corrosive. Has a stereotype truly ever served you in a positive way? Has a stereotype made your business more productive, team oriented, or effective in its mission? I highly doubt it.

I like to think I'm qualified to speak on the subject of stereotyping and generalizing because I've done plenty of it. It has caused frustrations and misunderstandings. I've had my share of screw-ups, but over the past 20 years, I have worked in a variety of industries, from finance to residential camping to hospitality and tourism. I have consulted on and facilitated programs for numerous Fortune 500 companies. Most recently, this has been at Biltmore and through the Biltmore Center for Professional Development (The Center) where I had the pleasure of working with Hannah Grady Williams. It was in this capacity where Hannah shattered my stereotypes and expectations. She helped open my eyes to new ways of approaching our various markets and client relationships. I'm forever grateful for the ways she helped me rethink my approach to leadership in general.

My personal focus has been on shaping business culture, building innovative talent management strategies and conducting organizational development interventions. All of this is done in service to a purpose that is greater than any one person and that will leave a positive, lasting legacy for generations to come. My philosophy, which Hannah shares, has always been "People First." Care for and develop your people and they will take good care of your customer. This generates brand loyalty and revenue: Your customer will in turn take care of the business, and then the business can reinvest in its people. Hannah shares this philosophy and has a deep desire to foster empathy in the workplace and between generations.

Through this insightful and illuminating book, Hannah Grady Williams is breaking stereotypes and providing a road map for generations to better understand one another and forge meaningful working relationships. Hannah is uniquely qualified to speak on this issue. As a member of Generation Z, she is a subject matter expert with incredible life experience. Hannah has approached this topic through the lens of a "workplace cultural anthropologist," shining a light on how those of us a little further down the road can see both the value and the vast benefits of leveraging Gen Z talent.

I like to think of Hannah as a "workplace cultural anthropologist" because there is no better way to describe someone with such a high level of curiosity, professionalism, and empathy. Her entrepreneurial drive is strong and she comes by it honestly. Hannah was indoctrinated into the world of start-ups from a young age by her family, when her dad handed her the phone at age 12 and told her to close a real estate transaction. She has gone on to form partnerships with leaders in health care and customer experience, and has started her own real estate and thought leadership companies.

Throughout my career, I've seen young people crush expectations time and time again. Their potential is endless. Their ideas and energy are infectious. Many can solve problems quickly; they can maintain a balance of optimistic vision and pragmatism. This goes well beyond a member of Gen Z teaching a more senior leader how to manage their social media campaign. The benefit lies in how these young people can elevate a team. They challenge us, and we're better for it. If you're uncomfortable or threatened by new ways of thinking or fearful of not having all the answers, you may want to avoid working with Gen Z. Of course, this approach must be undertaken at your own peril as this cohort is entering the workforce in a big way and you need them on your team if you want your organization to flourish.

Another blind spot for many companies is how they limit their diversity, equity, inclusion, and belonging (DEIB) perspective to ethnic and gender differences without giving much thought to age. Building a team that is also generationally diverse will reap countless benefits and produce the diversity of thought that drives competitive advantage. The key words here are *diversity of thought* and *perspective*. DEIB is not an end unto itself. It is about the different ways we see the world; this is critical in establishing a growth versus fixed mindset among your employees and your business. I have found that generational diversity (and a willingness to listen to and empower these individuals) should be a core tenet of every organization's talent strategy.

I'm incredibly excited about Hannah Grady Williams's book and the impact it will have on leaders and employees everywhere. I've counseled numerous people, from C-suite executives to front-line employees, struggling to navigate generational differences and misunderstandings. It has caused frustration and agony and wasted lots of time, energy, and money. This issue has led numerous people to leave organizations and others to see their teams collapse under the strain. We can no longer afford to operate this way. We owe it to ourselves and each other to find a new path. *A Leader's Guide to Unlocking Gen Z* will help you chart this path and navigate it successfully.

Chris Maslin

Chris Maslin
VP of HR and Organizational Development, The Biltmore Company
Executive Director, Biltmore Center for Professional Development

INTRODUCTION
DON'T SKIP ME :)

It was just after 8 p.m. on a stormy winter night. My sister and I brushed our teeth, jumped into our furry-footed pajamas, and leaped into bed with the eager expectation of a bedtime story from Dad. Mom usually read to us—*Anne of Green Gables, The Chronicles of Narnia, Oliver Twist*—and my nine-year-old self looked forward to those moments, while my sister begrudgingly listened (not much of a reader herself). Dad usually worked late into the evening handling tenant complaints and jumping on new real estate opportunities, but tonight was different. Mom was out of town and Dad was going to read us something new and exciting—or so he teased us about it all day...

"What will it be tonight? *The Giver? Little Women?*" I eagerly asked Dad as he walked into the room. To my surprise, he pulled out a different-looking book, one with a worn cover and faded lettering, and handed it to me. "No," he replied. "Tonight, we'll be starting *The Richest Man in Babylon*, and I think in future years you'll agree that books like this will change your life."

So began my coming of age. Following the completion of *The Richest Man in Babylon*, my father read us *Rich Dad, Poor Dad; The Millionaire Next Door*; and a plethora of other books, which I began to recognize as the pillar of my education, more so than formal learning. With my father's guidance, I knew I'd never see the world the same way. As the eldest of seven children, some people say I didn't experience much of a childhood, but from my perspective I got a jump-start on life that has launched me into an exciting place. I've come a long way. Now I have the pleasure of consulting businesses across the country in creating phenomenal employee experiences to achieve long-term strategic results.

Allow me to jump ahead in my story. After several years of managing growth for an incubator consulting start-up in Asheville, North Carolina, I had an epiphany. All around me, my HR partners were talking about the millennial generation—the young generation bringing so many changes to the workplace—but there was a problem: Few people were talking about my generation, Generation Z, and yet we are already in the workforce. Many of the challenges and successes that millennials bring did not, and do not, resonate with me. I continue hearing from my connections at employers' networks, chambers of commerce, and major businesses that the primary concern keeping them up at night is the recruitment and retention of high-performing talent, particularly with the challenges presented by new working environments, and yet few businesses are preparing their workforces for my generation—almost 73 million hardworking young people who could propel their initiatives. Additionally, many employers feel like college is not adequately preparing the next generation for the expectations of the workplace.

These employers and universities need someone to bridge the gap. Someone from my generation.

A Leader's Guide to Unlocking Gen Z is here to do just that—and to quell the idea that Gen Z is the same as our millennial predecessors. It's written with a simple intent in mind: **To give executives a road map for how to create an employee experience that enables them to recruit, retain, inspire, and engage the finest Gen Z talent.** In this book, I will not be delving into topics like "why Gen Z is named Gen Z" or composing lengthy paragraphs on the history of multiple generations in the workplace. This book will also not touch on the subject of marketing or selling to Gen Z consumers. These topics have already been covered in depth in other well-researched publications. Rather, *A Leader's Guide to Unlocking Gen Z* is intended to serve as a Gen Z employee experience guidebook, one that anyone can pick up and learn something brand new from in five minutes, and one that sparks conversations across the workplace between leaders from all generations and the Gen Z'rs they manage.

You may be wondering why I am positioned uniquely to speak to this niche topic, beyond my status as a Gen Z'r. Allow me to continue where we stopped at the bedtime story...

Following my dad-imposed exile to the world of financial stewardship novels, I began a self-imposed journey through the world of leadership and entrepreneurship books. When I was twelve years old, my father caught me reading Roger Dawson's *The Secrets of Power Negotiating* while riding along in the jolting back seat of his blue pickup truck, on the way to collect tenant rents. Dad was "the millionaire next door" and his greatest vision was to be the next Sam Walton—drive a beaten-up car and wear holey T-shirts while inconspicuously conquering the business world. I greatly admired him, and when he took notice of my desire to learn the world of business, I started working with him one day each week during middle school, which was easy enough because I was homeschooled.

One day, Dad abruptly handed me the phone and said, "There's a guy with a home for sale. You're going to close the deal. By the way, the phone is ringing." Terrified, I took the phone and fumbled through my first call, which, after a few negotiations and my dad's help, resulted in the purchase of a duplex. These experiences were invaluable and taught me that nothing in life comes easy, or without embarrassment.

When I was thirteen, my parents and I attended a seminar on the benefits of online education. I found myself enrolled the following semester in an online college program, which I ended up pursuing through the completion of my undergraduate degree. I graduated from both high school and college at age 18 with a bachelor's degree in international business, enabling me to enter the consulting world earlier than most.

During my senior year of college, I accepted an internship with The Biltmore Company in my hometown of Asheville. Biltmore Estate is nationally renowned as a provider of world-class "gracious hospitality" and customer service, welcoming guests from all over the globe to George W. Vanderbilt's private retreat in the mountains. But what guests remember most when they leave is not just the stunning gardens, massive home, and gorgeous winery—it's the people who showed them exceptional customer service during their visit. My initial curiosity about how Biltmore Estate could provide such consistently exceptional service with 2,600 employees developed into a fascination. The workplace culture and engagement strategies Biltmore has put in place have yielded results that have consistently landed among the top 10% of all companies. Biltmore has maintained an employee engagement rate that is three times better than the average organization measured by Gallup (Biltmore is considered "world class") and a retention rate five times better than the industry average. Additionally, Biltmore is widely recognized around the world for its delivery of "gracious hospitality" and has been named one of America's Best and Brightest Companies to Work For by the National Association for Business Resources in successive years. I spent my internship seeking to understand Biltmore's methodology, employee training approach, and leadership philosophies. Not long after my internship, the vice president of talent and organizational development pursued me to manage business development for a growing division of the company: Biltmore Center for Professional Development, the consultative arm of the company where Biltmore leaders train external companies across the country to apply the best practices of hospitality to their own organizations. This experience exposed me to the challenges, opportunities, and strategic direction of hundreds of executives across the US, representing dozens of industries and thousands of backgrounds.

While I am a Gen Z'r myself, I've had the unique opportunity to consult with, train, and advise vice presidents of human resources, C-suite executives, and start-up partners. My career has placed me in the opportune position to understand the needs, wants, and desires of these leaders. Through genuine curiosity and research, I've developed a passion for helping leaders of all backgrounds solve employee experience challenges and create a workplace where all generations thrive. Several of the most brilliant consultants and leaders I've had the pleasure of meeting along my consulting journey are featured in the pages of this book, and I believe you'll find their insights invaluable as well, as you begin to prepare your workplace for the next generation.

This project is the unfolding of years of curiosity, dozens of interviews, many mad nights of research, and a journey of empathy. I've spoken with professors, students, fellow Gen Z'rs in the workplace, executives, and leaders from all levels in their organizations, all of whom have questions about how they can work together to become the best versions of themselves and advance the success of their workplace. Additionally, I launched a LinkedIn learning series in early 2021 titled *Radical Empathy: Building the Bridge Between Gen Z and the Workplace* to lead a movement in bringing together generations and beginning dialogue around how we can better serve one another. In the series, I feature the voices of leaders and students who are equally passionate about spreading Radical Empathy for all generations, ethnicities, and backgrounds at work. This conversation is resonating with people from all walks of life, and tens of thousands of them have engaged with the movement. In fact, within the first three months of the series launch, dozens of leaders reached out to me expressing how grateful they were for the honest conversations about moving toward a better future.

As we take this journey together, I ask that my readers keep an open mind toward the perspectives each generation brings and take note of the small steps that can be taken to achieve greater harmony. I also encourage you to join the Radical Empathy movement and become a part of shaping the workplace of the future!

DISCLAIMER:

I want to provide the disclaimer that I recognize how challenging it can be to address and respond to a new generation entering the work sphere. With five generations coexisting in the modern-day workplace, it's no wonder there is confusion, misunderstanding, and faulty communication between colleagues of different eras. Throughout this book, I assume the premise that at the core of Gen Z and every other generation, we have more commonalities than differences, beginning with the fact that we are all, of course, human. We all share a human fear of the unknown, resistance to change, and emotional ups and downs, and we've all experienced the pain of failure and the excitement of success. While this may seem obvious, given the way many of us are tempted to speak about people from other generations, you'd think we were entirely different species! I firmly believe that because of our shared humanity, the things that separate us are external forces imposed on us and created by us.

GENERATIONAL INFLUENCES

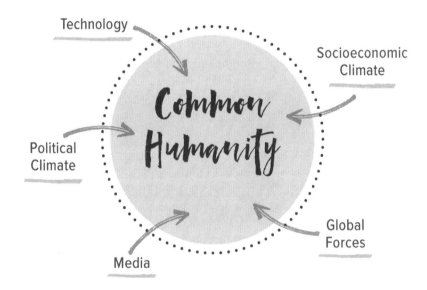

If each generation's varied exposure to socioeconomics, technology, political influence, and media are the only things separating us from our commonalities, the work to bridge gaps between generations may not seem as large a hurdle to overcome. Sometimes our common humanity can be overshadowed by what we think are large differences, when in actuality we are more alike than not, and each of us has the ability to view scenarios from another generation's perspective. I'm hopeful that this project will help shift perspectives for both those of you reading this book as well as my Generation Z peers.

If each generation's varied exposure to socioeconomics, technology, political influence, and media are the only things separating us from our commonalities, the work to bridge gaps between generations may not seem as large a hurdle to overcome.

That being said, in no way do I desire to make light of the hard work that goes into shifting culture for a new generation nor do I suggest that any company modify direction entirely based on the whims of Gen Z. Rather, the intent behind the recommendations presented in this book is to help leaders understand what motivates, inspires, and attracts my generation, and analyze which portions work for their distinct situations and the type of employee they desire to attract. Additionally, my generation has much to learn from those who have gone before us. There are numerous areas of growth and decades of wisdom we can glean from our millennial, Gen X, and boomer colleagues. My hope is that, through this project, we can find both commonalities and differences that allow us to collaborate, contribute, and communicate with one another to make our organizations and cultures flourish.

Before diving into the content of this book, I would encourage you to visit my website and take a quick "pulse check" assessment. This will allow you to gauge how ready you are for Gen Z to enter the workforce, including gaps and successes in your own hiring, recruitment, engagement, and retention operations. Some leaders I've spoken with are using this book as a 30-week enlightenment project for their organization, taking one chapter per week and seeing which lessons they can apply. Taking the initial assessment will allow you to reap the most benefit from this content and set goals along the way that are simple and easy to follow.

How Ready Is Your Workplace for Gen Z?
To take the pulse check, navigate to hannahgwilliams.com/assessment.

Now that you've taken the assessment, you're ready to jump into learning about Gen Z! We'll start by looking through the eyes of Gen Z, then discuss how this applies to your attracting, recruitment, retention, and leadership efforts.

Visit hannahgwilliams.com/downloads to access printable versions of exercises.

MEET GEN Z

Countless philosophers have stated that the foundation of understanding how someone behaves is empathy. So, for the sake of understanding the various perspective of Gen Z, I ask that you take a short journey with me. My generation brings a diversity of thoughts, opinions, and backgrounds. Often in narratives such as this, it can be easy to make broad statements about a generation that are not necessarily true of the individual. Therefore, as truly empathic leaders, I ask that you consider these varying perspectives and take the research presented here with a grain of salt.

I'd like to introduce you to some of my fellow Gen Z'rs (born 1995–2012). Each persona is inspired by one of my real-life peers, and they represent broad categories of the workforce and upcoming staff. As you consider the challenges and strengths of your individual employees, perhaps this will help you step into their shoes. We'll walk through the journeys of these Gen Z personas throughout the book to understand how they might respond differently in the workplace and how you can address their individual needs.

THE TRADITIONALIST

KABIR PATEL
(19 YEARS OLD)

Kabir lives in the North Carolina Triangle and is a thriving engineering student. As a second-generation immigrant, he worked endlessly during high school to receive a full ride to NC State's College of Engineering—heavily encouraged by his parents to find the stable career they didn't have when immigrating to the United States. Although NC State is renowned for its phenomenal engineering program, Kabir does not realize that his engineering career will likely include a major relationship-sales component for which the university's track does not include classes or training.

CAREER TRAJECTORY

During school, Kabir interned with several midsize engineering firms in Atlanta, GA, with the intent to take on a role as a junior project manager upon completing school. At this point, he presumes he'll stay at this firm for the next five to ten years, moving up the ranks. If he ever had a chance to take on international projects in his parents' home country of India, he would be delighted to give back by building infrastructure for the future.

HOBBIES

- Fly-fishing—His favorite spot is in Pisgah National Forest, where secluded nature leaves him to his own thoughts.
- Languages—Kabir is already bilingual (English and Hindi) but has a fascination for learning other languages. Right now, he's working on Arabic.
- Baking—His friends know him as the "pastry guy." Kabir has a knack for whipping up delicious baklava, croissants, and other goodies. He's had no formal training but plans to take culinary classes when he can afford them.

THE UNIFIER

DENISHA HENDERSON
(17 YEARS OLD)

Denisha grew up in the south of Chicago and, with her middle-class upbringing, she's fighting stereotypes of what it means to be a Black female in America. Her dad is an entrepreneur who inspired her to take advantage of whatever came her way in life. From an early age, Denisha was determined to engage in difficult dialogue with people from all walks of life, so she frequently participates in Jubilee (a YouTube channel) interviews discussing often-sensitive topics such as sexual health, racial equity, and the influence of religions on modern society. During high school, she started a blog connecting tourists with the best restaurants, entertainment, and attractions in Chicago, and within three years was making decent money from advertising with her 10,000 active subscribers. She is able to network well to build a reputation with local businesses. In addition, she uses her blog as a platform to better engage the community and bring people of all different backgrounds together. Right now, she's working at a local burger joint.

CAREER TRAJECTORY

Denisha knows her skill set could be applicable in many jobs. She could work in marketing or sales or even go to law school. Right now, she's graduating from high school and facing a crossroads: Should she continue growing her blogging business or go to college—or both?

HOBBIES

- Flute—Surprising to some, Denisha doesn't love jazz, even though her family has deep roots in the genre. Instead, she picked up the flute for fun and fell in love. She plays in her local orchestra, which holds concerts a few times each year.
- Flag football—Denisha can get rough and dirty with her friends. On the weekends, she's out with the boys playing flag football.
- Editing—Denisha's friends always had her editing their school projects, mostly because she loved doing it. Now she volunteers with Boys and Girls Clubs of America helping elementary and middle school students with homework.

THE COME-BACKER

CORBAN TRENTOR
(21 YEARS OLD)

Corban never liked social media. Growing up in northern Texas, he preferred to stay more isolated and not "put himself out there" like everyone else was doing. At age 19, he left home to live on the road, homeless for a couple of years. People always said he was a smart kid but made poor decisions, including a few brief bouts in the county jail. By the time he was 20, reality hit him. Living on the street wasn't the adventure he had anticipated, and it was time to shape up his life, set goals, and work hard to rebuild his reputation and stability. Beginning by enrolling in culinary school, Corban quickly found his passion for cooking and the rapid-paced life of the kitchen.

CAREER TRAJECTORY

Because of his experience on the street, Corban demanded of himself not to fall back into bad habits. Rather, he directs that energy toward bettering his skill set, with a goal of working as an executive chef in a high-end operation up north. To get there, he's pursuing the best experience possible, training under top chefs around the country, and hustling to make it work financially. Long term, he sees himself starting his own high-end catering business, with a focus on corporate events.

HOBBIES

- Kickboxing—On weekdays, Corban stays in shape with his buddies by kickboxing. He's not interested in competing, but it feels good to let out some steam after a hot, long weekend in the kitchen.
- Tattoo artist—Corban has designed a few of his own tattoos and even took a stab at tattooing his own arm. His friends thought it looked so good they wanted him to do theirs.

THE LACKLUSTER DREAMER

MINAR LIN
(25 YEARS OLD)

Born in Southern California, Minar has lived in seven different countries and speaks five languages. With one white parent and one Asian parent, she lives in between cultural identities. Now she works as a software engineer in a giant Silicon Valley firm as one of the "numbers." But there's this bug itching constantly in her ear: Isn't there something greater in life? Someone or something I can impact with my gifts? Even though her job pays well, the firm she works with has not figured out how to instill purpose in her work, so she's dreaming about something different.

CAREER TRAJECTORY

Minar has thought about her future deeply. Maybe she could run her own business? Maybe she could found a nonprofit? But she's feeling lost without direction because, while her technical skills are through the roof, she's struggling to find a mentor who will coach her toward her ultimate goals.

HOBBIES

- Coding—Several young girls have sought out Minar to teach them coding, so she's helping them on the weekends. It's great fun for all of them.
- Reading and Netflix—Minar is a diehard romance novel and Netflix series fan. She says she knows it's cheesy but can't help it.
- Photography—Minar has an excellent visual eye, and when traveling she's frequently toting her Canon EOS M50 Mark II. She's still a beginner but loves shooting landscapes.

THE QUINTESSENTIAL 'INTRAPRENEUR'

CLAIRE BEEZLEY
(24 YEARS OLD)

Immediately after graduating from the University of Michigan, Claire took a position with a midsize marketing consultancy firm as an analyst, and she loves her position. While many of her colleagues have left the firm to start their own businesses, Claire prefers the stability, benefits, and flexibility that her job offers, and enjoys the people she works with. Beyond her role as an analyst, Claire is able to get her voice heard and she headed up the employee engagement initiatives at her firm, having a say in the events the company puts on, and even the way benefits are structured.

CAREER TRAJECTORY

Because of the multiple hats Claire wears, her work is fulfilling and she never envisions herself leaving the firm unless something drastic happens. Besides, she plans to have kids someday, so with the stability and fulfillment of her work, why would she leave? She envisions a lengthy career with this firm, likely moving from analyst into a partner role—perhaps even purchasing the firm from the owners when they are ready to exit.

HOBBIES

- Dancing—On the weekends, you'll find Claire at the local swing club. In high school, she studied modern and jazz dance but now just dances for fun.
- Real estate—Claire is a savvy investor on the side. She just bought her first duplex and is living in one side while renting out the other, and has even done a couple of wholesale deals. She's a saver and, because of this house hack, her housing expense is only $400 per month.
- Sporadic travels—Claire is a single woman. Each year she buys a ticket to a remote international location without any other preemptive plans. Once she arrives, she figures everything out on the fly during her month-long vacation. Last year, she stayed in Israeli hostels, and the year before she was in Kazakhstan.

THE BABY MILLIONAIRE

RODRIGO GOMEZ
(15 YEARS OLD)

Rodrigo was a normal kid. He liked video games, so naturally, at 13, he started streaming his games on Twitch. Not expecting much of anything, he was surprised when thousands of people began watching his streams. Soon he was able to monetize through branded gear, start a YouTube channel, and build a massive following. Since he lives in Los Angeles with a millionaire's lifestyle, kids tell him all the time he's such an inspiration to them. He's doing what he loves and making a ton of money doing it, but his parents are concerned. What if Twitch fails or bumps him off the platform and he hasn't made plans to go to school? What then? They urge him to find some semblance of a normal job. He's trying to take their advice—what path will he choose?

CAREER TRAJECTORY

If Rodrigo does take his parents' suggestion, he's thinking about joining a fast-paced tech start-up. There are several in his area that are hiring high-potential students who understand tech, gaming, and video production, and they pay for their employee's school while they're working at the company.

HOBBIES

- E-sports—Rodrigo's passion is gaming, and he lucked out and turned it into a business. Even if he stops livestreaming, this is one of his lifelong hobbies.
- Music—Rodrigo is a huge music fan. He's at all the concerts for his favorite artists, some of which are The Weeknd, DJ Khaled, Bad Bunny, and Lele Pons.

Do you notice any similarities between your children, grandchildren, or young friends and these personas? The diversity of our generation is difficult to capture in a few paragraphs, but hopefully the common trends of high expectations, great skepticism, greater access to education, and a focus on entrepreneurship were clear. As we'll discuss throughout this book, these elements have created pros and cons for Gen Z'rs entering the workforce, and we'll use these personas to illustrate how broad categories of your Gen Z workforce will respond and adapt to culture, values, and policies your organization puts in place.

At this point, you might be thinking, "Yes, I see some of these characteristics in my children, but what makes those so different from millennials?" Let's discuss this before diving into the tactics of how to attract, retain, and lead Gen Z

THE DIFFERENCE BETWEEN GEN Z AND MILLENNIALS

Has one of your teens ever pulled this typical hotheaded rant on you? "Mom, Dad, you just don't understand me! You don't remember what it's like being my age!" I can certainly remember saying this to my own parents—and for anyone reading this who has parented teens, I know you can empathize. When your teens hurl these statements at you, you've likely thought, "Of course I remember what it was like being your age; of course I was stupid too. I'm trying to help you not make the same mistakes I did!"

Actually ... I would argue that your teen may be right. Why? Of course you remember being young, making careless mistakes, focusing on the wrong pursuits, and there's nothing new under the sun. But in a way, you don't truly understand what it's like growing up amongst a new generation—in fact, it's quite impossible to comprehend. Teens today are faced with very different challenges than the ones you encountered. It's similarly impossible for your teen to understand the challenges you faced when growing up, simply because the events that defined each generation are vastly different. Take, for example, the areas of commonality we all relate to: peer pressure, relationship issues, school burdens, etc. But when you were in middle school, did you have to actively fear for your safety every day? Did you graduate from college with a bachelor's degree and experience being rejected for a grocery-stocking position because jobs were so limited? Figure 1 distinguishes some of the common challenges Gen Z has faced in our young years from those of our parents.

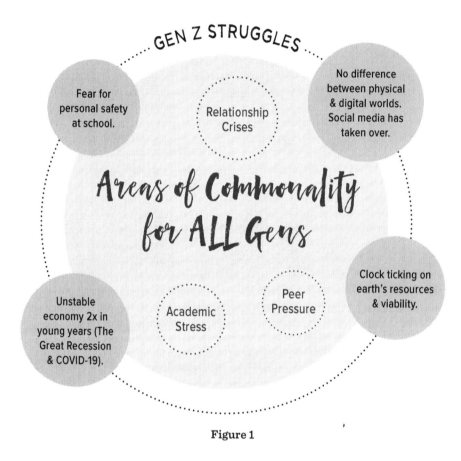

Figure 1

IDEALISM VS. PRAGMATISM

Let's zoom in even a bit more and simply compare millennials and Gen Z. Most researchers would agree that a defining moment for millennials (born 1981–1995) was 9/11, but Gen Z doesn't remember this tragedy firsthand, nor do we remember the advent of the internet. Beyond social and political events, the parenting styles of boomers (parents of millennials) and Gen Xers (parents of Gen Z) were vastly different. It's been said of the millennial generation that their boomer parents instilled in them a sense of optimism. The idea that "everyone is a winner" and that the group should be prioritized over the individual were common ideas millennials grew up with. As a result, millennials are highly collective and collaborative in their approach to work. Dozens of articles have been written on the civil, socioeconomic, and political factors that influenced this mindset, so we won't delve into it here. (If you want to learn more about these factors, I suggest reading *Gen Z @Work* by David Stillman and Jonah Stillman.)

However, Gen Z is vastly different. The situations that have influenced our perspective on life are the COVID-19 pandemic, school shootings, and the Great Recession, creating a generation that is hyper-realistic. Rather than a world full of only possibilities and success, we see a world where we'll have to work hard to get ahead, where stability is difficult to achieve, and where worry and anxiety are core drivers of success.[1] Ultimately, these factors have created a group of young people who have very different expectations of the workplace than their predecessors.

DIFFERING WORKPLACE PRIORITIES

You might be reading this book and thinking, "We've just now figured out millennials! Argh!" And I agree—it's rough to know there's yet another generation to adapt to. In fact, it's estimated that millennial turnover costs the US economy $30.5 billion annually.[2]

With companies losing many recruiting and training dollars to these efforts, I urge employers not to make the same mistakes with Gen Z. One of the easy mistakes to make is attempting to recruit and retain Gen Z the same way that your company recruited and retained millennials. Let's prevent that for your firm!

See if you can identify which of these workplace priorities in Figure 2 are important to each generation. Draw a line from each of the items on the left to the generation you think they match on the right. I encourage you to really try this—test your assumptions! You may be surprised.

(FYI, there's only one match per item in the left column.) Can you try matching which characteristics belong to each generation?

1. Prefer Digital Communication 2. Want a "Climb the Ladder" Career Path w/High Growth Potential 3. Desire to Stay with One Company for 10+ Years 4. Prefer Higher Salary over Work/Life Balance 5. Savers 6. Collaboration-Focused 7. Spenders 8. Individual/Self-Focused 9. Want In-Person Communication 10. Prefer Wearing Multiple Job Hats or Working Two Jobs Simultaneously	*Millennials* *Gen Z*

Figure 2
See how many you got correct! Answers are on the last page of this chapter.

Let's look at some of the data, because while there are many differences between Gen Z and millennials, there are also noticeable similarities. Glassdoor conducted a study of common phrases Gen Z and millennials used when describing pros and cons about their workplaces. Interestingly, they found that the most common phrases Gen Z uses as pros to describe the company they work for are "work environment," "flexible hours," and "good pay." Some of their phrases— "easy job," "employee discount," "free food," and "easy work"—do not appear at all in the millennials' list.[3] Take a look at the most common pros and cons for Gen Z vs. millennials.

You'll see some of Gen Z's fears manifesting themselves in these charts. How many did you get correct? When I conduct this exercise in live workshops, most leaders are surprised by the stark differences between the two generations, and I can see why. In all honesty, you'll see some of Gen Z's fears manifesting themselves in these results, and if you also look at the common "pros" and "cons" for Gen Z versus millennials (see Figures 3 and 4), you'll notice the core distinctions. Notably, good pay is much more important to Gen Z on a broad scale than to their millennial peers. Where millennials focus on culture and work/life balance with greater fervor, Gen Z wants a solid work environment that compensates them well for the work they do and offers flexibility and stability.

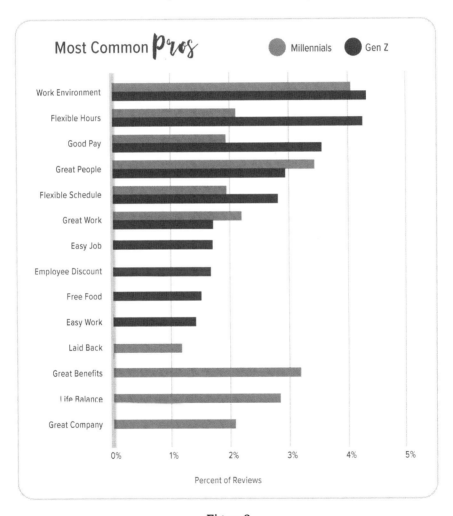

Figure 3

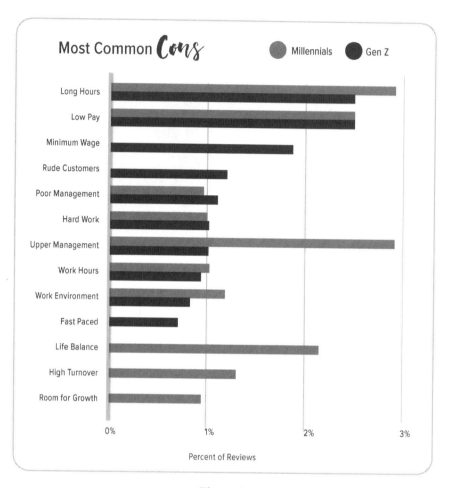

Figure 4

There is currently much more research available on the millennial generation's values because Gen Z is so new. However, I hope some of the immediate differences are evident. Employers who want to attract Gen Z should consider prioritizing pay over benefits and flexible hours/spaces over rigid and expensive office environments, and they may want to give a nod to small perks that attract Gen Z to the company in the first place (free food, etc.). There is still much research to be done that will influence the data, particularly as Gen Z'rs move into management themselves.

For example, given Gen Z's current employment in pre-college jobs, attaining leadership or upper management positions in a company is not nearly as concerning as the immediate desire for higher pay. And work/life balance is not even a top 10 concern for Gen Z, while for millennials who are already starting families, balance and flexibility are mature responses to current life needs. You may also not be surprised by Gen Z's concern about "hard work." See Figure 4. At first glance, this may seem like we aren't willing to put in effort. However, as I hope will become clear throughout this book, Gen Z is simply a highly efficiency-focused generation, and when innovation is too slow or the proper tools aren't provided to complete work efficiently, we easily write the work off as "too difficult." There is a highly innovative, productive, and self-driven workforce that's waiting for you to tap into it—not begrudgingly, but as a competitive advantage.

We'll break down these areas further as we embark on this journey of understanding and leading Gen Z'rs, so let's start at the very beginning of the employee journey: How do you attract the brightest Gen Z talent to your company?

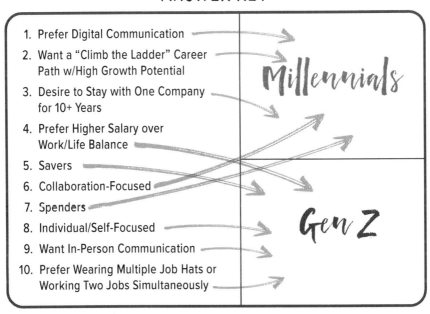

Section I
ATTRACT

> **GEN Z'RS TAKE IMMENSE PRIDE IN SHARING WHERE THEY WORK AND THE PURPOSE BEHIND THEIR DAILY TASKS.**

CHAPTER 1:
BE A PART OF OUR NARCISSTORY

It's been said of human beings that we are continually on a quest for a meaningful life. Generation Z is no exception—in fact, finding purpose and meaning in not only our personal life but also our work identity is of the utmost importance. As we enter this discussion about attracting Gen Z, let's think like a chief marketing officer would about how we can meet Gen Z where they are and speak to what they're seeking in the workplace. Beginning with the basics, any skilled marketer would know that corporate storytelling is important to connecting consumers with a product or service, but let's talk about storytelling from a slightly different angle. Instead of telling the company's story, let's discuss how a company can become a part of a Gen Z'rs life story (or "NarcisStory," as I call it) as a powerful attraction tool. As I'm sure you'll quickly notice, this concept is an important foundation of how Generation Z thinks and will be instrumental in attracting, retaining, and leading our generation of talent.

WHAT IS A 'NARCISSTORY'?

As a result of our surroundings, Gen Z'rs' natural tendency is to be a bit narcissistic, sometimes selfish, and, depending on our maturity, self-absorbed. But isn't this the human condition? Hardly anyone would disagree that social media has amplified my generation's self-consciousness and self-focus, but I would posit this is not all negative—particularly when the resulting demands cause workplaces to shift toward more proactive engagement with all areas of the human experience, rather than simply focusing on shareholder value. Here's the definition of a NarcisStory:

> *The reputation of a person, amplified by interests, activities, and associations by which they want to be defined.*

Essentially, a NarcisStory is the reputation that a person creates naturally through their social media presence, fashion choices, or activities they participate in. Many Z'rs do this subconsciously. It's too easy to create a personal brand through Instagram filters these days, so while some Z'rs formalize their "brands," others have created them based on their personal preferences and may not even know how they are perceived. Why is understanding these important for employers?

Well, when you hire a Gen Z'r, you are no longer just hiring an employee—you are hiring someone with a brand and reputation, and it's your job to be part of their NarcisStory, not the other way around.

EXPECTATION DISRUPTION

To understand exactly how integral the concept of NarcisStory is to Gen Z, let's take a step back into generational history. Those of you from the boomer generation remember the expectation from your parents to attend college, get a solid job with a good company, and "pay dues" as you moved through the ranks. With an awaiting pension plan and stability, it didn't make sense to leave the company you'd been with for many years. Gen X children came along and questioned the necessity of the traditional college path, but their parents had saved diligently for many years and assuredly told them no one would take them seriously without at least a bachelor's degree, especially as college was becoming more accessible. Of course, you can imagine the resistance millennials faced from their boomer parents when they wondered if a college degree was worthwhile—you see, most boomer households were prepared to send their millennial children to school, no matter the cost.

When you hire a Gen Z'r, you are no longer just hiring an employee—you are hiring someone with a brand and reputation, and it's your job to be part of their NarcisStory, not the other way around.

A different conversation has occurred with Gen Z. Gen X parents are watching their children found online businesses and take internships during high school, essentially creating alternative paths for themselves before the question of college even seriously arises. Unlike past generations where children were expected to attend college, get married, and take on the best job they could to support their growing family—even if this meant punching a clock for 40 years at a potentially mind-numbing job—**Gen Z expects their work to be an extension of their identity**. Gen Z'rs take immense pride in sharing where they work and the purpose behind their daily tasks. Beyond this, Gen X watched their parents go into immense debt sending their millennial children to school, and they don't want that either! As a result, the conversation has begun to shift around traditional college paths as both Gen Z children and their Gen X parents look at alternative methods.

This has impacted Gen Z in a powerful way. It's almost as if Gen Z is bringing the "American dream" back to life. Rather than settling into the flourishing economy with a white picket fence, a traditional job, and a family with two parents and two kids, Gen Z is hustling and exploring a multitude of opportunities while making their own unique way in the world. Much like the immigrants coming to the New World, the internet has enabled Gen Z'rs around the globe to gain access to new markets, build connections with people of other languages, and build a brand from a very early age. We are pioneers of a new era. We aren't here to copy the journeys of our predecessors; rather, we are stepping out and creating our own unique story in a new age.

PERSONAL BRAND AND EMPLOYERS

What does this mean for employers? To recruit Gen Z talent, companies must balance messaging that shares their own story with messaging that allows Gen Z to see how their personal story can be enhanced by associating themselves with that employer. From my generation's perspective, anything we choose to do in life becomes one piece of an intricate, colorful journey of the person we want to become. In fact, work itself is seen as a tool for self-development, not the be-all and end-all in and of itself. Think about attracting Gen Z'rs like a marketer would think about attracting consumers: from the perspective of storytelling, and how you can fit into the Gen Z NarcisStory.

Anything we choose to do in life becomes one piece of an intricate, colorful journey of the person we want to become.

This shift in thinking is important for employers to make when seeking to hire Gen Z. While previous generations may have seen their career as a method for earning enough money to spend on personal enjoyment, Gen Z is okay with blurring the lines between work life and personal life because both are seen as enjoyable, fulfilling, and part of our story. Research by HubSpot supports this, indicating that only 38% of Gen Z'rs are focused on work/life balance in their ideal job, whereas 47% of millennials indicated this as important.[4] Essentially, Gen Z'rs are more willing to focus on "work/life integration" rather than "work/life balance," where the two spheres are separated. Perhaps this concept of Gen Z's need for a compelling story is best illustrated visually:

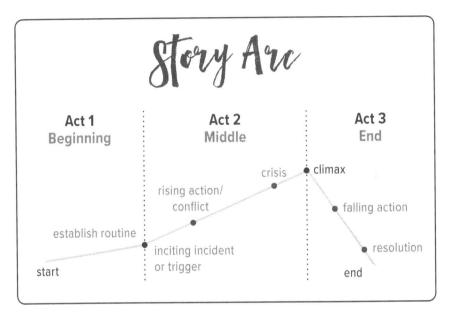

Figure 1

Think of how a story works. It is the one thing that can hold a human being's attention for hours, and it's because of the way the story is written; it not only generates excitement and anticipation but also contains crises that the protagonist faces before finding their ultimate path and a satisfactory resolution. These elements make a story relatable and beautiful. In a world infiltrated by social media, Gen Z'rs often craft lives that paint stories in a similar way. How does this translate to the workplace? It's simple: Gen Z'rs are reviewing the potential job they would accept with your company based on how well it aligns with the story they want to live out, and specifically how the crux of the story relates to their personal journey. For example, most Gen Z'rs have a crisis and/or passion they are seeking to solve or fulfill in life, and they expect the "rising action" or "climax" of that passion to be shared by the company they choose to give the majority of their waking hours to serve. Here are a few examples of crises or passions that Gen Z'rs might expect to find in their workplace:

Gen Z's are reviewing the potential job they would accept with your company based on how well it aligns with the story they want to live out.

CRISES:
- I want to minimize my impact on the world. The environment is hurting from what humans have done to it—I am compelled to be a part of the solution.
- Other people are suffering. I live to help them.

ON A LIGHTER NOTE:
- I know what it's like to live with acne. I want to help other women feel beautiful.
- I used to be terrified of going to the dentist. As a hygienist, I get to create amazing dental experiences for kids that weren't available when I was their age!
- As a child, I visited beautiful places. Now I want to be a part of creating family memories for someone else!

LIFE PASSIONS:
- I grew up in a single-parent household living in poverty. I want to be successful and show that anyone can create something out of nothing.

- I want to revolutionize a complacent industry—I live to disrupt.
- My life goal is to bring happiness to the world. When I'm able to help others make memories, it excites me.
- I live to build the world of the future. To innovate. To make it more efficient. And to ultimately leave a better future for generations to come.
- It's important that my work stimulates my intellect—I want to be seen as someone who never turns down a challenge.

For many Gen Zr's, doing something meaningful or impactful that leaves a mark on the world is a way of justifying our existence, and companies that can tap into this innate desire for the Gen Z'r to build a unique and special story will attract us. I hope you can see from the examples above that not all these crises or passions are glamorous. In fact, the messaging you convey to a potential employee is equally as important as the actual work they'll be conducting. For previous generations, glamorous mission statements may have cut it; but for Gen Z, we'd just prefer you to be authentic. We want to understand what you do and why it matters—and in fact, if your mission statement is inauthentic or overzealous, my generation may not take it seriously. Let's take one of our personas and talk about how speaking to the Gen Z NarcisStory will play itself out:

> **GEN Z MUSINGS**
> *Seriously? This company says its mission is to be innovative, but they haven't even updated their website since 2012. BS.*

The messaging you convey to a potential employee is equally as important as the actual work they'll be conducting.

THE LACKLUSTER DREAMER

MINAR LIN (25 YEARS OLD)

Scenario: Your company is trying to attract young, forward-thinking, but discontent, talent. You've found that this talent is similar to our Lackluster Dreamer: Someone with a high degree of education and technical skills but who is discontent working for a large institution where they are treated like a number. Like Minar, they are unhappy in their current position and look to entrepreneurship as a potential solution but aren't necessarily ready for or capable of making the leap into owning their own business.

Objective: Attract talent like Minar for your company's software engineering positions, away from larger employers.

CHALLENGES:

- You can't compete on pay—you won't be able to offer a salary as high as her current position.
- You can't compete on benefits.
- You are in a remote location without the prowess of Silicon Valley and can't compete on reputation alone.

Let's step into Minar's shoes and really think about the problems in her current position so we can understand how to attract her and set ourselves apart from the competition.

MINAR'S NEEDS:

- She doesn't feel heard. She just feels like "another number." Minar wants to flourish in a position where she feels like she's adding true value.

- Her work isn't meaningful. It doesn't fit within the legacy she wants to leave for her life and live out each day. Minar has many other gifts that her current employer doesn't leverage. She's there for one job.
- She needs stability and good pay, but if she had to give up some of that pay to have a mentor who would take her under their wing, she would do it.

Now, let's build a few strategies to attract someone like Minar to consider applying at our firm using the NarcisStory technique. Of course, when building out a similar strategy for your firm, you'll want to laser-focus on the specific channels where your top talent is searching and apply these techniques to your personal situation, company size, and resource reach. Here are just a few ideas:

- **Identify the Crisis:** Remember how Gen Z is motivated by intrinsic passions or crises that we want to be a part of solving? Sit down and brainstorm a few crises your company helps solve or passions you help employees relate to that you believe would relate to Minar. For example, perhaps it's: *I live to build the world of the future. To innovate. To make it more efficient. And to ultimately leave a better future for generations to come.* For Minar's situation in a large institution, she probably doesn't realize the importance of her work to a larger cause, so because she is a natural innovator, the limited box she's been put inside is constraining. You can pique her interest in your company by speaking to this inner passion.

- **Preach Stories on Your Career Website:** Take the passion/crisis you've identified and ask any Gen Z staff member you already employ how your company allows them to meet this need in their life. Film this aspirational story and share it on your career website, TikTok, or other social media channels.

Please note a very important distinction between a NarcisStory campaign and a normal career campaign. Most video career marketing is not going to be as effective with Gen Z'rs because the language looks something like this:

"At (INSERT COMPANY NAME), I feel valued because I work on a great team, there are great benefits, and leadership cares about me. Come join my team!"

While this messaging is often effective, it's overused. And more specifically, this is NOT the messaging we're talking about here. Here's an example of a better script that illustrates what tapping into the power of NarcisStory looks like, as told by a current Gen Z employee:

"Going to work in Silicon Valley right out of college, I was sure all my dreams would be fulfilled. Instead, I discovered I was just a number and that I functioned almost like a robot. But that's NOT my passion. My passion is to help people use tech to create a better life for themselves. You see, when I left Silicon Valley to work for (INSERT COMPANY NAME), I realized that being a software engineer could actually be fulfilling. Every day, I leap out of bed to create the next innovative idea that will change the world and make it better for the next generation. I know I'm not the only one who felt like a number. If this is you, come join my team and cut through the bullshit. It'll be hard some days, but we're in it together to make the world a little better each day."

Do you see the difference in this language? It's authentic—and it's not focused on the company, it's focused on the Gen Z'r's story. If Minar sees this, she's likely to at least view the position or even apply without even glancing at salary initially. You've captured her attention and it's not based on pay or benefits; rather, it's based on connecting with the power of her NarcisStory.

SIMPLE STEPS YOU CAN TAKE:

I encourage you to walk through the above exercise with one position you're trying to fill. Implement the NarcisStory technique by focusing on the position and the applicant's innate desires, then see if your thinking shifts. Here's a template:

SCENARIO Where is your talent coming from?	
OBJECTIVE What position are you trying to fill?	
LIMITATIONS/ CHALLENGES Based on your company's resources, what limitations might you face?	
MESSAGING This could be a video, printed/online marketing collateral, social media content, etc.	

Note on exercises: You'll notice as we go through the book that most chapters end with an action-oriented activity like this one. To get the most out of the content, I highly suggest you pause and complete the exercise. Additionally, many of these activities are helpful to conduct with your team! I've developed a resource list, included in the back of the book, to direct you to facilitators who can help lead the exercises. These exercises can be powerful in a group setting.

 Visit hannahgwilliams.com/downloads to access printable versions of exercises.

> "GEN Z'RS RESPOND TO LEADERS WHO ARE ENGAGED IN THE BEST, BRIGHTEST, AND LATEST CONCEPTS."

CHAPTER 2
CREATE A PERSONAL BRAND

A popular YouTube channel for all ages, Yes Theory, launched a creative project over the summer. Their mission? To land a subscriber their dream job.[5] They chose to feature Ivan, a recent college graduate with a business development and sales focus. The company where he dreamed of working? A gaming start-up with fewer than 75 employees at the time, with a vision of becoming the most valuable and relevant gaming lifestyle brand in the world. Of course, the mission was inspirational, but why was Ivan so drawn to this company? Simple answer: Matthew Haag, the company's CEO, also known as Nadeshot, is one of the most respected personalities in the gaming industry—and Ivan's hero. Yes, the company culture, vision, and direction were all important, but Ivan had his eyes set on learning from Matthew. Without questioning Matthew's leadership ability or any skills beyond his competition success and celebrity, Ivan was a devotee of Matthew's and wanted to learn from the best of the best.

FIRST STEPS TO BUILDING A PERSONAL BRAND

Like Matthew demonstrated, to attract the best Gen Z talent, leaders at any level can build their personal brand and become an icon that Gen Z can admire and aspire to become. As we spoke about in the previous chapter, Gen Z seeks to live out fulfilling life stories, and there is a massive opportunity for leaders—no matter the level within the organization or the size of the company—to engage a Gen Z audience by generating a name and content that challenges, equips, and inspires them to see themselves in your shoes one day. How can you build a personal brand online? Here are a couple of practical ways:

- **Effectively use your LinkedIn, Instagram, and even TikTok profiles.** If you are someone with a small but growing following, this might mean posting original content a few times per month through blogs or videos, or even posting a story on LinkedIn or Instagram. Of course, for a personal brand, this content should not be focused on recruitment; rather, it should showcase your personal interests, passions, and challenges. Who knows? You might have the dream career or life a Gen Z'r is looking for when they scour LinkedIn. Think you have a less-than-interesting job? Trust me—I've seen some college students as enthusiastic about paper science as the average male would be about the Super Bowl. There's a candidate out there who admires what you do. Look to Gary Vaynerchuk, Jon Tesser, and Sara Blakely for inspiration. Or on a smaller level, leaders like Maryam Salehijam and Brandon Bornancin are leveraging their personal platforms to attract top-quality talent and have

> **GEN Z MUSINGS**
>
> *That's bussin. This guy has 10k followers on Twitter and his posts really make me think differently about work. He says not to settle and to find something I'm passionate about. It makes me want to work hard and find a place I can grow.*

the opportunity every day to get in front of their target market. Once they post a position, it's "all hands on deck" to manage the application influx.

- **Hire an intern to manage your social media.** Let's face it—most busy leaders do not have time to manage their social media platforms or post consistently. Why not hire a marketing/social media intern who can post for you and develop your content plan? You'll want to identify your niche and the type of content you like to post, and it will take dedication to get off the ground. Once your bright intern gets to know your tastes, however, they can take pictures of you, take snippets from books you've written or enjoy, or sit in on important meetings and put your heart and strategy into words for others to benefit from.

- **Be an early adopter whenever you can.** Gen Z'rs respond to leaders who are engaged in the best, brightest, and latest concepts—for example, if you adopt a new feature on a social media platform when it's launched, we will see you as innovative. If you partner with a community organization or social trend, even when it may not be popular in the professional world to do so, Gen Z will be attracted to what you stand for.

Really, this concept is simple, and while it takes effort, even small changes in how you use personal branding platforms will help Gen Z'rs find and appreciate your work. In the next chapter, we'll dive into some of the pitfalls the internet can also bring to recruiting.

SIMPLE STEPS YOU CAN TAKE:

- **Follow Jonathan George on Instagram and LinkedIn**—his company, Unleash Your Rockstar, helps anyone discover how to build and refine an attractive personal brand.
- **Pick one of the three strategies in this chapter and try it out!** Are you tempted to skip over this chapter and exercise? I don't blame you. Posting consistently on social media is a lot of work. Trust me, I know. That's why those who do it have a competitive advantage! Here's a simple exercise to get your juices flowing if you want to test this out.

WHAT'S YOUR NICHE? Your niche is based on your specialties. Are you passionate about leadership? Project management? Customer experience?	
WHICH PLATFORM WILL BE MOST BENEFICIAL FOR YOUR TARGET EMPLOYEE?	

I've created a sample content calendar template you can use to begin posting, and you can download it (along with other end-of-chapter exercise resources) at hannahgwilliams.com/downloads. Simply plan out your content in advance (or have an intern do it) and post a few times per week. I've added sample content ideas in the following chart to provide inspiration for your own downloaded version of the template.

MONTH: MARCH

	TIPS FOR YOUR TARGET AUDIENCE These types of posts include strategies, data, or info to help your audience in whatever niche you select.	INDUSTRY RESEARCH These posts point to articles or research in your niche.	COMPANY/ LIFE UPDATES Update your audience on company growth/ accolades to build your reputation.	PERSONAL THOUGHTS/ MUSINGS Everyone benefits from seeing the personal side of you. This shows your humanity.
IMAGE	Graph of new career path we are testing. Add description of the latest test results.			
VIDEO				30 seconds of a TEDx Talk I heard recently that inspired me to change how I spend my time.
TEXT			Write LinkedIn post about our company policy on entrepreneur-ship. Use the success story of Matt, who started his side hustle last year.	
POLL				
ARTICLE		Original article titled "5 Misno-mers Students Should Know Before Getting Their HR Manage-ment Degree."		

 Visit hannahgwilliams.com/downloads to access printable versions of exercises.

> **FOCUS YOUR EFFORTS ON PROACTIVELY BUILDING A BRAND IN THE PLACES GEN Z IS LOOKING.**

CHAPTER 3
WATCH YOUR REVIEWS

If your company quickly adapted your strategies to attract millennials, the topic of online reviews is certainly on your radar. However, the importance of employer reviews is a bit more nuanced for Gen Z.

TO REVIEW OR NOT TO REVIEW?

Websites like Glassdoor provide candidates with a look behind the scenes at a company's culture, pay, and pros and cons of working there. While the intent of these sites was initially to foster transparency, Gen Z views them through a different lens. You see, we are the first generation to grow up in a world where the internet has always existed. Since online reviews have been around for years now, my generation has lived through an era where robotic, fake reviews and paid (and certainly biased) information is a norm—we have "Spidey sense" for nongenuine content. We've seen stories like "The Shed at Dulwich" make headlines, where a random bloke in London was able to turn the shed in his back yard into the highest-rated restaurant in London on TripAdvisor.[36] Stories like these have made us very skeptical about the validity of online content, even though we are spoon-fed curated information more hours than not in a day. It is nearly automatic for Gen Z to exclude the nonsensical low reviews and overzealous high reviews posted on any site—whether Google, Yelp, or Glassdoor—and this certainly translates to the job search. Because of this, it's even more important for employers trying to attract Gen Z to watch the activity occurring on Glassdoor and thoughtfully consider the anonymous employee critiques as invaluable data that can be used to improve hiring and engagement strategies.

What else should you consider when it comes to reviews and Gen Z? Honestly, don't worry too much about them. Be sure you are making consistent efforts to gain authentic reviews from employees, but don't stress it. Focus your efforts on proactively building a brand in the places Gen Z is looking (Instagram, TikTok, LinkedIn, etc.) and building personal brands among your leaders, and the healthy balance will serve you well. If you are a smaller company that needs to build reviews, or a firm that's gone through an ownership transition and needs to rebuild its online reputation, you'll also want to think about how you incentivize (or don't incentivize) reviews on platforms like Glassdoor.

INCENTIVIZING REVIEWS TO ATTRACT OTHER Z'RS? THINK AGAIN...

Only 36% of Gen Z'rs were slightly likely to post a review if offered an incentive.

Not only has our upbringing taught Gen Z to be skeptical about the information we find in reviews, but also we can feel slightly manipulated when asked to post a review in exchange for a gift card or other incentive, even though this is a widely used strategy by businesses on both the consumer and employee fronts. In fact, the Pollack Group conducted a study⁷ of nearly 500 Gen Z'rs and found that only 36% were slightly likely to post a review if offered an incentive, while the remaining 64% would not post one. In fact, it's a generational faux pas, and we perceive that many online review providers, such as Yelp, are tinged with corporate influence, which is associated with our parents' generation. The takeaway? Employers should be strategic about how they ask Gen Z candidates to review their company on Glassdoor and other sites. There are several simple steps you can take to up your Gen Z review game.

> **GEN Z MUSINGS**
>
> *What's Yelp? Oh... it's that thing I never click on when looking for reviews... I just skip to the next link. Can't wait till Google doesn't give me that result anymore.*

SIMPLE STEPS YOU CAN TAKE:

- **Take Glassdoor reviews seriously, but don't sweat the volume:** This is where your candidates are looking first—and this is not just a job for HR. In fact, one of the key categories on Glassdoor is "approval of the CEO." What does this mean for the company? Every single leader in your company is responsible for the reputation of the CEO, even if it's how policy that is "passed down from on high" is articulated and supported by mid-level management in the firm. If you're an HR leader reading, you're probably thinking, "Glassdoor is untrustworthy! Reviews are fake and usually written by disgruntled employees after they've left, or people who've only interviewed!" But Gen Z'rs don't consider these factors. Your firm must base strategy on what is visible to the candidate, not on what you wish was available online. Whatever your level or position within your firm, read the reviews on Glassdoor and see if there are modifications in your departmental strategy that can support and correct the issues—and celebrate the successes of what employees love about the company! Then do the next step.

- **Evaluate your company and build an action plan:** Use the following rubric to rate yourself in each of the Glassdoor categories. You're the only one looking, so be honest with yourself about where your company is and where you want to go! Then take the simple total score, which is your current Glassdoor rating in that area minus what you/your team thinks the rating should be. For example, if your Glassdoor score for Work/Life Balance is 3.2 and you believe it should be 4.5, you have a disparity of 1.3 points.

	CURRENT GLASSDOOR RATING (Between 1.0 and 5.0)	WHAT YOU THINK THE RATING SHOULD BE	WHAT % OF THE REVIEWS YOU BELIEVE TO BE FAKE (5–10% is Glassdoor standard)	TOTAL: Difference between YOUR rating and the Glassdoor rating
CULTURE & VALUES				
DIVERSITY & INCLUSION				
WORK/LIFE BALANCE				
SENIOR MANAGEMENT				
COMPENSATION & BENEFITS				
CAREER GROWTH				

Based on this simple exercise (and factoring in which area you believe has the most credible reviews, depending on the size of your company and number of reviews), in which area of your company do you believe there is the largest disparity between online perception and reality?

List your top two:

1: _____

2: _____

- **Build a strategy to address the gap in these areas—ETHICALLY:** Ultimately, reviews are a manifestation of the culture of a company, so when I say "strategy" here, I truly mean a strategy to help you gain honest online reviews. The rest of this book is devoted to helping you unlock retention, engagement, and leadership strategies that, over time, develop healthy culture, and in turn affect reviews. No review strategy will change the way your employees feel; however, if you feel there's a large disparity between your online presence and where your company is today, you need to intentionally ask for reviews.

- **Ask for reviews:** In your next series of employee reviews or surveys, keep an ear out for employees who are highly engaged—not just those who do good work and love your benefits, but those who truly connect with your company values and live them out each day. If they fit this category (generation doesn't matter as much here), ask them if they would post a review on Glassdoor. Don't incentivize the review. Ask them to be honest. The key here is to ask! Don't assume employees will post on Glassdoor if they are engaged. Many of your employees live in what I call "the zone of indifference," meaning they are neither disengaged enough to write an extremely poor review on Glassdoor nor raving fans who are posting all over social media about how great it is to work for your company. You need to step in at the right moment and request they write a review on Glassdoor. You can build your employer reputation little by little.

 Visit hannahgwilliams.com/downloads to access printable versions of exercises.

"BEING UPFRONT, TRANSPARENT, AND INTENTIONAL ABOUT SETTING EXPECTATIONS IS CRUCIAL TO STRONG PERFORMANCE FROM A GEN Z CANDIDATE."

CHAPTER 4
UNDERSTAND THE "GEN Z TRINITY"

"So many problems in the world could be solved if people would learn to Google a little better," my friend Maryam Salehijam mused during our first Zoom call together. I sat in a local Balkan café sipping espresso and eating a Balkan burek that was far larger in person than it appeared on the menu. Maryam joined from the comfort of her Honolulu home. Having lived in eight countries on three continents, Maryam experienced her early years very differently than I experienced mine, beginning by growing up in the Middle East as a Muslim woman and pursuing her first law degree at 17. She completed her PhD in international law by the time she was 26, but after experiencing the degrading nature of being a woman of color in law within the US, she left the industry to make changes from the outside. Now she is the head of go-to-market strategy for Galliot, a fast-scaling software development firm.

"You see, here in America, people don't speak from a basis of curiosity. Instead, they just want others to reaffirm their presumed positions on a topic. That makes it extremely difficult to have a conversation. As a Muslim woman who grew up in the Middle East, I have people tell me, 'Wow, it must have been difficult finding food to eat, right? You're just in the middle of a desert, right?' If these people would just do a bit of Googling or remember their middle school history, they'd recall that Mesopotamia was the cradle of life and is rich with resources. And if every sentence didn't end with 'right?' with that all-knowing head nod that prompts the recipient to agree rather than push back, perhaps we could have an educational dialogue." I couldn't help but agree with Maryam's position, because I similarly find that most Americans exhibit a strong tendency of listening to dominate rather than listening to understand.

Most Americans exhibit a strong tendency of listening to dominate rather than listening to understand.

This problem is impacting how we discuss sensitive topics such as diversity, inclusion, and even ethics in our businesses. After speaking with hundreds of leaders throughout my research, I've discovered that when leaders of older generations walk on eggshells, they actually hurt the problem more than help. While we will certainly make our own slew of mistakes, I find that my peers in Gen Z are much more open-minded about understanding how to help the problem instead of first resisting it. Companies that don't adapt to the key needs Gen Z has in this important area are going to fall behind the curve in attracting young talent. I call these vital elements the **"Gen Z Trinity."**

What is the Gen Z Trinity? It's the name I've coined to describe the three crucial values a company must live out to attract top Gen Z talent: **Ethics, Authenticity and Transparency,**

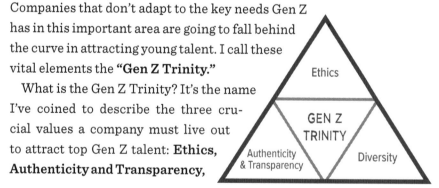

Figure 1

and **Diversity.** Let's break down the values to understand why they are crucial to your attraction strategy for Gen Z, but also why they are core values to Gen Z'rs and should permeate all areas of your culture.

ETHICS

In previous chapters, we discussed the importance of your company's story helping Gen Z'rs live fulfilled lives, and it should go without saying that positive business practices are foundational to this fulfillment. The term *ethics* can be subjective, so for the intent of this section, let's think of ethics as *values a company defines to govern, systematize, and defend their standards of right and wrong.* In other words, we're not talking about broader societal ethics that are illegal across the board—e.g., corruption in leadership, scandals, theft, etc., all of which are important. Rather, I am referring to the code of ethics and values an organization has the power to tailor based on their personal convictions to attract the talent they are seeking and achieve the goals they desire to accomplish. 77% of Gen Z'rs prioritize employers whose values are in alignment with their own, with a key piece being that Gen Z forms opinions of a company based on not only the quality of their products/services but also their ethics, practices, and social impact.[8] What does this mean for employers? To win the hearts and loyalty of Gen Z, an integral part of your company philosophy should revolve around making the world a better place through social, economic, and/or environmental activism.

Gen Z forms opinions of a company based on not only the quality of their products/services but also their ethics, practices, and social impact.

I know some of you are thinking, "Not this again! So now I'm going to have to purchase paper straws or the 'save the whales' Z'rs won't work for me . . ." That's not what we are talking about. To be clear, these philanthropic efforts should always be in alignment with your core values, never deployed just because the younger generation requires it. A great example of thoughtful activism is The Biltmore Company's policy around philanthropic efforts. A thriving company and a pinnacle of the Asheville, North Carolina, economy, The Biltmore Company has a history of philanthropy dating back to the time of its founders, George and Edith Vanderbilt. During my time at Biltmore, we received thousands of requests each year for aid from local charities, individuals, and nonprofits. How did we screen the requests? We took the core values (Community Service, Hospitality, Integrity, Profitability, Teamwork, Authenticity, Quality, and Leadership) and identified the causes that were most authentic to our brand and that would make the most impact in the long run. Eventually, leadership narrowed the causes they support down to a few key areas that the Vanderbilts were most passionate about and supported during their time as master and mistress of the estate back in 1895, such as education and low-income housing.[9] Young people who were attracted to the idea of supporting the local community's education and sustainability were the first to apply! And the ones who cared more about tech innovation or animal rights, for example, weren't naturally attracted to the work of the Vanderbilts because those passions weren't at their core.

Overall, the most important part of corporate ethics is to be authentic with the causes your firm supports. For example, during the 2020 Black Lives Matter protests, Gen Z'rs such as Ziad Ahmed, founder of JUV Consulting, called out companies who posted "BLM" on social media but then made zero changes in their corporate leadership to support their statements. When it comes to ethics, select causes authentic to your brand and then put wholehearted effort into supporting them.

AUTHENTICITY AND TRANSPARENCY

What's one of the most annoying interview questions you can ask a Gen Z'r? How about: "How much would you like to be paid?" Questions like this can throw anyone for a loop, but for Gen Z it's an immediate red flag that this company has an antiquated employee policy. How is anyone supposed to answer that question, much less a Gen Z'r who is likely applying for their first position and has very little interviewing savvy? To Gen Z, a lack of transparency—whether with regard to pay, policy, or the reason why decisions are made—is an immediate turnoff. What would be a better question for the employer to ask? Try something like: "Our pay range for this position is $40,000–$50,000 based on qualifications like experience and education. Based on the interview we've had, we can offer you $42,000 plus benefits, with room to grow up to and beyond $50,000 based on performance. Does that work for your needs, and is this what you were anticipating?"

Being up front, transparent, and intentional about setting expectations is crucial to strong performance from a Gen Z candidate. The importance of this is manifested in all areas of the employee experience—including hiring, coaching, and engagement—as we'll discuss in other chapters. To attract top Gen Z talent, transparency needs to be a core cultural element that is evident from the first time a Gen Z'r interacts with your brand, all the way through their employment with you. Here are some ways you can be authentic in the attraction process:

- **Be honest with job postings:** If you are hiring for an entry-level position, don't require multiple years of experience. Be honest if you truly require a candidate with experience or a more robust background. Trust me, this sets off immediate red flags for Gen Z about the culture of your firm.

- **Don't attempt to relate to us when it isn't authentic:** A great example of this is the push for employers to suddenly have a large social media presence simply "because." I will go so far as to say that Gen Z can smell inauthenticity, and if your company is posting poor content on social media simply for the sake of posting, it is worse than if you never had social media to begin with. There are many small companies who could devote resources to much more effective employee attraction strategies than social media—visiting local universities and building real connections, volunteering in local nonprofits and building a positive word-of-mouth reputation, etc.—while being authentic to their brand.

> *Gen Z can* smell inauthenticity, and if your company is posting poor content on social media simply for the sake of posting, it is worse than if you never had social media to begin with.

DIVERSITY

If you're like me, you are tired of hearing about "diversity in the workplace." It's as if this ambiguous concept (along with the term "culture") has become a buzzword that permeates every HR meeting and conference. In the modern-day workplace, not only is diversity a highly controversial subject, but also diversity initiatives are often politically heated and misunderstood. It has been shared often with me that many generations don't recognize the blind spot they have around this particular issue, so I encourage you to keep an open mind in this section. Let's talk about diversity, and then why it's so important to Gen Z when attracting them to your firm.

EMPATHY FIRST

First, let's have a moment of empathy. I asked my friend Maryam, mentioned earlier in the chapter, why the assumptions people make about her and other people of color are so harmful—after all, they are just some words, right? Her patient response interestingly had less to do with her and more to do with the impact assumptions have on the other party. "When someone makes an assumption instead of asking a question, they are permanently burning a bridge between themselves and me. I no longer see them as someone worthy of time," Maryam relayed with evident passion in her voice. "If that individual believes I am only there to confirm their false beliefs, I can't take them seriously. Wouldn't our conversation be more effective if they said, 'You know what, I know nothing about Islam; tell me what it's like growing up in the faith' instead of presuming they know all about Islam simply from watching American television?" As a white woman myself, I have not experienced exactly what Maryam has, and yet the number of times I've heard someone say, "Women are just too sensitive about how men treat them" or "Black/Asian/young people just don't get it" is all too frequent. To add my own comments to Maryam's perspective, when we believe the media when it says the "right phrases" or "politically correct terms" are going to solve the underlying problem, we are lying to ourselves. You see, most people have a colossal power to be forgiving when someone missteps and says "deaf" instead of "hearing impaired" or "mankind" instead of "humanity"—it's not so much the language used as it is the heart behind it. As Maryam says, always ask instead of assume.

When we believe the media when it says the "right phrases" or "politically correct terms" are going to solve the underlying problem, we are lying to ourselves.

DIVERSITY FOR GEN Z

It's important to know that when Gen Z talks about diversity in the broad spectrum, we don't mean making sure there's one Black person hired for every five white people. **Rather, we are talking about a cultural mindset that celebrates the inclusiveness, encouragement, and differences that every gender, ethnicity, socioeconomic background, physical and/or mental disability, and color brings to the workplace.** In other words, all we're asking is that every individual responsible for hiring celebrate that it doesn't matter what a person looks like or what their background might be, and that the person hiring make an intentional effort to find people who are different from them. With only 52%

of the 68 million Gen Z'rs in the US being white, compared to 82% of the 76 million members of the baby boomer generation,[10] it should come as no surprise that Gen Z expects to see a workplace where their colleagues look, act, and think differently than they do. In fact, according to a massive study conducted by Intel, inclusion is a deciding factor in employment for Gen Z.[11] You see, to a Gen Z'r, we are simply asking the question "If only 52% of my generation is white, then why are 90% of my colleagues white?" Even though there are educational and financial barriers many groups of people experience, Gen Z is asking the tough questions and demanding that both companies and the education system address the root of the issue.

> **GEN Z MUSINGS**
> *Well, that's odd. This company says they support diversity, but there's only one woman of color on their board, which is BS. That's as bad as not supporting the right for women to vote. Don't think I want a career there...*

We are talking about a cultural mindset that celebrates the inclusiveness, encouragement, and differences that every gender, ethnicity, socioeconomic background, physical and/or mental disability, and color brings to the workplace.

OTHER TYPES OF DIVERSITY

Because "diversity and inclusion" is a buzzphrase, here are some factors you may not have considered. Have you ever thought about the skills a formerly incarcerated person could bring to your workspace? What about someone with physical immobility? What about a first-generation immigrant who worked while trying to earn their high school diploma and never went to college? The unemployment rate of a formerly incarcerated person is over 27%,[12] essentially five times higher than the unemployment rate for a normal citizen in times of economic stability. Companies who have recognized this massive labor pool are reaping the benefits of incredible skill and an eager workforce. Consider Slack, a business communications platform widely used across the world, whose coding team is largely composed of formerly incarcerated employees. Through a partnership with The Last Mile, an organization that teaches coding in prisons, Slack created a "quality engineering" program that hires these individuals and leverages their creativity and passion, while filling their hiring gap and solving the difficult hiring challenge faced by so many companies in America today.

This is a wide-ranging topic, but I hope that these examples illustrate that diversity is an organizational posture, not a fad. Organizations that take full advantage of the immense opportunity to attract talent of all backgrounds will not only realize a competitive advantage but also build a brand that attracts top Gen Z talent.

Diversity is an organizational posture, not a fad.

SIMPLE STEPS YOU CAN TAKE:

I'm going to assume that if you're this far into the book, you're probably an open-minded and caring leader. Perhaps you're the owner of your business, or maybe you're a leader passionate about learning how to serve others. Connecting the Gen Z Trinity to your business's future may seem natural—or it may seem incredibly daunting. I want to encourage you wherever you are in the journey and help you think about Ethics, Authenticity and Transparency, and Diversity from a personal and practical point of view each day.

EXERCISE 1: STICKY-NOTE REMINDERS

One practice that anchors me in my daily life is to put intentional reminders of wisdom I frequently forget in places I frequently see. I put sticky notes on my bathroom mirror, the bottom of my monitor screen, and several other places I glance at multiple times per day to remind me of what's true. Here's what I suggest to you: Take one of the phrases below from the Trinity that challenges you, then write it on two or three sticky notes and put them in places where you'll see them daily.

- Listen to understand; don't listen to dominate.
- Do my company's actions align with the causes we say we support?
- I am my best self when I am authentic, and my staff can tell the difference.
- I celebrate the differences that every gender, ethnicity, socioeconomic background, physical and/or mental disability, and color brings to my workplace.

Did you write it down? Keep it up for a month, reminding yourself of the challenge you've embarked on to become an empathetic human being.

EXERCISE 2: INVITE SOMEONE TO DINNER

Friends, I challenge you with something simple that goes far beyond work. Fill out some information about yourself on Figure 2—your race, your background, etc. Then I want you to think of someone completely opposite from you and invite them to dinner. Yes, you heard me right. Perhaps you are a well-educated businesswoman with a master's degree in organizational psychology, living in an upper-class suburban neighborhood in Chicago, but you grew up in poverty and know what it's like not knowing where your next meal is coming from. Perhaps you should invite to your home a recent immigrant who owns a small Asian grocery store and has known prosperity in America but speaks only broken English. Whatever your background, truly think about the person or family you want to invite and celebrate their differences. Get to know them personally! This will impact the way you see the Trinity in your workplace in a much more personal light. Decide who your dinner guest should be by filling in Figures 2 and 3.

YOU:

RACE	
EDUCATION LEVEL	
WHAT WAS YOUR SITUATION GROWING UP? POVERTY? SUBURBAN? MIDDLE CLASS?	
TITLE	

Figure 2

YOUR GUEST:

RACE	
EDUCATION LEVEL	
WHAT WAS YOUR SITUATION GROWING UP? POVERTY? SUBURBAN? MIDDLE CLASS?	
TITLE	

Figure 3

ADDITIONAL IDEAS TO SPARK YOUR THOUGHTS ON DIVERSITY:

- **Engage early with potential candidates in diverse areas:** Some of the most forward-thinking companies have deployed programs to mentor high school students, particularly those in underserved communities. Organizations like Deloitte LLP send professionals to work with these students after hours on their school projects, while building relationships that last[13] and positioning Deloitte as an attractive employer for Gen Z candidates from all backgrounds once those students graduate from college. What if your organization could take a similar approach? Depending on the size of your company, launching a formalized program may or may not make sense, but consider the creative ways your organization could partner with high schools in underserved areas. Perhaps you could bring students into your workplace to help them understand the corporate environment or pay your existing employees for their volunteer time e-mentoring high school students through partnerships with organizations like MENTOR.[14]

- **Consider a hiring program for disabled or formerly incarcerated workers:** Join companies like Slack and Justice Java that build an attraction and recruitment strategy around underserved populations. You might consider partnering with a company like Cornbread Hustle, a staffing agency for second chances that was founded by Cheri Garcia, a formerly incarcerated young woman.[15] Garcia's story is phenomenal, and her passion to help the underserved get back on their feet is a mission any company could get behind.

- **Host a workshop to generate honest dialogue:** There are far too many "diversity and inclusion" workshops that accomplish little in terms of change. Instead, bring someone in who can speak to The Future of Work and shed light on the important Gen Z Trinity conversations, including brand authenticity. Best of all, experienced facilitators can generate powerful dialogue that can create more meaningful connections. Of course, I'm happy to guide you toward the best facilitators in this area—just shoot me an email (see About the Author for contact details).

 Visit hannahgwilliams.com/downloads to access printable versions of exercises.

"SIMPLY PUT, GEN Z EXPECTS TO BE ABLE TO WORK AND FUNCTION REMOTELY AS EASILY AS WITHIN THE OFFICE."

CHAPTER 5
APPEAL TO OUR DIGITAL LIFESTYLE

Let's talk about another Gen Z buzzword—technology. You see, Gen Z is used to hearing that our generation is "defined by technology," but here's what most people get incorrect: We don't actually appreciate technology the same way other generations do. You see, while we may be tech natives, we are not necessarily tech lovers. Just as a face-to-face conversation was a fixture for our grandparents—an afternoon stroll down the street to Aunt Julie's home for a slice of pie and a jovial conversation after school was common (at least here in the South)—so is a text or Snapchat for Gen Z. It's simply part of our daily life. It's a necessity, not a luxury. Because of this, the technological savvy of a company is nearly imperative to our successful functioning, not because we love technology but because it's what we're used to and we don't know how to function without it in many ways. According to research conducted by Jonah and David Stillman, 91% of Gen Z'rs say that an organization's technological sophistication would impact their decision of whether or not to work for a firm.[16] So you might be asking, "What does it mean to be technologically savvy as a company? How much does Gen Z care? At what point does the culture or great leadership surpass the technical savvy as a top hiring factor?" Let's start with the basics.

We may be tech natives; we are not tech lovers.

TECHNOLOGY BASICS

It's important to realize that if an organization does not have a dynamic presence online, with a website at minimum, in the eyes of Gen Z it doesn't exist. Step into the shoes of the Gen Z'rs we discussed at the beginning of this book and consider the world we've grown up in. We don't remember a world without the internet. We are the first generation to witness that for nearly every physical store there is a digital counterpart. In fact, we live in a world where separating the physical from the digital is nearly impossible—when we shop in a physical store, it's for the experience, not the actual product or service we could buy. We'd rather enjoy the physical experience in the store, walk down the street, and place an order from that store on our smartphone. How does this translate to the workplace? Simply put, Gen Z expects to be able to work and function remotely as easily as within the office. To us, a Zoom conference is the same as face-to-face, and we expect to be able to conduct our work smarter rather than harder. Access to technology enables a savvy Gen Z'r to accomplish more work with greater efficiency than could be achieved previously, and we believe we can add immense value to the workplace because of this and help our colleagues from different generations up their game.

THE UNIFIER
KABIR PATEL (19 YEARS OLD)

Take our "Traditionalist" Gen Z'r, Kabir Patel, as an example of how this plays into attracting Gen Z to your firm. During his internship at a midsize engineering firm in Atlanta, Georgia, Kabir discovers one day in the field that his mentor, Pete, is responsible for not only designing major components of the retaining wall project for a new luxury apartment complex the firm is working on but also selling the developer on additional builds, and that part of his compensation is based on new sales. Kabir is surprised to learn that despite the sizable commissions associated with developing new business, Pete does not have an organized CRM system to manage his relationships to produce new business. Kabir interviewed last summer with a similar-sized firm in Ohio that had a robust business development team and equipped their seller-doers with access to the CRM system to funnel new leads into the pipeline and grow relationships. He begins to wonder if he should reconsider his employment with the firm in Atlanta when he graduates next spring...

As you can see, technology is a vital component of attracting Gen Z simply because there are some antiquated systems we don't know how to use or that are less efficient. If you're still using a fax machine, attracting Gen Z'rs is probably not going to be easy.

STEPPING UP THE TECHNOLOGY GAME

Because of the impact of COVID-19 in 2020, organizations had to rapidly adapt to the new digital reality; however, most firms still have a long way to go. Organizations that adapted to the new realities brought by the pandemic began using web conferencing for meetings, implementing work-from-home policies, and using technology to promote safer workplaces for when employees returned to work. However, the most innovative companies are permanently rewriting the rules around where, when, and how we work. This new reality (that for Gen Z was almost expected anyway, with or without the pandemic) gives businesses a massive opportunity to hire globally and attract a more diverse pool of talent. The strength of the new remote workforce is evident in its increased diversity of thought and skill sets.[17] Companies that sustain this approach and remain innovative in their working and recruitment practices will be attractive to Gen Z candidates.

The most innovative companies are permanently rewriting the rules around where, when, and how we work.

TAKING TECHNOLOGY EVEN FURTHER

While they can be expensive, innovative companies are deploying new technologies such as augmented reality and virtual reality to attract and recruit Gen Z candidates and overcome hiring challenges such as the antiquated emphasis on experience rather than skill. Take Accenture, for example: As a software company, Accenture focuses on attracting candidates with exceptional skill sets, even if they have limited experience. Through data science and machine learning, they are able to predict a candidate's potential for success with their company in both soft and technical skill sets.[18] To a Gen Z'r

> **GEN Z MUSINGS**
> *Amanda, look at this! If I make it into the second round of interviewing in this company, they have me jump into VR to see how I'd interact with customers if I got the job. AND, if I'm hired, they do my training the same way! That's so much better than a textbook orientation.*

who may or may not be committed to earning a four-year degree (we'll discuss this in later chapters), this type of recruitment methodology is highly attractive. It also indicates the company's commitment to technological advancement, which is intrinsically valuable to Gen Z.

To summarize the importance of technological sophistication to a Gen Z'r, depending on the industry you are in and the tasks the Gen Z'r is expected to execute, technology is a critical area that Gen Z can assist you in, but also one that our generation expects so we can produce the best work for you. To an overwhelming number of Gen Z'rs, showcasing your technological innovation is important in the attraction process. For those reading this whose firms don't have funding or a supportive culture to be technologically innovative the way you'd like to be, don't worry—small changes can make a massive difference.

SIMPLE STEPS YOU CAN TAKE:

- **Adopt just a bit more technology:** Simply adopting technology that is innovative for your industry, even if it is behind the times when compared to a gaming or tech company, is a step in the right direction. For example, perhaps you work in a high-touch hospitality industry, such as country club management, and want to attract the most qualified serving staff. Simultaneously, you've decided to implement an after-dining member feedback experience, where members can quickly give feedback on their dining experience while paying their bill. A Gen Z candidate will see your adoption of this technology as innovative and may choose to work for your club over others in the region. You can use this bit of technology to attract candidates to your club by featuring your technological approach to member service within your hiring and recruitment. The bottom line? Changes can be small and may require little effort.

- **Focus on culture first, *then* technology:** Don't be that company that thinks simply adding technology is going to attract Gen Z. Tech is just one component of a more robust strategy, despite 91% of us saying the sophistication of your tech will be a factor in our employment decision. Focus on building a supportive culture first, then enhance your firm with efficiency-focused technology. If you focus on tech first, we may be attracted to the "hype" like moths to bright lights, but after being hired we'll see through the ruse. However, keep in mind that we will assess the agility and adaptability of your business based on the technology you've adopted. Also, the level of effect technological sophistication has on a Gen Z'r's employment choices is heavily impacted by region and competition. As any smart team would, consider what your competitors are offering and which elements will make the greatest difference for your hiring efforts.

- **Let your Gen Z'r assess what technology you or they need:** If you're a smaller company without a dedicated IT team, your Gen Z'r may be a blessing from heaven. Ask them what tech could make your processes more efficient, and most will be happy to give you a straightforward answer! Also, ask the Gen Z'r what technology they could use to help make their job easier, even if it's not a company-wide initiative, and it will go a long way. One benefit of the modern education system is access to a broad range of tech tools that Gen Z is accustomed to using and that will translate easily from school to the workplace.

 Visit hannahgwilliams.com/downloads to access printable versions of exercises.

"54% OF GEN Z'RS HAVE EITHER ALREADY STARTED OR WANT TO START THEIR OWN COMPANY, CREATING AN EXTREME NEED TO CONVERT POTENTIAL ENTREPRENEURS INTO 'INTRAPRENEURS' FOR YOUR FIRM."

CHAPTER 6
INSPIRE INTRAPRENEURS

As I write this book, I am deeply immersed in multiple spheres of work. While launching my consulting business, I am simultaneously building a separate brand as a recording artist, working as the vice president of business development for my family's property management business, and building a start-up company with my husband, which we plan to launch in five to six years. While I may not be your typical Gen Z candidate, the message remains the same: Gen Z'rs are entrepreneurially driven. You likely have a child (or know one) who has built a personal online brand and is monetizing it—perhaps through a blog, a YouTube channel, or an Instagram brand—and in fact, this is the new norm for my generation. According to a recent Nielsen study, 54% of Gen Z'rs plan to start their own business and, as of the time of the study, 24% of those interviewed already had.[19] Take, for example, Nudestix, a makeup company co-founded by Taylor Frankel, a 22-year-old who built her personal brand on YouTube and then launched a company with her sister and mother. Or take Dylan Gambardella, a now-24-year-old entrepreneur and founder of Next Gen HQ, a marketing and consulting firm that helps companies create marketing campaigns that resonate with Gen Z. This entrepreneurial mindset was birthed from access to the internet and technology unlike what any generation before us has had and the onset of the "gig" economy.

With these successful side ventures, many Gen Z'rs want to have the stability of a company job while keeping the creativity and autonomy of entrepreneurship. Enter the "intrapreneur." Most business owners have heard the term *intrapreneur*, coined by Gifford Pinchot in his 1978 white paper titled "Intra-Corporate Entrepreneurship," defined as "employees who do for corporate innovation what an entrepreneur does for his or her start-up."[20] To attract Gen Z employees, you'll want to think about this from two angles: Does your company support the side hustles that your young employees will likely have, and how well do you leverage the entrepreneurial talent of your Gen Z employees by fostering intrapreneurship?

> **GEN Z MUSINGS**
> *Is it just me or is it odd I'm not allowed to run my side hustle while I'm working here? Like, I'm not going to give up my YouTube channel for this job...*

Take a look at Figure 1 and check off the statements that apply to your company. There are many considerations that come with the new generation of side-hustlers, and if you checked off fewer than five items, you should do some intentional thinking about whether your company really supports entrepreneurship. If your firm isn't prepared, it could cost you over half your candidate pool. These entrepreneurially minded young people will thrive at your firm and may even think about maintaining their side hustle as a side hustle rather than a way to escape your firm after slogging through a few years of work for you—if you support and encourage their ventures. Otherwise, you can bet they won't lose any time in building a business that takes them away from you. Encourage their vision and they will become intrapreneurs for your firm.

> **CHECK THE BOXES THAT APPLY TO YOUR COMPANY:**
>
> ☐ Do you offer flexible work hours (e.g., could someone leave the office at 3 p.m. on a Tuesday to finish a personal project, then pick up work where they left off from 7 to 10 p.m. that evening at home)?
>
> ☐ Do you have flexible working locations?
>
> ☐ Does your company policy allow and encourage side hustles rather than prohibiting or discouraging business ownership?
>
> ☐ Do you have a favorable policy for how IP ownership is handled when an employee invents/creates a procedure/strategy/product/service while working for your firm?
>
> ☐ Do you have coaching/accountability procedures in place if side hustles begin overshadowing job responsibilities?
>
> ☐ Have you developed an understanding and criteria for how your brand is impacted by the social media of your employees' side hustles? And do you encourage side hustles with robust social media presence?

Figure 1

HIGHLIGHT INTRAPRENEURSHIP

As an employer, you may be discouraged by the fact that 54% of Gen Z have either already started or want to start their own company, removing the most driven talent from your pool of candidates. The reality is that while many Gen Z'rs plan to begin businesses, competition is rapidly increasing as the internet becomes saturated and breaking through the noise becomes more difficult. These Gen Z'rs may be able to start businesses or work a gig job, but fewer will make a full-time living off them and will still need to work a traditional career. I encourage you to see these statistics as incredible opportunities to appeal to Gen Z's entrepreneurial mindset as a competitive advantage for your organization and build workforces that allow Gen Z'rs' entrepreneurial spirit to thrive while they work for your company alongside their own.

Build workforces that allow Gen Z'rs' entrepreneurial spirit to thrive while they work for your company alongside their own

---

Imagine an army of young people who already have successful side hustles or have founded a start-up in the past, using their natural sales, marketing, copywriting, and overall business knowledge to grow your company! Even better, imagine they bring the same passion, drive, and fire they needed in the days of beginning their start-up to your firm. To attract this type of young talent, you'll need to assess how receptive your culture is to them. Here's a basic exercise:

YOU CAN LIKELY PINPOINT A FEW PEOPLE ON YOUR TEAM WHO EXHIBIT THE QUALITIES OF AN INTRAPRENEUR, BUT HOW DO YOU ATTRACT MORE SIMILAR CANDIDATES? CHECK THE BOXES THAT APPLY TO YOUR FIRM:

☐ Do you set aside time for your employees to "play" or set aside time for creative musings and personal projects?[21] (And, of course, do you highlight this on your recruiting pages?)

☐ How much of an employee's week do you allow them to devote to personal development? (This could be reading, writing, attending training sessions, leveraging online videos, learning about cross-departmental functions, shadowing other roles, etc.) Check this box if it's 10% or more of their time.

☐ Are new employees allowed to serve on meaningful committees or teams that will build their cross-departmental relationships?

☐ Do you have a budget dedicated to testing and/or executing on the ideas brought to you by employees?

☐ Do you have a "sponsorship" culture where upper-level managers are responsible for sponsoring the ideas/initiatives of up-and-coming intrapreneurs each year?

☐ Do you host training and classes on intrapreneurship or entrepreneurship?

☐ Do you offer incentives (could be financial, shares of stock, extra personal development hours, etc.) for tinkering with creative projects?

☐ Are your incentives and is your company structured/arranged for tinkering over longer periods of time, without pressure for quarterly results? In other words, is there creative space and time instead of a hurried rush?

☐ If you're honest with yourself, do you have the culture of innovation and entrepreneurship you want to have?

Figure 2

If you checked off five or more of the above, you're doing great! Be sure you're highlighting these important items on your recruitment channels and talk about them at job fairs or any other recruiting outlet you're using.

INCREASE FLEXIBILITY

To encourage a flock of entrepreneurially minded young people to apply for your jobs, you'll want to highlight the flexibility your firm offers. When creating recruitment messaging, highlight the specific ways in which you grant autonomy in everyday work life—but be honest. In order to showcase your company's autonomy, you may have to make internal changes to support your claims. This is an area where many companies struggle, often placing emphasis on long hours rather than intentional, project-based effort, and holding fast to a traditional 9-to-5 work schedule. Companies must recognize that these are "areas of rigidity" that a Gen Z'r will quickly disdain. Policies like this run counter to a Gen Z'r's entrepreneurial drive and mindset, and I would strongly encourage you to carefully self-assess your firm using the checklists above before stating you have a flexible and entrepreneurial culture.

SIMPLE STEPS YOU CAN TAKE:

Complete the Entrepreneur and Intrapreneur checklists in Figures 1 and 2. If you checked fewer than five on either checklist, do exercise 1. If you checked more than five on each, do exercise 2.

Exercise 1:

Choose one of the items you checked earlier in the chapter that you feel your company does very well. In your next team meeting, have your team jump onto your social media, website, and recruitment collateral and assess the company's performance. How well did you showcase that element on your recruiting platforms? Give yourself a grade of 1 to 7 on each element in Figure 3 (if you don't use one of the below, just mark N/A).

RECRUITING METHOD	GRADE (1-7)	RECRUITING METHOD	GRADE (1-7)
Instagram		LinkedIn content	
Indeed/Glassdoor/etc. profile pages		Video collateral	
Career website		Print collateral	
Candidate follow-up emails		Job descriptions	
Company LinkedIn page		TOTAL SCORE	

Figure 3

Add up your grades. Add up the number of platforms you use (subtracting all "N/A" platforms), then divide your total grade by the number of platforms.

TOTAL SCORE	
TOTAL NUMBER OF RECRUITING METHODS	
YOUR SCORE	

Refer to the end of the chapter to assess your score.

Exercise 2:

If you're already doing well in creating a culture that supports intra/entrepreneurship, let's make sure you're showcasing it in your recruiting efforts. If our "Quintessential Intrapreneur" avatar, Claire Beezley, was looking at those channels, would she immediately recognize that she would have these things if working for your company?

- Her real estate side hustle would be supported, and if she had to take calls during work to secure another deal, it would not be looked down on.
- She'd be encouraged to grow with intra/entrepreneur classes and training and be given leadership training and opportunities.
- She'd be given creative space to bring her skill set into your workplace to improve it.

Evaluate your recruitment marketing collateral in Figure 4 on a scale of 1 to 7.

QUESTION	YOUR GRADE (1-7)
How well do your recruitment channels highlight that employees can "bring their side hustle" when working for your company?	
How well do your channels highlight the chance to expand one's network while working for you?	
How well is your flexibility showcased? (time, working location, etc.)	
How well are your creative incentives showcased?	

Figure 4

Assess Your Score:

6-7	**Excellent**—You are on a great track showcasing this benefit! Try a few of the other items you checked and see how you're doing.
4-5	**Good**—You're doing well but still have room to go. Consider posting one additional time per month or creating one additional piece of collateral that highlights your intra/entrepreneur-focused culture.
3	**Average**—You're doing okay, but you should probably think about your strategy if you want to attract entrepreneurial talent. Review your recruitment strategies and discuss places to highlight your company's features with your team.
BELOW 3	**Lots of Work to Do**—Gen Z'rs looking at your advertising likely don't realize you offer any benefits for intra/entrepreneurs. What needs to shift?

 Visit hannahgwilliams.com/downloads to access printable versions of exercises.

"GEN Z'S VOCALITY, CREATIVITY WITH TECHNOLOGY, AND NEED FOR PERSONALIZATION ARE POWERFUL ASSETS TO ANY COMPANY."

CHAPTER 7
ENABLE EXTREME CUSTOMIZATION

No one can put their finger on exactly what caused it, but there is something extremely hip about thrifting for Gen Z. Yes, you read that correctly: thrifting. According to the Association of Resale Professionals, the thrifting industry is growing at a rate of 7% per year and generated approximately $10.2 billion in revenue in 2019.[22] YouTubers like Adelaines Camera Roll, Micarah Tewers, and bestdressed have garnered millions of subscribers and views with their videos about how to find the best thrifting locations, methods for putting together chic and trendy outfits using Goodwill and Salvation Army finds, and shopping online thrift stores like thredUP for incredible deals on unique pieces—even ones that are several years "out of style." Why do Gen Z'rs want to thrift? Beyond the obvious reason of saving money, Gen Z actually prefers to shop thrift because they are likely to find unique items that no one else has—items that will make them stand apart from the herd as their own, unique identity. Gen Z has a need for extreme customization, whether in fashion, music, or entertainment tastes.

PERSONALIZATION FOR GEN Z VS. MILLENNIALS

Contrast this with the millennial generation. You likely remember the early 2000s when Aéropostale graphic T-shirts swept the market as the hottest new thing in clothing. The teenagers with the sweatshirts with "Aéropostale" printed across the middle were the "in crowd." Large swarms of Aéro millennial teens would swarm malls and schools in their matching T-shirts, sweatshirts, and sweatpants, all hoping to blend into the pack. For Gen Z, blending in is quite the opposite of ideal—we'd rather stand out, and selecting pieces of clothing that fit our "personal style" rather than simply what everyone else is wearing is a way of showcasing that uniqueness.

This innate preference for customization translates to the workplace. I certainly won't pretend there aren't some odd, seemingly useless things our generation cares about more than we should, but when we've grown up in a world where brands have developed machine learning and AI to personalize our every purchase and interaction online, it's no wonder those same expectations show up in the workplace. For example, studies are showing that Gen Z will expect to be able to customize their workspaces, job descriptions, and even benefits plans. We'll discuss this more in a moment.

ELIZABETH SOLARU
Director, Luxury Business Emporium

PERSONALIZATION AND THE WORKFORCE

To better understand how this need for extreme customization translates to the workplace, I interviewed Elizabeth Solaru, founder of the Luxury Business Emporium, London, England, and a bestselling author whose work has been featured in *Vogue Japan*, on the BBC, and in *Martha Stewart Weddings*. As a business owner of one of the highest-award-winning luxury cake companies in the world, Elizabeth has a unique perspective on how the newest generation is transforming both the consumer and talent game. "Brands at the forefront of Gen Z'rs' desire for personalization are Gucci and LVMH," Elizabeth offered during our conversation on a lovely spring afternoon while describing to me the brands that have recognized the shift from millennials' tastes to those of Gen Z. "Gucci's collaboration with North Face is an example of continuous evolution," she said. "Their ability to tap into the ugly fashion zeitgeist has demonstrated their understanding of their own foundations and guidelines. They have been rigorous about testing each major offering or collaboration to see how Gen Z'rs react to their brand." But from Elizabeth's perspective, it's not just the consumer market that's shifting rapidly toward customization. She believes Gen Z is going to transform the future of recruiting simply based on their consumer preferences, which luxury brands are already having to adjust to. "Gen Z's vocality, creativity with technology, and need for personalization are such powerful assets to any company," she said. "Gen Z'rs are the leaders of the tribe who have shown their ability to outwit, outplay, and outlast." I believe Elizabeth is spot on. When it comes to Gen Z'rs deciding which firm they want to work for, the more a company can showcase their adaptability and ability to customize the process, the more appealing the workplace will be for Gen Z.

> *"Gen Z'rs are the leaders of the tribe who have shown their ability to outwit, outplay, and outlast."*
> —Elizabeth Solaru

SOME OF THE AREAS WHERE GEN Z WANTS EXTREME CUSTOMIZATION:

- **Workspaces:** For Gen Z, gone are the days of the cubicle and the open office layout. Beyond dozens of studies showing that an open office layout diminishes productivity, Gen Z values privacy and a flexible layout that can change based on their working needs.[23] Companies are embracing "activity-based workspaces" in which the goal is to have an agile office that creates an environment that gives employees more autonomy, freedom of choice, and a platform to be as productive as possible.[24] Think coffee shop with the addition of private office space. There are tables for collaboration, nooks and crannies for solo reading or learning, and couches for a change of pace midday, but also offices for privacy with a focus on solo work, which Gen Z greatly values. The idea here is to give Gen Z the ability to "customize" their workspace for the day, whether they are thinking deeply in their office privately or lounging on the couch to read for personal development.

- **Job Descriptions:** According to research by David Stillman and Jonah Stillman, 56% of Gen Z would rather write their own job description than be given a generic one, and 62% would rather customize their own career plan than have the organization lay one out for them.[25] What does this mean? In the upcoming section about coaching and mentoring Gen Z, we'll dive into how to work with a direct report in customizing their career path, but for now, think back to Chapter 1, where we demonstrated how Gen Z sees work as an extension of themselves. It should come as no surprise that by joining a company, Gen Z is seeking to learn skills and disciplines that translate across roles—they don't want to be stuck in the same career path their entire journey. When we say we want to customize our career path and/or job description, we're essentially saying we want to leverage our talents in many different areas, not just the job we were hired for.

- **Benefits:** In Gen Z's mind, one size should never fit all, and this translates to your benefits package. As we'll discuss later in the book, benefits such as health insurance are more important to Gen Z than to millennials. And rather than office beanbag chairs and pool tables, Gen Z would prefer benefits that flex with their lifestyle choices. For example, the most agile companies are adopting lifestyle spending accounts (LSAs),[26] which annually allocate a certain sum (for example $1,500) to each employee to spend on personal development, gym memberships, or even therapy—essentially any product or service that contributes to employee well-being and health. The company pays only for what the employee uses. This flexibility allows a Gen Z'r to invest in themselves, fosters engagement, and allows them to make their own choices. Again, one size never fits all in Gen Z's mind.

> **GEN Z MUSINGS**
>
> Alyssa, this is awesome! I thought when I first started at this company, I'd have benefits like my parents do . . . they get tickets to a theme park or something. But this is SO much better. I don't have to pay for my own yoga classes now, and I can even afford therapy that I was putting off paying for!

Have you done a bit of mental gymnastics? I hope so. There are many creative ways to appeal to Gen Z's need for customization, and I encourage you to get creative!

Instead of a simple forward step on this chapter, I leave you with a few thoughts as we move into recruiting Gen Z. So far, we've discussed how Gen Z's "NarcisStory" is at the center of our life decisions, including employment, and that appealing to our story in your recruitment messaging will attract us to your firm. You can take simple steps toward appealing to our inner drive, no matter your role in the company, by having a personal brand yourself. We are attracted to leaders who embrace our values and who we know we can learn from. Companies that embrace our desire for diversity, authenticity, and ethical behavior in the workplace will immediately stand out, particularly the ones who tap into our innate need for (not love of) technology and build policies that support our entrepreneurial efforts. You see, each element is a balancing act. Overall, attracting Gen Z will mean remaining constantly relevant or, as Elizabeth Solaru so eloquently put it, "In these times, it's not survival of the fittest; it's survival of the most adaptable."

Be adaptable and you'll be an experienced player in the Gen Z attracting game.

Section II

RECRUIT

"GEN Z GOES TO FAMILY AND FRIENDS FOR ADVICE ON MAJOR DECISIONS BEFORE WE TURN TO THE INTERNET."

CHAPTER 8
USE CULTURE-CENTRIC RECRUITING

When I was 5, my father was a fledgling entrepreneur. Having won numerous awards in Shotokan karate and fencing, he was a well-known instructor in the martial arts world and opened a karate school with plans to expand the business over the course of several years. As a young child, I remember his working late into the evening and visiting him each night in the dojo where he'd stay after hours taking care of paperwork while my sister and I played with giant balls and punching bags. Unfortunately, Dad hadn't yet realized that owning and operating a martial arts school was not a lucrative business, and our family struggled to make ends meet. Dad and Mom worked odd jobs late in the evening, and Mom picked up a part-time position working at Biltmore Estate Winery's gift shop, where I have memories of frolicking about tasting samples and begging Mom for bunny-shaped artisan pasta.

Christmas came swiftly that year, and all I wanted was an Easy-Bake Oven—remember those little ovens that were all the rage? Well, my sister wanted her own as well. You see, Mom had taught us both to enjoy cooking and baking, but somehow it was much more special if we had our own ovens. Disappointingly, my parents told us they weren't able to buy Easy-Bake Ovens but "maybe next year" they could. To my 5-year-old self, this was a major letdown. Little did I know what was coming...

In early November, I have a distinct memory of attending a Christmas party somewhere with massive indoor plants and tall ceilings. My sister and I each sat on Santa's lap and shared our Christmas gift wish list with him—of course we both said Easy-Bake Ovens, knowing full well that we wouldn't receive them that year. But to my amazement, as I jumped off Santa's lap, an elf at the party handed me my very own Easy-Bake Oven and my sister got one too! We whooped with excitement and laughter, forgetting the cookies and hot chocolate at the party waiting for us. It was one of the best Christmas memories ever.

Years later, I asked my parents where that Christmas party had taken place. To my surprise, they responded, "That was the employee Christmas party at Biltmore Estate." Every year, Biltmore hosts a Christmas party for its 2,600 employees and their families, during which the children of every single employee receive a special gift from the family owners—no matter the status or tenure of the employee. This tradition dates back to the 1800s, when Edith Vanderbilt did the same for her employees. My family was invited because my mom worked a minimum-wage part-time job in their gift shop, and because of that, my sister and I received one of the most special gifts we could have asked for, and that my parents couldn't afford.

When I was scouting out potential employers during college, you can probably guess which company immediately came to my mind. How could it not when I was seeking owners and a culture that cares and gives willingly to their staff? It was a no-brainer, and I would have done anything to work for Biltmore. In fact, to this day, when leaders ask me how Biltmore would handle a particular challenge, I sometimes catch myself saying, "This is how **we** solve this problem" before realizing I no longer work there. Biltmore's mission and purpose have become so integral to my own "why" that they are almost inseparable. I like to call this phenomenon "culture-centric recruitment" and it applies at any point in the employee journey, whether it's a child with no concept of what a "job" means yet or an employee dissatisfied with their current position and looking for a change. You can leverage your culture to find exceptional talent.

FEAR OF MISSING OUT (FOMO)

Culture-centric recruitment is powerful for Gen Z. Why? First of all, Gen Z goes to family and friends for advice on major decisions before we turn to the internet,[27] so the word of mouth generated by cultural moments (like my Easy-Bake Oven story) resonates with us. Second, as you can probably guess, a by-product of the social media–fueled world in which we've grown up is fear of missing out (FOMO). Let's see an example of this:

THE BABY MILLIONAIRE

RODRIGO GOMEZ (15 YEARS OLD)

Take Rodrigo Gomez, our "Baby Millionaire," who has been successfully streaming on Twitch for years and has made quite an incredible living doing so. As we all know, one of the natural dangers of being a public figure online is the trolls and commenters who can't seem to let up on the negativity. You see, while Rodrigo is successful and plans to be a gamer for quite some time, he's seeing many of his peers go to college and land exciting jobs that involve traveling. Questions like "Am I missing something?" and "Is gaming all I'm capable of, or could I use my digital media skills elsewhere?" are going through his head. He doesn't want the impact of the negative online presence forever.

> **GEN Z MUSINGS**
>
> *Mom, you know I've got a fine job, but look at what Jacob's getting to do. He's on a cruise ship literally half the year and gets to go to Barbados and Alaska and all sorts of places. I like what I'm doing but I'm stuck in an office.... Ugh, but he gets paid so much less. But maybe I should switch...*

You see, if we witness your compelling culture from an early age, there is a psychological urge to ask, "If I stay in my current role, what am I missing out on at that company?" You can tap into this FOMO, so I posit this question to you: In today's competitive job market, are you missing out on culture-centric recruitment opportunities to take advantage of word-of-mouth recruiting and FOMO?

THE IMPORTANCE OF CULTURE-CENTRIC RECRUITING

Not only can you tap into this strategy as a competitive advantage, culture-centric recruitment is such an important strategy for recruiting Gen Z that I urge any company that wishes to remain relevant in the next five to ten years to be actively strategizing how to get face time with young talent earlier. According to Yello's most recent report, nearly 62% of Gen Z is going to referrals first in their job search. Yet less than 33% are looking on social media![28] This data is quite contrary to the ways most companies spend their recruiting dollars. I actually just joined the board start-up Make a RPL in Johnson City, Tennessee, to solve this problem. They have built an app to connect students with corporate mentors—not only does it help students find dream careers but it also enables employers to find talent in the competitive hiring market, and have a much higher likelihood of retaining that talent once they begin.[29] Let's get practical with how you can implement culture-centric recruitment strategy immediately in the Simple Steps.

SIMPLE STEPS YOU CAN TAKE:

Think about opportunities you have to create "shareable cultural moments" among your staff as an early-career (or even early-age!) recruitment tool. I'll list a few examples below and then let you get creative for what works in your company's unique situation.

BUCKETS OF SHAREABLE CULTURE MOMENTS

"DAY IN THE LIFE"	EMPLOYEE EVENTS	COMMUNITY IMPACT/ VOLUNTEER MOMENTS
Are there milestones your employees are proud of? Professional development certifications? Quarterly goal-meeting celebrations? Think about ways you can encourage social media sharing.	What company events could you invite not just staff but also their families to? How do you include kids in the experience? Here's an idea—if your employees travel, why not encourage families to join them?	Could your organization partner with the local food pantry? What if parents were encouraged to bring their kids to the company-sponsored volunteer time?
Could you hire a career influencer? This would be a young person from your existing team with a decent social media following (i.e., 1,000–1,500 followers) who you could pay to become an ambassador for you. They'd vlog or post on Instagram 3–4 times per week about what it's like working in their role! You'd have a chance to share exciting scenery and how they overcame challenges, and showcase the successes of their co-workers and the support network they have.	What if you have a day when kids come into the office and learn various skills, like balancing a checkbook or handling a client meeting, or visit various business functions? Set up intentional time to connect the brand with the kids. Who knows . . . they might remember the experience into adulthood.	

Now fill in some of your own ideas. What upcoming events or experiences could you highlight throughout your recruitment and attraction process to create shareable moments?

"DAY IN THE LIFE"	EMPLOYEE EVENTS	COMMUNITY IMPACT/ VOLUNTEER MOMENTS

 Visit hannahgwilliams.com/downloads to access printable versions of exercises.

"TIKTOK, TWITTER, AND YOUTUBE ARE BECOMING POPULAR PLATFORMS GEN Z USES TO RECORD AND DELIVER VIDEO RÉSUMÉS TO POTENTIAL EMPLOYERS."

CHAPTER 9
ENCOURAGE NONTRADITIONAL RÉSUMÉS

Recent graduate Jonathan Javier, a self-proclaimed "underdog," didn't understand why he wasn't landing any positions in the tech firms he applied to. After graduating from the University of California, Riverside, he found the job-hunting process excruciatingly competitive, as Ivy League graduates pulled ahead, and submitting hundreds of résumés didn't seem to matter—the application button didn't work. Frustrated but ambitious, he decided to take a different approach. Instead of going the traditional route, he began creating LinkedIn content—both video and written—in his niche. Then he connected with top leaders in his target firms on LinkedIn and requested a phone call to learn their story. After the call, he simply asked to share their insights with his network so others could benefit from their advice. Once he posted the video or story, every person in THAT leader's network saw the content and clicked on his profile. Jonathan then followed up with a personalized connection request, and over time has built a following of over 100,000 followers on LinkedIn! Through this strategy, he received offers from Snapchat, Cisco, and other top tech firms. Today, he's the CEO of Wonsulting, a firm with a mission of turning underdogs into winners and has helped tens of thousands of clients/mentees receive offers from top companies like Google, Deloitte, and Goldman Sachs. The lesson? The recruiting game has changed, and job seekers are becoming creative.

In today's highly saturated job space, it's more difficult than ever for entry-level candidates to stand out. Add the massive shifts brought about by COVID-19 and it's even more challenging for companies to justify hiring entry-level candidates, making the job space even more competitive for young talent. What are some other ways Z'rs are meeting the challenge of getting hired? Turning to all forms of social media, of course. TikTok, Twitter, and YouTube are becoming popular platforms Gen Z uses to record and deliver video résumés to potential employers while simultaneously building their own brand. For tech, gaming, and social media marketing companies, these Gen Z candidates stand out as "go getters"; however, not many industries have adopted this new trend and they are missing out. There are a number of benefits to the video résumé:

> **GEN Z MUSINGS**
> *That company I just applied to said I didn't fit that position but to keep trying. I know what I'll do! I'll create a video about how much I want that job and post it to social media, then get all my friends to tweet about it!*

- **Videos showcase personality:** What's the worst part about a written résumé or cover letter? I believe recruiters and candidates alike would say the lack of ability to distinguish personality and potential team fit from a résumé is frustrating. While nothing can replace a phone conversation or formal interview, a video résumé is a quick way for employers to check for cultural fit and for a candidate to demonstrate their personality.

- **Videos can better demonstrate soft skills:** Understanding a candidate's communication style, ability to work within a team, emotional intelligence, and other soft skills is not easy from a paper résumé. Certainly, if someone is an effective writer (or hires a professional to assist with their résumé), they may be able to showcase their personality better than other candidates, but even this can be difficult to convey and also challenging for an employer to interpret. Countless articles and college classes have been launched to help candidates get over the hurdle, but in case the soft skills of a candidate don't transfer into a written cover letter, why not encourage young talent to use a medium that is in their DNA as Gen Z'rs? Through video, candidates are able to demonstrate their soft skills—for example, footage from their college debate tournament or "a day in the life" during their recent internship—of creativity, humor, and communication style.
- **Video engages more senses:** As the video résumé increases in popularity, technologies will adapt to leverage keyword searching (or listening!), word crawling, etc. However, if your company adopts this trend in its infancy, video résumé will be a welcome change of pace for hiring managers. When done well, they are visually engaging and compelling to watch.

VIDEO INTERVIEWING

In the age of COVID-19, apps like Slync[30] have launched, which enable candidates to record and deliver 35-second video résumé to recruiters. And if your company is extra-ready to adopt targeted hiring practices for Gen Z, services like Jobma have you covered. Jobma allows hiring managers to easily interview, record, and review candidates in a single platform, increasing the speed of hiring for candidates and reducing the immense costs associated with filling positions.[31] Having been a hiring manager myself, I believe one of the most important parts of interviewing is collaborating with other hiring managers to gain different perspectives, but scheduling can be a pain. Hiring via video interview is one of the easiest ways to reduce time spent driving and allows you to make faster decisions.

So I pose this question: Is the traditional résumé the only way? Well, for some companies, it might be. For others, perhaps a hybrid approach between digital and written content is appropriate. And for others, migrating fully digitally will position them ahead of the hiring curve, but also make them an "alpha test" for challenges that arise as new technology is adopted. As you work toward attracting Gen Z talent, I encourage each employer to examine their options and find ways to encourage young talent to participate in video content creation—it's the way of the future.

SIMPLE STEPS YOU CAN TAKE:

- **Consider the future of hiring:** Just like the traditional résumé, eventually the number of video résumés will be completely overwhelming for intake managers to handle. If you want to get ahead of the curve, your company could consider not encouraging video résumés but rather leveraging video in the first-round interview by having candidates submit video introductions. This way, you control the number of videos hiring managers are watching, yet still leverage the power a video offers.

- **Check out TikTok:** If you want to see great examples of video résumés, search TikTok for "resumes" and "video resumes." This will give you a glimpse into the creativity that video résumés offer and the types of candidates creating them. You might be surprised to find that apps like TikTok are filled with great educational and business content—not just teenagers dancing.

- **Test the video résumé (for now):** Next time you have an open position, try marketing video résumé submissions! Encourage candidates to submit a video accompanying their résumé. The ones who submit will set themselves apart from the rest of the candidates.

- **Modify your interview evaluation rubric to accommodate video résumés:** Video résumés likely will not replace written ones for a while, if ever. Practically speaking, it may not make sense for companies to fully convert and instead have candidates continue to submit both a written and a video résumé. I suggest HR teams consider how to integrate video résumés into the existing hiring rubric and how to support them. For example, adding a small rubric to evaluate the professional appeal of the video could be helpful. I've included some ideas in Figure 1; however, I strongly suggest you customize these to your evaluation rubric to gain the most value from the exercise.

QUESTION	RATING SCALE (FOLLOW COMPANY GUIDELINES)
How creative is the video? (Consider: Does it show that the candidate "means business"? Do they use any interesting or informative props? Are there parts of the video that make you laugh? Do they have your attention completely or do you start feeling bored 30 seconds into the video?)	
How professional is the candidate and the video execution? (Consider: Where did they film? Does their vibe seem to suit the professional nature of your culture?)	
How well does the candidate show their values in the video?	
How personalized to the role/your company does it feel?	
How well do the evident values of the candidate align with your culture?	
How well does the candidate express themselves verbally?	
Would the candidate add value to your team (not just be a "good fit")?	
Does the video capture and maintain your attention?	

Figure 1

 Visit hannahgwilliams.com/downloads to access printable versions of exercises.

"OFFERING IN-PERSON CAREER CENTERS CAN BE A FANTASTIC WAY TO ATTRACT GEN Z TALENT."

CHAPTER 10
MEET US WHERE WE ARE

Let's get technical for a minute. For all the non-tech experts out there (including myself), you might share Spock's sentiment: "Computers make excellent and efficient servants, but I have no wish to serve under them." Seriously, though, don't be worried—Gen Z may be digital natives, but most of us enjoy having technology intuitively work for us without understanding all the details, and we greatly prefer to leave the technical details up to the experts. Leveraging recruiting technologies is not only a great way to appeal to the Gen Z talent pool but also significantly decreases the costs and timeline of hiring. With the average cost of recruiting at over $4,200 per candidate and climbing,[32] companies leveraging technology in the hiring process are positioning themselves ahead of the curve for not only hiring Gen Z talent but also hiring great talent in general.

RECRUITING TO FIT OUR LIFESTYLE

Let's take our "Come-Backer," 21-year-old Corban Trentor, as an example of the hiring journey.

THE COME-BACKER
CORBAN TRENTOR (21 YEARS OLD)

Corban is on the road frequently, driving from city to city, a result of his culinary career choices and desire to grow his skills. While he's got a few top-name restaurants in mind as places he'd love to work in Chicago, he recognizes the need to gain experience first. One of his favorite pastimes during culinary school is hopping from local dive to local dive with his buddies, sampling avant-garde appetizers and craft cocktails as he goes. One particularly innovative stop happens to have on the table a "text to apply" sign for line cook positions. Curious, Corban figures, "Why not apply?" After all, he's not set on a home base in any particular place. The return text says, "Check out the list of available positions or visit our in-person career center, where you can speak with a specialist about your career goals!" He's pumped—you see, Corban's never been really into social media. He'd rather speak with a human and highlight his skills in person. The next morning, Corban hops over to the career center. After speaking with a specialist, he realizes that this management team not only operates this restaurant but also has a series of local digs around the area. There is opportunity for growth and even a long-term career, which Corban wasn't expecting. Intrigued, he jumps on the phone to apply for a line cook position.

RECRUITING TECHNOLOGIES AND METHODS

Much like Corban, your candidates expect your recruiting experience to meet them where they are. In other words, not every Z'r is prepared to sit down at a laptop and complete a full-blown application in the moment. Instead, you can put opportunities in front of us—on the go—and pique our curiosity. Here are some tips used by technology companies:

- **Use text-to-apply**—Many companies are already using text-to-apply services for nonskilled positions. While fast-food chains, hospitality companies, and driving services have seen the value in the speed of texting for several years, the majority of firms haven't taken advantage of this powerful method to connect with candidates in skilled positions. Imagine if your recruiting team could screen candidates and build relationships with them over text before scheduling formal interviews. The benefit is that younger talent is regularly on their phones and will respond much faster to an informal text than an email, which for many is perceived as a formal method of communication.

- **Offer in-person career centers**—Yes, you read that correctly—offering in-person career centers can be a fantastic way to attract Gen Z talent. In fact, 54.55% of Gen Z would prefer to go to a school or corporate career center! Contrast that with only 11% of millennials who used that method. Despite the rise in virtual technologies, Gen Z employees still seem to prefer in-person communication, with students indicating that while a company's website is their

> **GEN Z MUSINGS**
> *Finding a job is HARD, man. I don't even know how to fill out an application most of the time... nobody taught me. But look at this! This company has a career center where I can walk in and talk to someone and they'll help me figure it out. Oh, and they'll even help me find a position that fits my skills! I'll head over there tomorrow.*

primary source for information, 51% would prefer to speak with their school's career counsel or attend a hiring event (51.14%) rather than search for jobs on sodial media.[33] You can imagine in the competitive and blurry job market, Gen Z often feels lost in the massive pool of candidates, so we prefer face-to-face guidance where we can connect with real decision makers. Take this a step further: Make dual use of your career center by allowing existing employees to seek guidance from staff on how to grow their career at your company.

- **Integrate AI to automate the hiring process:** If you want to go even deeper, integrate artificial intelligence to help move candidates through the funnel more efficiently. Depending on the size of your business, you might consider services like Fetcher or XOR. If you want to automate even more of the hiring experience and test for specific skills using science and research, you might want to look into Pymetrics, a company that has designed a fit-based recruitment system based on job/skill relevance. As they describe it: Imagine if Netflix recommended movies to their audience based on the Rotten Tomatoes score. Well, everyone would get the same recommendation. Instead, their system—like Netflix—recognizes the tastes of each individual person and recommends movies based on that preference. Rather than assuming job attributes are always good or bad, they recognize that every role and candidate are unique, and everyone has a fit within some role with some company.[34]

- **Develop your people:** I interviewed Keith Glover, a learning and development professional in higher education, whose mantra is "Developing your people is your greatest recruitment tool." What a powerful statement. "You see, somewhere along the way, we taught leaders to pretend they are listening," Keith shared with me, "and when leaders only pretend, rather than truly listen to the needs, wants, and desires of their young talent, they miss key opportunities to generate word-of-mouth referrals from their staff." I couldn't agree more with Keith—who is a prime example of a mid-level leader within an organization who is taking personal initiative to bring the best-qualified talent to his organization—and I echo his sentiment. Because Z'rs are so strongly drawn to challenges and personal development, leaders who personally listen to and develop their young talent will successfully recruit their similarly minded friends.

- **Hire a "career influencer":** If you're an average company, you're likely spending between $3,000 and $5,000 recruiting each new entry-level hire, according to SHRM data.[35] By calculating your average CPH (cost per hire) using this equation, you can evaluate how much your company spends in total on recruitment marketing/hiring:

$$\text{CPH} = \frac{\text{Internal Recruiting Costs} + \text{External Recruiting Costs}}{\text{Total Number of Hires}}$$

Of course, many of these expenses include background checks, personality tests, and other expenses that will likely remain consistent no matter the strategy. However, depending on the size of your firm, you are likely spending hundreds of thousands to millions of dollars on recruiting efforts. As a 1,000-person firm with 15% turnover, you could be spending $450,000 to $750,000 just on filling entry-level positions that have turned over, not including new acquisition costs as the firm expands. These numbers are heavily oversimplified, but the principle remains: Recruiting is expensive. Even worse, for Gen Z, the job hunt doesn't take place on social media! Most of the advertising your firm is likely expending is falling on deaf ears if you're trying to recruit young people.

A CAREER INFLUENCER?

Rather than taking a traditional approach, what if your company were to hire a few "career influencers"? Here's what I mean: Could you identify a few Gen Z'rs on your existing team—it doesn't matter the role—and pay them $15,000–$30,000 on top of their current salary to be your inside influencers? It's not difficult to find young people with a small following of 1,000–2,000 people on Instagram who are already posting content. All you'd be doing is paying them to vlog and post relevant content a few times per week related to a "day in the life" at their job. To successfully execute this strategy, I suggest having your young influencer work with a small team to curate relevant content, and I'd suggest including the following:

> **GEN Z MUSINGS**
>
> *Oh wow! Rodrigo from school landed a job at this company last year and he's been posting on Instagram about it. I DM'd him and it sounds like he's really enjoying it and the pay is great. I'd definitely trust his word over some job board.*

- **Someone (or a few people) from marketing who is familiar with social media engagement for consumers and could advise the team on strategies.** If you don't have someone, I would engage a consultant to serve in this role (my contact information is included in the resource section at the end of the book and I can make recommendations for you). Given the number of posts you'll be sharing, creativity is important so that the content doesn't become boring.

- **Someone from HR.** You don't want to run into legal concerns featuring your employees on social media. I strongly suggest involving a dedicated individual from HR who approves content before it's released.

- **The influencer.** You can try a few. They need to be comfortable in their own skin, and also have bought into your company's purpose, as they'll be representing the true "day in a life," which may include the rough patches as well.

Why could this recruiting method be so influential for Gen Z? First, as we've discussed, Gen Z demands authenticity in the workplace. Your advertisements shouldn't be perfect; rather, they should educate potential hires on the reality of the workplace. Second, they are inspirational! Who wouldn't want to follow the "leading voice" for a local health care company if they are in school for nursing? And last, this method is very likely going to bring you better candidates.

Whether it's leveraging text-to-apply, building AI into your hiring processes, or even using the power of social media to influence your candidates' career choices, you have the power of technology and innovation at your fingertips.

THOUGHT: THE FUTURE OF RECRUITING

Remember Jonathan Javier from the previous chapter? LinkedIn has named him the #1 account to follow for career advice. During our interview, he shared, "Résumés are going to be obsolete soon. The future will be for those who've created personal brands with personal relationships." Even further, Jonathan believes companies will have an enormous responsibility to address viral posts. "Last week, a job seeker decided to 'Spotify-theme' her résumé to land a job at Spotify and it went viral. After literally millions of people saw her résumé, imagine what would have happened if Spotify hadn't hired her? They would look terrible. It would be less expensive to hire her for $80,000 per year than deal with the PR mess. You see, the hiring game has been put in the hands of the job seekers and it's going to be up to companies to respond."

As your firm thinks of out-of-the-box recruiting methods, consider that the future of recruiting is going to look very different as Gen Z'rs uncover more and more ways to get in front of your brand and leverage it to make a name for themselves.

SIMPLE STEPS YOU CAN TAKE:

- **Follow influencers with ideas:** Recruitment techniques and the use of technology are continually changing. Follow me on LinkedIn for recruitment and hiring tips as technology ebbs and flows—I post three tips per week to help you recruit and lead Gen Z talent, including articles, videos, and quick tips. Other influencers in the recruitment/hiring sphere you should follow include Jonathan Javier, founder of Wonsulting, for underdog recruiting, and Lou Adler for performance-based hiring.

- **Open a conversation with Gen Z'rs:** Is your company still using "in the box" recruiting methods that aren't as effective as you'd like them to be? I've given a few creative ideas in this chapter for how you can step outside the box—now it's your turn. Try this exercise to brainstorm ideas:

Instructions: Bring in a group of Gen Z'rs from your local college. How to attract them? Offer them a free lunch to do a daylong internship and networking opportunity at your company. Maybe you have a group of five to ten who come to explore your company. Ask them to come up with some crazy ideas for how to recruit people into your firm.

Give them sticky notes, markers, and buzzers. You can do creative things like this:

- Bring three samples of your social media posts. At the sound of the buzzer, ask them to point to the first one that catches their attention.

- Give them three of your job descriptions. Ask which one is most appealing or which they would choose to apply for and why.

- Have them jot down on sticky notes, as fast as they can in 2 minutes, the types of things they are looking for in an employer. You could turn this into a relay! Have them run to the opposite wall and post the sticky notes and see how many they can pin up in 5 minutes.

- Make up your own ideas!

Take the learnings from this day and apply them to the technology you decide to select for recruiting, based on your target audience. Sometimes just spending time and having spontaneous fun with a group of young people will give you ideas of how they think and what they'd appreciate in the workplace.

 Visit hannahgwilliams.com/downloads to access printable versions of exercises.

> **IT'S IMPORTANT TO SPEAK TO THE NARCISSTORY WHILE ALSO SHOWING THAT THE JOB IS SERIOUS AND STABLE.**

CHAPTER 11
ELIMINATE HIRING NUISANCES

The great thing about a new generation entering the workplace is that it pushes the standards of every company to become better and better. Among my peers, I've developed a list of "hiring nuisances" over the years—in other words, this single chapter will be filled with more opinion than data—and I encourage you to listen to the voices of Gen Z'rs who are living in a competitive marketplace and wish to see companies eliminate these hiring practices:

- **The chicken or the egg: How are we supposed to get multiple years of experience in order to qualify for an entry-level position?**

Have you ever come across a job description like the one in Figure 1? Or maybe your company is guilty of posting one? (Don't worry, we'll talk about how to remedy this!)

ENTRY-LEVEL DATA ENGINEER

Location: Omaha, NE
Categories: Algorithm Development, Analytics

This entry-level data engineer will perform digital modeling, simulation, analysis, performance optimization, and machine learning tasks to support technology research and development. This position will be on an agile team that performs software testing, performance evaluation, digital simulation, and processor-in-the-loop simulation using hardware-acceleration techniques on dedicated high-performance computing clusters for our sponsors.

> *A student reading this thinks, "I can learn that. No problem. It's just building on what I learned in school."*

Job Duties
- Develop algorithms and apply machine learning/deep-learning methods to EW applications
- Run simulations and algorithm optimizations
- Curate data and write automation scripts
- Write and perform software tests supporting software verification and document outcomes
- Perform other duties as assigned

Travel Requirements
<10% travel

> *"I definitely have those! I'm trained in C++ and we used machine learning at my last internship."*

Required Minimum Qualifications
- Experience with machine learning and/or genetic programming methods through employment, coursework, internship, student employment, or freelance
- Experience with Python and C++

> *Then they get here and think "WHAT? I have all the qualifications but they won't accept me because I don't have a master's? Welp, never mind then."*

Education & Length of Experience
- A master's degree in electrical engineering, computer engineering, computer science, or a related technical field and five years of relevant full-time experience after completion of a bachelor's degree; or
- A doctoral degree in electrical engineering, computer engineering, computer science, or a related technical field

Preferred Qualifications
- Experience with Evolutionary Multi-objective Algorithm Design Engine (EMADE) tool set
- Experience with Modeling and Simulation (M&S)
- Experience with Matlab, Fortran, or Ada

Salary Range: $35k–50k

Because this position is entry level, we will have a variety of growth opportunities available. We'll chat about this during your interview.

Figure 1

Does this position sound entry level? Does the pay sound like it matches the role? Millions of young people who have all the skills listed in the Required Minimum Qualifications section do not apply for these jobs because they lack five years of experience, so they are stuck in a rut. Without experience they can't get jobs, yet companies won't hire them without experience. Unfortunately, these types of requirements disproportionately impact the hardest-working students.

- **Experience requirements eliminate a large pool of candidates.**

The "starving student" has been around for as long as the college institution itself; however, for Gen Z'rs, this phenomenon exists on an entirely different level. The cost of college in America is increasingly on the rise, and an undergraduate degree is no longer an incredible achievement; it's almost an expected rite of passage to apply for any job. Students find themselves entering master's programs straightaway to attempt to stand out in the hiring process, or opting for technical schools, as we'll discuss in future chapters.

Another rite of passage? The internship. The problem: There is a massive pool of students who've taken nontraditional approaches to education and, rather than being rewarded for their creativity and hard work, the American hiring system punishes them.

A good friend of mine from a middle-class family was accepted to a four-year university an hour and a half from his hometown. Despite his strong grades, Eric qualified for very few scholarships. To avoid putting financial pressure on his parents, he decided to pay his own way through school and finish as quickly as possible. Loading on classes, he reduced his mathematics degree path to three years and decided to live at home during his enrollment, which meant a long commute to school every single day. To pay his way through his undergraduate program, he took on several part-time jobs and even started a side hustle doing graphic design work for local businesses. Exhausted from studying late, Eric got up every morning at 5:30 to drive through the winding mountains of North Carolina for 7:30 classes, leaving time to park in the commuter lot on the far side of campus and walk to class. Sometimes he'd sleep in his car so he didn't miss class the next morning or a study group for his group projects. After a hard three years of hustling, he could see the finish line! He walked the stage, then excitedly started applying for data/math positions. But he received rejection letter after rejection letter (if he heard back at all). Fast-forward two years and my friend Eric is still working multiple part-time jobs and has not been able to land a full-time position, with most companies citing his "lack of experience" as the reason they won't interview him. Eric had committed the cardinal sin: He didn't prioritize an internship.

I know that many of you reading this can relate. Some of you may have worked your way through school just like Eric. Some of you may have foraged out of garbage cans for food during school or donated plasma to pay for a basic meal. But times have changed—no longer is crossing the finish line with your undergraduate degree enough. I would argue that our system punishes the hardworking, entrepreneurial students among us, many of whom were not fortunate enough to afford moving to another city or the time to complete the "proper internship." I urge hiring managers to consider the population of creative individuals, who shouldn't be excluded from the hiring pool. They should be given a shot.

- **Why won't companies respond to our applications?**

What is the #1 complaint about the hiring process I hear from my Gen Z peers? They rarely hear back from hiring managers. It continues to amaze me the number of companies that lack proper response mechanisms, especially when attempting to hire young talent, who often base their decisions on first impressions. While organizations cite lack

> **GEN Z MUSINGS**
>
> *Welp, I never heard from that company, so I guess that's a good sign I didn't need to work there anyway.*

of time or an overwhelming volume of candidates, the truth is that there are ways to remedy those internal issues and grant candidates a hiring experience that, at the very least, thanks them for submitting an application and lets them know you've chosen other candidates.

Whatever steps you choose to take, now you know the top hiring nuisances from your Gen Z'rs. Taking a few small, intentional steps, even if it's not an entire policy overhaul, can make a huge difference.

SIMPLE STEPS YOU CAN TAKE:

- **Take the #onemorecandidate challenge:** As a leader and individual hiring manager, the next time you've released a job description, consider interviewing one "atypical" candidate. For you, this might be someone without an internship. Or maybe it's someone who has worked at a few fast-food restaurants while getting their computer science degree, but something in their cover letter piqued your curiosity. Maybe it's even someone who doesn't have the required years of experience listed on your job description. Give them a chance—who knows, you may find the hardest-working, most agile and willing-to-learn employee you've ever hired! Every time you hire for a new position, simply bring in one additional person for the interview that you typically never would have considered. See what happens. You might be surprised!

- **Revise your job descriptions to speak to Gen Z:** Here's a checklist to start using for hiring for the jobs meant for Gen Z'rs. As you've learned from other chapters, it's important to speak to the NarcisStory while also showing that the job is serious and stable.

CHECK THE BOXES THAT APPLY TO YOUR COMPANY:

☐ Is the job title descriptive? (Is it intentional? Does it accurately describe the role? Does it embrace the company culture without being "cute"?)

☐ Is the typical "Requirements" section phrased as "How You'll Make an Impact" or "How You'll Make a Difference"? (Use compelling language to connect to the NarcisStory and show your candidate how they can make a difference, not just what's required of them. Be honest about minimum qualifications Gen Z will need to be successful in the role.)

☐ Is the description approachable and simple/concise? (Does it use language like "we" and "you" instead of "the candidate" or "the employer"? Is it organized in easy-to-read bullets instead of a glob of text?)

☐ Is the "required experience" truly needed?

☐ Does it include a 30-/60-/90-day checklist or a way to measure success?

☐ Does it use multimedia (e.g., company videos, a visual job description, visual quotes from other employees)?

☐ Does it highlight growth/professional development/mentorship opportunities? (Be honest here, but highlight what your company can offer.)

☐ Is it honest about salary and what's expected in terms of time commitment? (Remember, Gen Z can smell inauthenticity from a mile away!)

☐ Overall, does the description feel human? Is it trying to be "too clever" or does it feel authentic?

You can see a description that would speak well to a recent Gen Z graduate in Figure 2.

> *The title is descriptive, not cheesy, cute, or inauthentic.*

DATA ANALYST, COMPANYABC

Location: Seattle, WA
Categories: Analytics, Data Science

> *Highlights how the employee will make a true difference. They are involved in something bigger and aren't just generating reports.*

CompanyABC may look like a fashion company, but under the surface we're a micro-economy that runs on data. From product to marketing to finance, every department at CompanyABC relies on data to make business decisions. As a data analyst, you are more than just a person who makes reports. You will be empowered to partner with business owners to investigate issues and recommend solutions for our most pressing challenges.

If you're our ideal candidate, you will be a storyteller who can paint narratives with data along with the investigative chops to get to the core of issues. The problems you work on will be some of the most pressing to our business, ranging from the supply and demand of our marketplace, to understanding the impact of new product features, to optimizing our marketing and inventory operations.

> *The candidate will see that from the very beginning, they will be challenged and must work hard to prove their worth.*

This role will be part of a team of analysts, data scientists, and engineers. You will have not only regular exposure to our varied business teams but also direct access to the executive team, as well as many opportunities for growth.

> *The bullet points make the description easy to read.*

How You Will Make a Difference:
- Be an excellent communicator who can drive the full cycle of analytics workflow, from requirement gathering, to data collection, reporting, and visualization
- Identify and analyze trends and shifts in customer behavior, both independently and in collaboration with business stakeholders
- Have a keen eye for detail and ensure that numbers always add up
- Have strong presentation skills with the ability to create beautiful charts and slide decks

You Have:
- 1–3 years' experience in an analytics- or data-related role (or can demonstrate skill through school projects, internships, and accomplishments)
- Excellent SQL and data modeling skills
- Fluency with Excel functions (pivot tables, VLOOKUPs, SUMIFs, etc.)
- Tableau or similar dashboarding tool experience
- Outstanding communication skills and experience presenting results

> *Experience is very reasonable for the role—notice there is no undergraduate degree required; rather, demonstrated abilities are highlighted.*

What to Expect:
Apply through our website, www.companyabc.com, or any affiliate job boards and you will receive a confirmation email. If we feel you don't meet the requirements for this position, we will send you an email. We won't leave you hanging.

If we think you meet enough of our criteria, one of our in-house recruiters will reach out to schedule an introductory call.

> This is honest. The salary is listed and shows support for employee well-being.

> Notice how growth opportunities are highlighted, but the reins are given to the candidate, with guidance offered.

Compensation/Benefits:
- Competitive salary: Commensurate with skill set, experience, and the position. What you made at your last job should not dictate your worth. CompanyABC is committed to a basic living wage threshold and holds its own $50k minimum salary standard for entry-level positions. This role earns $55k–$65k.
- True opportunity for growth—We don't believe in time served or waiting for your manager to get promoted or leave. Carve out your own path, at your pace—if you want to "play on the jungle gym" instead of climbing a ladder, we'll help you learn the skills you need to succeed in various divisions.
- Individual and team bonuses based on performance
- Comprehensive health benefits
    » Several options for company-paid medical, dental, prescription drug, and vision plans. CompanyABC pays 100% of the premiums for individuals and offers great discounts if you want to add spouse/children/families.
- Wealth benefits:
    » 401(k) option and equity (stock options) because every employee should be an owner
    » Flexible paid time off
    » We coordinate with each other to make sure work and play find a healthy balance.
    » A combination of set and floating company holidays—so you can choose the days most meaningful to you
    » Designated paid time off to serve (jury duty) and VOTE as well!
    » Mentorship opportunities—Grow within your field, gain valuable skills and experience in a new one, or become a change agent for those around you—all on company time
    » Paid parental leave—for moms, dads, and everyone in between

> The stability of health insurance is very important to Gen Z.

Our Commitment to You:
- We will continually innovate and find new ways to stay meaningfully connected in this virtual world.
- We will value your fresh eyes and listen to your perspective.
- Are you a night owl? Got kids/pets/family obligations? We commit to valuing your output, not the hours you put on the clock.
- We believe culture is defined by people and not by place. We promise you'll have a flexible workplace, both in schedules and location.
- We commit to making a meaningful and intentional difference in the community through philanthropy and community outreach.

Figure 2

> This section is a creative way to demonstrate to Gen Z candidates that the company is empathetic. They see the perspective of their employees and are there to serve them.

- **Fix the application response problems in your hiring experience:** It may take time to build a culture where hiring managers respond to all applicants, but thankfully there's technology for this problem. Look into the technologies we discussed in the previous chapter and find one that allows hiring managers to respond simultaneously to pools of applicants you aren't planning to bring in for an interview. The least your firm can do is send an automated decline, no matter how small or strapped your business is. Word of mouth travels far.

 Visit hannahgwilliams.com/downloads to access printable versions of exercises.

> **CONSIDER HOW GEN Z LEARNS AND RETAINS NEW INFORMATION TODAY AND HOW DIFFERENT IT IS FROM PAST GENERATIONS.**

CHAPTER 12
FOCUS ON SKILLS OVER EXPERIENCE

In the spring of her senior year of high school, Malavika Vivek had four choices: attend Caltech, UC Berkeley, or Carnegie Mellon, or become a solutions architect at software company Avasoft Inc. She chose Avasoft.

Vivek had been working for the company part-time while at an engineering-focused magnet high school in Edison, New Jersey. When she was offered a full-time position, she couldn't pass up the opportunity. "I definitely thought about going to college because those schools are all really good," Vivek shared. "But in the end, I knew I would learn more discovering things on my own and working in the real world." Vivek is not unusual as a Gen Z'r deciding to take a nontraditional career path, and it should come as no surprise, considering that the cost of college tuition is increasingly on the rise.

According to a recent *Forbes* article, the average student loan payment was $32,731 in 2020,[36] with a collective US student loan debt of $1.56 trillion. TD Ameritrade has conducted significant research on thousands of

Gen Z'rs and young millennials and concluded that about one in five say they may choose not to go to college. Many others see a less conventional path through education as a good idea. Over 30% of Gen Z—and 18% of young millennials—said they have considered taking a gap year between high school and college.[37]

> **GEN Z MUSINGS**
>
> *Everyone's asking me if I'm going to college, so I'll probably go... but you know what? It doesn't even make sense. Emma's dad, Jim, offered me a chance to learn the brewing process at his brewery and maybe take over management someday. He'd pay me great and I don't even need more school... that'd be awesome.*

DON'T JUST GO TO SCHOOL... DO SOMETHING!

Beyond these statistics, consider how Gen Z learns and retains new information today and how different it is from past generations. I am an example of a Gen Z'r who took the nontraditional path of completing my BS degree completely online in less than two years during high school. Despite the agility often present in online programs, my international business textbooks were from four to five years before my class took place! The information was outdated and uninformative, so I turned to YouTube and the media to truly learn the happenings of international business, digesting the content in micro-bits. What did I do as soon as I graduated? Started my own small international business, of course!

In the winter of 2017, I began researching how Amazon sellers worked through the platform to generate passive income online. While I knew it was a risk, I invested a few thousand dollars in myself, enrolled in an online program, and began researching a product to sell. I quickly realized that the market was oversaturated. Despite this, I pushed through and found a product: decorative floating wooden wall shelves that were increasing in popularity. Competition was fairly low on Amazon as long as I could get a product to market quickly, and I eagerly located several suppliers in Hong Kong who worked with different varieties of wood and had them send quotes and samples. After several weeks of negotiation and product design with the suppliers, I found shelves that worked! Beautifully designed, they were vastly improved versions of the ones already on the market both in quality and functionality. I placed an order for 500 units and learned about international importing regulations, taxes, and how to work with Amazon fulfillment services to bring my product to market. After months of my hard work and hustle, the shelves arrived and customers began ordering. It quickly became apparent that the quality of these shelves was NOT the same as the sample product. Long story short, I ended up closing the business and disposing of the remaining 475 shelving sets. It felt horrible. I had spent $12,000 on a failed business when I didn't have that type of money to spare. I felt like a failure.

But then I realized something: I had just spent $12,000 on the best education of my life. For the cost of practically one semester at school, I had done all the things that schools merely talk about. I had negotiated with international suppliers, learned online marketing and branding, built a business plan, and faced the challenges of controlling supply chain quality when outsourcing. Contrary to my gut reaction, I had succeeded. I failed fast, failed cheaply, and in the process, I learned lessons for a lifetime.

I had succeeded. I failed fast, failed cheaply, and in the process, I learned lessons for a lifetime.

I share this story to give you a bit of insight into the minds of Gen Z'rs. We aren't unique in our trial and error with entrepreneurship, but rather than gaining this education later in life after working a traditional career, we are gaining it in micro-bits throughout our young years and actually prefer to learn this way. We've learned from YouTube creators, Khan Academy, and Skillshare. For employers, this means that hiring the best and brightest talent may look very different in the future. Within many fields, the most qualified and valuable talent may not be the candidate with the most formal education; rather, it may be someone who has spent their life on a journey of learning during their young years rather than attending a four-year school.

CAPITALIZE ON LESS EXPERIENCE

If you are a leader seeking to capitalize on this trend toward less education, more experience, and more results from driven Gen Z'rs, here are suggestions from Scott Ledford, director of human resources at General Shale. His company's highly technically skilled team is often schooled untraditionally. Take Bubba, for example: Bubba is from Corbin, Kentucky, but has become the standard for hires across General Shale's operation based on his incredible technical acumen. He had no automation credentials when he was hired, yet he's become the go-to employee for robotics and programming, having learned during his journey at the company. Equally strong are his warm personality and helpfulness, so much so that other plants jockey for him. I'm sure the majority of you reading this story can relate—sometimes the most unlikely hire becomes your greatest asset. Based on experiences with employees like Bubba throughout his years at General Shale, Ledford's advice is "Don't assume people aren't capable if they don't have a degree." Instead, he suggests all HR teams ask these questions:

- What are we really looking for in a new hire?
- Are there programs we could reevaluate?
- Could we rethink our willingness to train and develop these high-potential employees internally? Instead of recruiting from colleges, could we recruit from high schools?

Ledford's opinion is that there won't be an alternative in the future. If companies do not pivot now toward the nontraditional education paths that Gen Z'rs are seeking, they will become irrelevant in the future.

SIMPLE STEPS YOU CAN TAKE:

Do some spring cleaning: I challenge you to identify three positions you're currently hiring for and do some cleanup. Take one of the job descriptions you revised in the previous chapter! Follow these steps:

1. Take one job description at a time and remove the education requirement.

2. Pull a cross-functional group together of four or five people—not just HR, and not just from the division you're hiring within—then have them read the job description. Have them each write on a piece of paper, without discussing with other members in the group, what they think the experience/education requirement should be for the position. Have them put their answer in a basket.

3. Take the basket and read people's answers aloud. Have a discussion about why each person thinks the role requires the education/experience they listed.

4. Reveal the education/experience requirement HR has deemed appropriate for that job.

5. Challenge the group to creatively brainstorm (with sticky notes or a whiteboard) a few ways the experience requirements could be modified to include a more creative pool of candidates.

For example, say the team is hiring for this role:
Marketing Manager (HR's Experience Requirement)

- Three to five years of experience in a marketing manager role or an equivalent combination of education and experience
- Bachelor's degree in marketing, business, or related field

But . . . here's the information you know about the role:

- The "manager" position does not actually involve managing people—leadership or management experience is not required.
- Metrics are important to the position. The focus is output, not just creativity.
- Your goal with the role is to create personalized, high-touch connections with your customers so they feel your brand is intimate. You need a true connector—someone who can make the brand relatable.

Instead of hiring your typical manager with 3–5 years' experience, what if you could modify the requirements to include candidates like Denisha Henderson (the Unifier)? Consider her qualifications:

High-schooler who has run her own online blog with 10,000 followers for four years and has shown steady growth, creative copywriting skill, and exceptional communication ability. She's never led a team (but that's not required for this role); instead, she has experience delivering results on her own blog and having high-touch connections with her followers. She's teachable, has natural skill and entrepreneurial drive—but she's never been to college.

This may be a true challenge for your team and goes against a lot of how businesses currently function! Try to think outside the box about experience, education, outputs, and what you are truly looking for in a position when completing this exercise. Then, based on the output of this session, revise one or two job descriptions and you'll be certain to attract more motivated Gen Z talent.

 Visit hannahgwilliams.com/downloads to access printable versions of exercises.

Section III
RETAIN

Alert: Companies, our inexperience could be your greatest asset.

> "MY GENERATION DEMANDS THAT OUR GROWTH TRAJECTORY BE CUSTOMIZED TO THE INDUSTRY WE ARE IN AND THE UNIQUE RETENTION CHALLENGES YOU FACE."

CHAPTER 13
RETHINK YOUR EMPLOYEE JOURNEY, PART I:
The Jungle Gym Model

THE LACKLUSTER DREAMER
MINAR LIN (25 YEARS OLD)

Minar Lin is eager to start her new job with a fast-growing midsize engineering company in Phoenix, Arizona. She bit the bullet, accepting a position for far less money than she was making in her previous job, and has made a career transition into marketing. More important to her is the opportunity to "apprentice"

> under her new boss, Molly, and gain access to training opportunities she never had. However, on her first day of orientation, one line of questioning won't leave her mind: "Where do I go from this position? Do I have to knock out Molly's position to grow in this organization? How long will I be stuck at entry level?" You see, Minar is already thinking about growth and the path to get there from day one or earlier.

You want to retain Gen Z'rs? Let's rethink the employee journey/growth models in your organization. In a Gen Z'r's eyes, your organization likely has one of two problems. Either:

1. **Your organizational structure is too rigid.** Someone has to get knocked out of a position—or leave the company—before we can grow to the next level. (Trespassers here tend to be industries with typically rigid high-education requirements, such as health care, PR, financial services, and legal.)

OR

2. **Your growth model is too confusing.** If I start working at your company, I want to know where I can realistically be in two years if I stick with it and prove myself. I need clarity—and often internal education—and specific milestones, where I can distinctly see the specific steps I'm achieving along the journey while making visible progress. (Trespassers here tend to be lower-education-required entry-level positions such as manufacturing, hospitality, and construction.)

At first, these perspectives may seem contradictory, but what I'm proposing is that there is no single growth model that fits every company. Rather, I urge you to understand where your retention model is not serving your business well. Gen Z is not demanding less structure specifically—in fact, as we'll discuss in further chapters, we tend to be less risk averse than other generations, and structure is actually very important to us. My generation demands that our growth trajectory be customized to the industry we are in and the unique retention challenges you face. In addition, we want growth models personalized to us. Let's walk through how this may present itself in practical terms. In this chapter, we'll address the growth model that is ***too rigid***.

Most companies have a growth model that looks something like the following—let's use the journey Minar might have seen as a typical marketing professional in the average engineering firm as an example:

THE LADDER

"The Ladder" growth model indicates that growth in your company is linear, and usually one has the opportunity to move up the ladder after two to five years. After Minar "pays her dues" as a marketing specialist, she has the opportunity for a paid promotion to manager, then director, and so on throughout the course of her career. From Gen Z'r Minar's perspective, there are several problems with this vision of growth:

- In order to grow at the company, often someone has to get knocked off the rung above her before she can grow.

- Too much of her potential growth is based on timing. If someone in the VP of marketing role happens to be close to retirement, she just might have a shot at the role. However, if she's in a director role and the VP just got hired, she may have to wait years before stepping up.
- There's often a lack of creativity in the ladder to encompass her interests. She may not want to be in marketing forever, but her marketing skills could translate very well to other parts of the company and vision.

Rather than the traditional growth ladder, my generation would prefer something more akin to what I call "The Jungle Gym." The firm Minar

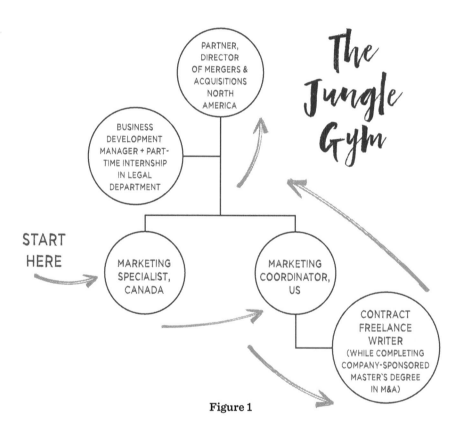

Figure 1

chose to work for offers opportunities like this model in Figure 1, which captures what growth may look like for her.

THE JUNGLE GYM

Look odd? Allow me to explain. For Gen Z'rs, sometimes our idea of growth is not an increase in pay or rank; rather, it's a development in our ability to use our gifts and talents to create the life we want. Remember how important the NarcisStory is to our generation? Well, for some of us, we chose a degree path because we didn't fully understand what we wanted to do during college. Let's continue with our example of Minar moving into a marketing role. When she was compelled to make the decision to transition from a Silicon Valley testing position, she didn't know what marketing roles particularly entailed or the work involved. Perhaps two years into her career, she has developed a fascination with the mergers and acquisitions division of the company. Because of the rigid growth trajectory the firm is on, she has decided to look at other firms where she could be offered a path toward M&A management. You as her manager catch wind of her plans but want to retain her—what should you do? As the Jungle Gym diagram conveys, perhaps she'd respond well to stepping into a part-time role while the company pays for her master's in M&A so that once she graduates, she can step into a role focused in her new area of expertise.

Why would I stay at a company and climb a ladder that, even if I followed all the steps, offered no certain possibility that I would achieve my career goals?

You may be reading this as a millennial or traditionalist and find this type of thinking odd. Why would someone take a decrease in pay and status to switch career paths? Furthermore, why would they "intern" after returning from school? Think back to how a Gen Z'r operates. If I'm on a mission to create a compelling NarcisStory for my life that, when I look back, I feel confident was what made me happy and fulfilled, why would I remain in a marketing role that I didn't love? Why would I stay at a company and climb a ladder that, even if I followed all the steps, offered no certain possibility that I would achieve my career goals? Also, if as a Gen Z'r I need some sense of stability, why wouldn't I stay at a company I love (rather than going through the job-hunting rat race again) if that company redesigned my growth path to fit my needs and add value for them? This is Gen Z reasoning. In Figure 2, you'll see a depiction of the different generational mindsets when it comes to white-collar career pathways:

GEN Z	MILLENNIALS	WHAT OLDER GENERATIONS THINK ABOUT THE GEN Z MINDSET (but confuse it with that of millennials)
If I'm learning and growing and getting to use all my skills, I'm good with jumping "down" the ladder or moving up! If I'm working part-time while starting my own gig, that flexibility is perfect. But if this company doesn't support where I want to go in my career or with my own business, I'm not staying. Can't imagine why anyone would!	It's important I keep moving up the ladder and my title and pay reflect that. My hard work should pay off, or I'll find a company where there are more growth opportunities.	Kids don't seem to be content with their roles. It doesn't take long for them to want a promotion, even if their job hasn't increased in difficulty. When I was their age, I had to work my way up and earn the respect of upper management, and I had to be patient. I got to where I am because I stayed long enough at this company, paid my dues, and worked my tail off, even when times were tough. We need to teach our kids better.

Figure 2

If your firm is to retain young talent, you must be open to varied models of growth that may seem extraneous or downright ridiculous to you. It's part of meeting Gen Z's expectations, and I think you'll be surprised how mutually advantageous listening to our needs in this realm can be for your company. In the next chapter, we'll discuss what to do if your growth structure is ***too confusing***.

SIMPLE STEPS YOU CAN TAKE:

- **Identify the problem:** Is retention of young people a real problem in your organization? You need to identify why it's occurring. If you don't already conduct an employee engagement survey, you need one. This is the first step. And no, I'm not talking about asking your employees once a year, "Would you recommend our company to a friend?" I'm talking about investing time and energy in measuring your employee engagement as compared to others in your industry. For starters, I would suggest consulting Gallup to build a survey that fits your needs.

- **Analyze your employee survey:** If you already conduct employee engagement surveys, great! Now you need to (1) make sure your survey results are categorized by age, and (2) add questions to understand when your Gen Z employees are considering leaving, what is causing them to leave, and what might compel them to stay. If there is a trend of Gen Z'rs considering leaving due to "lack of growth opportunity," you should consider the next suggestion.

- **Rethink your organization's structure:** A simple first step might be presenting the contrasting Ladder and Jungle Gym models to your HR team and beginning a dialogue around the importance of growth flexibility for retaining Gen Z. Any data you can provide from your employee survey pointing to the problem will help make a convincing case as to why you should modify the structure. Once you have buy-in, if you're struggling to develop a model to meet your needs, you'll find there are excellent consultants who can help you brainstorm, or you can even build your own Jungle Gym model with flexible mechanisms. In a workshop, you can hash out the various problems associated with moving roles around, or the possibilities that increasing flexibility could present.

Visit hannahgwilliams.com/downloads to access printable versions of exercises.

> **ADAPT YOUR STRATEGIES FOR THE NEXT GENERATION, AND OTHER COMPANIES WILL BE FORCED TO KEEP UP WITH YOU.**

CHAPTER 14

RETHINK YOUR EMPLOYEE JOURNEY, PART II: Consider the Video Game Model

Let's consider the second problem in growth trajectories—maybe your challenge is not rigidity, but instead that young talent doesn't have a clear sense of direction when they start working for your company. If you're in an industry like manufacturing where there aren't dozens of divisions and no true "jungle gym" to play on, let's look at a different employee growth model—I like to call it the "Video Game" model—which a partner of mine helped me develop to solve major retention challenges in blue-collar positions. To effectively use this model, you need to be a company with duplicates of the same role (e.g., manufacturing, food and beverage, construction, etc.) where most employees begin in a minimum-wage position often without a college degree (but who possibly hold a trade degree).

Here are some of the problems you likely face in retaining Gen Z'rs:

- Your company likely has a traditional "pay your dues before getting promoted" culture. Usually, this means that new hires get the grunt work—cleaning the machines, serving the hard-to-deal-with guests, working long and hard hours with little choice in which shift they work, etc. New hires (particularly young ones) who do only grunt work may become frustrated by their lack of progress and leave within the first few weeks.

- Your employees are likely coming from a rigid high school or community college background where their life revolved around deadlines, assignments, and performance. The pro of this? Your workplace likely revolves around those same metrics! You need people who can work off deadlines, who have a clear assignment, and who are expected to perform each day/night—and your new hires are likely very used to this system. The con? Unlike college, once someone consistently performs those duties over and over, there is no guarantee of growth or advancement.

Let's dive deeper into that last point. In school, your average Gen Z employee was used to completing assignments on time for the sake of a grade. If they got good grades, they progressed to the next grade. If they did this consistently, they'd end up with a diploma. The key here? In school, there was always a clear expectation of "if I complete X, then Y is the reward." The extent to which your workplace may offer this currently is "if I complete X, I continue getting paid." For most Gen Z'rs, this is not enough to retain them. They could work for any other firm that could offer the same promise. So how do you differentiate your experience?

To answer this question, I spoke with Dave McAuley, founder of Summit Leadership and a good friend of mine. Dave is an expert in revisioning talent models and has worked with dozens of companies to increase their retention based on the principles he teaches. He has a passion for solving talent models, and we'll hear from him again when discussing the efficacy of the gig economy later in this section.

DAVE McAULEY
Founder, Summit Leadership Foundation

QUESTION: WHAT DOES THE RECRUITING MODEL OF THE FUTURE LOOK LIKE? WHAT SHOULD COMPANIES ANTICIPATE?

DAVE: I believe that a shift toward skilled labor over white-collar jobs will be a defining factor of the Z generation—and if this is the case, a massive trend of the future will be certificate programs that are company sponsored. If you look around, the idea of certificates is already happening in real estate, franchises, and many other industries—whether it's a pizza joint or a gym. Franchise owners will train employees through the ranks and teach them to run their own business, including leadership skills and everything they need to get up and running on their own. These are the types of models I believe we'll see moving forward in less traditional spaces such as engineering, avionics, or plumbing. Less education will take place in traditional schools and more will be company sponsored based on the extreme need for skilled labor, essentially meeting the demand for labor while hiring staff who can't necessarily afford to attend even a two-year degree program.

Once enough companies adopt the model and implement their own certificate programs, there will be reciprocation of those certificates between employers. If an employee has a certificate from a reputable company, when they eventually transition to a new firm, that company will be able to look at that "degree" the employee has earned and recognize they've "stuck it out"—which is primarily what employees look for from most undergraduate degrees currently.

While the current academic structure is becoming obsolete, one of the problems universities are going to see is that they are continuing to cripple themselves with endowments. Colleges are losing credibility with the next generation because of the handicapping debt that results, their lack of relevance with the modern world, and, honestly, the fact that there aren't as many reasons to attend school anymore. Add the impact of COVID-19 on top of that and the next wave of Gen Z'rs who are not already enrolled in college are considering remote options more so than in the past.

QUESTION: WHAT MODELS CAN COMPANIES ADOPT NOW TO GET AHEAD OF THE CURVE?

DAVE: I'm working with a manufacturing company and a construction firm that are both doing something revolutionary. They're bringing in entry-level folks who don't want to go to college and launching them into a two-year certificate program. For six hours of their eight-hour day, employees are doing the hard labor like stacking wood (the jobs no one with tenure wants to do), but for two hours of their day, the company invests in teaching them skilled jobs—like how to work an excavator, drive a forklift, or do basic plumbing skills. These activities are led by a mentor in the company so that entry-level employees get a taste of what it's like to work in various divisions. Throughout the process, they interact with managers who care about their growth. As the employee learns new skills each week, they get a bump in pay as the company's way of demonstrating they've become more valuable to the firm.

With this model, not only are these employees escaping thousands of dollars of college debt, but also they are doing meaningful work from day one, not just grunt work. They are paying their dues, but the company is also investing in training and growing them. To me, this is a model we've got to look at more and experiment with in other industries as well. In the future, your employee could end up with a two-year certificate in general construction skills or manufacturing to add to their résumé, which could eventually be the equivalent of finishing a two-year program with a community college.

Dave is highlighting a model that I believe will be central to the future of retention and employee journey modeling. Besides the clear benefits he's outlined, there's yet another solution this approach provides. As we discussed earlier, employees coming from school often require a clear sense of how to get from entry-level tasks like cleaning machines to managing people (or whatever their career goal is). Here's where the Video Game model comes into play.

WHY VIDEO GAME?

Think of how video games work: There's a clearly defined set of steps players have to complete to reach the next level. Because of the clearly defined levels, there's a sense of certainty that comes with playing—essentially, you always know you're on your way to achieving the desired outcome. With 90% of Gen Z'rs considering themselves gamers—and 42% of us spending over two hours per day playing video games[38]—it should be clear that any company that can apply similar tactics is sure to have buy-in from Gen Z. Let's look at an example of how a game works. In the popular game Fortnite, players earn Experience Points (or XP) by completing kills, by surviving a certain number of minutes in the game, or by ranking at a certain level within each "play." Once you earn a defined number of XP, your reward is revealed—you might unlock coveted "skins" like Drift and Ragnarok or earn the ability to play against more talented gamers. What if we applied these same principles to the employee journey? And what if we even gamified it? Let's see what the Video Game growth model could look like for a manufacturing firm in Figure 1.

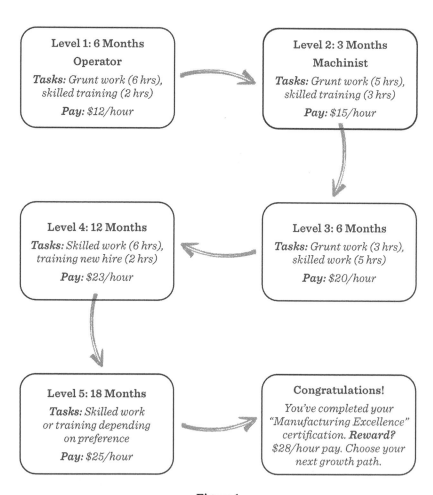

Figure 1

You can even make this fun! Create "levels" like a game would and provide ways to earn "points" that equal increases in pay, access to greater responsibilities, and more time doing skilled work. Once an employee has completed the two-year program, it's up to your team's imagination to envision the next few years, based on your labor needs. Could you have multiple career path options for those looking to grow more? For your employees who are content doing the same job for many years but need consistent increases in pay, could you simply offer a pay growth path? What about those who want to be managers-in-training or seek higher education? These are all options your company can determine based on your unique needs.

Once your team begins thinking about labor models this way, the sky is truly the limit. You'll be able to mold your Video Game model levels to your employees' expectations and your company's goals. While we may be several years away from the adoption of certificate programs, perhaps you can be part of the shift! Adapt your strategies for the next generation, and other companies will be forced to keep up with you.

> **GEN Z MUSINGS**
>
> Gen Z 1: "Man, they expect me to do that much hard work for 9 hours straight on my feet for $9/hour? Don't think I'll be doing that for long. It's not even worth the pay; it's kinda just a temporary thing until I've got enough saved for that new car..."
>
> Gen Z 2: "You should come work with me instead. I'm washing dishes, too, but if I stick at it for 8 weeks, my company guarantees a $2 pay raise and I get to spend 10 hours per week training as a line cook. Plus, I even got permission to start a TikTok channel of me working in the kitchen! Then if I stick around 6 months, they promote me again. I've got my whole plan laid out for the next few years if things go well."

SIMPLE STEPS YOU CAN TAKE:

Take a few minutes to sketch out what "levels" in the Video Game model could look like for your business (fill in the Figure 2 chart). If your company has multiple facets and divisions, think about one position this could be pilot tested within. For example, if you're a hotel chain, think about the path for your entry-level front-desk agent. If you run a warehouse, think about the path for your entry-level stockers. If you're a grocery store, what about for your cashiers? Not every company will have the luxury of thinking this way, but with a little creativity I'm sure most of you reading this paragraph could find some way to gamify your employee journey to grow and energize your employees.

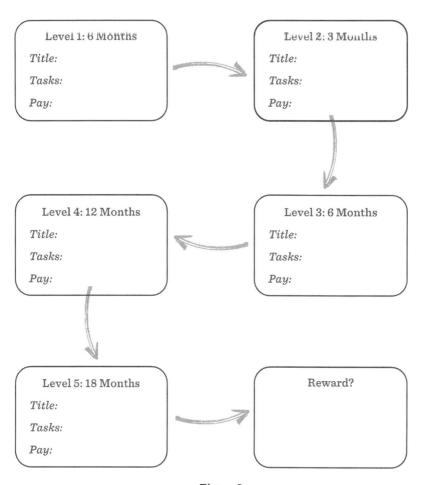

Figure 2

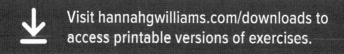

> **IF YOUR COMPANY IS NOT SOMEWHERE WE SEE OURSELVES IN SEVERAL YEARS, WE KNOW BY DAY ONE.**

CHAPTER 15

RECOGNIZE THE IMPORTANCE OF DAY ONE

You've built hiring frameworks that are attractive to Z'rs; now think back through all the jobs you've ever had. Think about the best first-day experience you ever had. What about it was so memorable? Was it the donuts and coffee? Was it the warm way you felt when your co-workers welcomed you? Was it the straightforward nature of how everyone handled processes smoothly and the evident preparedness the company demonstrated?

Now think about the worst first day: What about it was instantly unpleasant? Was it the confusion you felt when you stumbled around the building trying to find the door you were supposed to enter through? Was it the sloppy, unorganized way your boss flitted from phone call to task without much time to listen to your questions?

Let's think about those experiences in terms of today's job market. Imagine you are a young, unestablished person who has hundreds of options—if you don't enjoy working for this company, you could pick up a couple of part-time gigs while building an online personal brand and starting your own business. You could work as a Starbucks barista and get two years of free college.[39] You could even work on a cruise line in the kitchen and travel around the Baltics capturing Instagram-able moments your friends are sure to envy. In other words, your options are almost endless.

THE IMPORTANCE OF DAY ONE

Perhaps when you first graduated, you were willing to give a company several years to let you find your place in its structure and build your credibility with the company. While Gen Z is less apt to "jump ship" as quickly as millennials on average, we've still grown up in a world with a strong sense of FOMO. In other words, if your company is not somewhere we see ourselves in several years, we know by day one. Let's take a moment to review the key characteristics of Gen Z to understand why the first day is so important.

- Gen Z is **experience led**. We are constantly analyzing and crafting our own narrative to build the life we want to have, and we have a strong fear of missing out on the excitement of life.

- We are **realists**. We don't expect life to be easy, but we do expect to be genuinely, authentically treated in the workplace and for our voice to be heard.

- Gen Z is **driven**. We expect to achieve individual success, not be dependent on our employer, parents, or friends to define what success looks like for us. And if we fail, we know there's only one person to blame. Because of the technologically advanced world in which we've grown up, sometimes we are also impatient. (It's the reason advertisers are making videos shorter and shorter: to appeal to our attention spans.)

So when it comes to the first day of work, we expect excellence from the beginning. In our mind, a company should be prepared to bring their best effort to our first day, set up expectations correctly, and be authentic with the experience we should expect from working there. Let's walk through some key strategies you can use to prepare for Gen Z's first day of work.

SEND PRE-DAY ONE INFORMATION

By the time Gen Z arrives on the first day, we should already have a clear expectation of job duties, purpose, and what our journey at your company could look like if we work diligently. But all those items are big picture. You may have presented an exceptional employee package and journey to your new Z'r, but if they show up on day one and can't find the entrance, it's already a poor experience. Pay attention to the little things! Most companies have a pre-onboarding process (if you don't, please pause right now and do some research), but here are a few items you can add to make the experience better for Z'rs:

- **Send swag:** Get your new hire excited before day one! If you want to be exceptional, send your employee a "prep box" with items they'll need the first day on the job, to build anticipation. Include a letter from the team (or you, the manager) and welcome them. A handwritten letter goes a long way with Gen Z, who is used to communication being digital—this will stand out.

- **Schedule pre-day one online training:** If you have online training the new hire can complete before day one, send it to them in advance! Don't have them sit in a room on a computer all day. Pay them to learn before they show up at work (and please always pay for training).

- **Send directions:** If you work at an exceptional company that offers all-employee training in mission, values, and overall vision before day one with a new hire's individual team (think Marriott, Zappos, Disney), you are probably already sending extensive communications to prepare employees for what's to come. If you aren't quite there yet, at least make sure your employees have directions once inside the building—or better yet, go greet them at the very front! Send dress code information. Prep the employee with any handbooks or benefits packages in advance. Help us feel prepared.

CREATE AN EXPERIENCE, NOT JUST ANOTHER TRAINING: MAKE IT MEMORABLE, RELATABLE, AND SHAREABLE

Remember how Gen Z is continually seeking memorable experiences to create a better life? Now's your chance to be part of that with day one on the job. Let's talk about an example of a fantastic day one experience.

During my first year at Biltmore, I had the opportunity to lead the two-day orientation the company hosts for new hires before they begin working on the estate. The first day consists of a refreshing day in the classroom where new hires meet one another, enjoy snacks and drinks, and engage with their instructor on fun and interactive activities to learn the mission, values, and overarching policies of Biltmore. Bill Cecil, Biltmore's CEO and one of the family owners, visits every single Biltmore Estate Staff Training (B.E.S.T.) class to speak with the new employees and add a personal touch to the day. The second day is spent on the estate, where new hires are treated to "a day as a guest." They tour Biltmore House and Gardens, eat lunch in one of the farm-to-table restaurants, explore the grounds of Antler Hill Village, and conclude with a wine tasting hosted by a Biltmore sommelier. Despite the luxurious and caring treatment employees receive from their very first day, what continually amazed me was this: As an instructor, I witnessed employees walk out of day one of training saying, "This is how *we* do things at Biltmore." Not *they* do things, but *we* do things. Stew on that for a moment.

FOCUS ON EMPLOYEE RETENTION STRATEGY

So often in our businesses, we talk about converting our customers and clients into "raving fans," and we mull over strategies that move the needle on customer loyalty only minute percentages. Why don't we take the time to be just as strategic about our employees? What if every new hire you brought on from day one identified with your mission and values as their own? What if you could build a culture where even 50% of your employees walked into work every day with the mindset of "I'm here to accomplish my very own goals, which align with the mission of this company, and every day I leave, I know I've made the world a little better"? How would that impact your retention? What about your overall employee happiness? What about your bottom line?

Of course, this principle does not just apply to Gen Z but to humanity, as we are all seeking to fulfill a greater purpose in life. However, as we'll see in subsequent chapters, speaking to the purpose and fulfillment in work is becoming even more crucial as a retention and engagement tool for Generation Z. Think about it: When a young generation experiences the stresses we have early on, we grow up a little bit faster. A company that can connect with young people early in their journey and make a lasting impression will leave a legacy. Even if you don't give a child the Christmas gift of their dreams, as Biltmore did for me, you can still instill authentic care in your culture and you will build loyalty as a powerful recruiting and retention platform for your firm. I promise.

Here are some creative ways I've seen companies create experiences for young talent:

- Send a $5 coffee or tea gift card specifically so we can pick up a drink on the way to training. Food and drinks make any first day better.

- Gamify orientation! There are fantastic resources available on how to gamify training and teach adult learners effectively. One of my favorites is the book *Adult Learning: Linking Theory and Practice* by Sharan B. Merriam and Laura L. Bierema. Besides having an instructive and enjoyable education period, you can even leverage technologies like the live quiz app Kahoot to create quiz competitions that make the day more fun. Depending on the age makeup of your orientation (this will likely only work if you have mostly Z'rs in the room), split the class into a few groups and have them make competing TikTok videos role-playing what they've learned! (If you don't know where to start with this, your Gen Z class likely will.) Focus on what's trending on TikTok—it could be "a day at work" or even "shock factor." The group that gets the most combined likes in one hour wins. You can even create a unique hashtag that's used just for social content your employees create.

- Set the stage by appealing to our FOMO. I trained new hires for three years and was used to the sluggish way employees walked in for what they presumed would be a boring orientation. They'd slump down in their seats with a coffee, ready to drudge through the day. Instead of "here's where the bathrooms are," I led off by asking this question: "Do you know how rare it is that you're sitting in this room? Take a guess at how many applications we receive every year." Students would respond. "1,500? 500?" Then I'd ask, "And out of those, how many employees do you think we hire?" Usually, they'd guess a lower number: "200? 150?" When I revealed that Biltmore received over 18,500 applications per year and out of those fewer than 400 were hired, you should witness the look of surprise on their faces. "You are part of the 2.1%." A definite attention-grabber.

> **GEN Z MUSINGS**
> Dude, you won't believe how amazing it is I got this job! They only hire 2% of the people who apply. I had no idea...

- This goes without saying, but: Treat us like adults. Set the stage for training to be a fun, interactive time of learning, not time to pore over a manual. And don't forget the small things! A nice catered lunch, snacks throughout, and interactive group activities can go a long way in breaking up the day and helping us feel special.

If you can make orientation memorable, trust me, you'll have us talking to our friends about it. You'll have us generating hype around it. And best of all, you'll have young employees who become raving fans of your company and whose core mission and purpose are the same as that of your business.

SIMPLE STEPS YOU CAN TAKE:

- Pick one of the onboarding practices we've discussed that you aren't using yet. If you aren't HR staff and don't have the power to make sweeping changes across the organization, at least practice what you can on a small scale! Maybe for you, it just means taking half a day to truly introduce your new hire to the team, walk the facility with them, and get to know them, instead of just jumping straight into on-the-job training. It can make a massive difference.

- If you already have a formalized and effective training structure, consider integrating some Gen Z–specific experiences. Have you gamified your learning or is it still in textbooks? Are you discussing growth opportunities with your employees from day one in front of the entire cohort? How about this: Do HR/T&D trainers do all the training or do you have employees from different divisions get involved? This can be a great cross-training opportunity for operational employees and can speak volumes to the passion your employees carry, which is appealing to Gen Z.

 Visit hannahgwilliams.com/downloads to access printable versions of exercises.

"YOUR GEN Z'R NEEDS TO KNOW THAT YOU UNDERSTAND THEIR PERSPECTIVE AND ARE ON THEIR SIDE!"

CHAPTER 16
PERFECT THE FIRST WEEK

Your new hire has now been through overall orientation. They know your company's vision and direction, and they feel empowered to begin work. It's time for them to spend a full day with their manager and team. As we discussed in the previous chapter, it can be tempting to thrust your new hire into the work immediately—that is what you're paying them for—but this is not how you build loyalty and confidence with Gen Z. Your new hire needs to know you have their best interests in mind from day one and that you are vested in their overall well-being, not just how they'll perform for your company. How can you build this sort of trust from the very start, beyond being a kind and genuine person? It all begins with alignment.

In *The Alliance: Managing Talent in the Networked Age* by Reid Hoffman, the author describes several key ingredients to retaining and nurturing any talent, not just Gen Z'rs. The principles he shares are relevant to any generation,[40] and will make a major difference for your company when hiring young people because we are more apt to leave quickly if we don't see ourselves thriving in the future. Based on principles from *The Alliance*, let's continue the employee journey through day one and discuss what a manager should do to build rapport with the Gen Z'r.

SET EXPECTATIONS UP FRONT

If your company is focused on building a highly successful team of young people, your Gen Z'r needs to know that you understand their perspective and are on their side! Sit down with your young new hire on the first day (over coffee or lunch is a great idea) and set expectations up front with them. One of the most senseless lies many leaders have been led to believe is that you can somehow manipulate your young hire into feeling staunchly loyal to a company by vaguely alluding to how far they might be able to scale the company ladder if they stick with it. Gen Z'rs can smell the inauthenticity of this tactic and the often-empty promises of growth. Instead, you'll build commitment and genuine trust with your new hire by validating their expectations of tenure.

THE UNIFIER

DENISHA HENDERSON (17 YEARS OLD)

You're having a conversation with Denisha Henderson. In the four years since we met her in the introduction, she has graduated from college and is working for a small nonprofit while studying for her LSAT. Her side-hustle blog is growing, but she's chosen to pursue a more traditional path, at least for now. Her intuitive manager, understanding that Denisha has goals far beyond the business, sits her down during the first week and reveals her expectations candidly. "I don't expect you to stay here forever," she shares. "In fact, even if you are here for only a couple of years, I want to support you and be by your side for however long you're with us. When you choose to move on, I hope what you've learned here prepares you for the next step in your journey, including law school! I'm on your side and I know you'll give 110% effort every day that you're with us. That's the reason I hired you."

By having this conversation, Denisha's manager has done several important things: (1) She is openly committing to developing the whole person she is mentoring, not just nurturing her skills for the company's benefit, which will build immediate trust with the new hire. (2) In Denisha's mind, she's thinking, "Wow, my manager understands me and my goals. She's invested in me, not just what the nonprofit can extract from me." (3) If her manager continually reinforces this sentiment, Denisha will not hesitate to tell her when she is considering transitioning to another role/company. Her manager will have the opportunity to get advance notice of the transition or to help guide her toward another opportunity within the company that better suits her skills and growth.

> **GEN Z MUSINGS**
>
> *If I choose to leave this company, I'm definitely going to give them as much notice as I can. I want to help them find a replacement even. My manager obviously cares about me.*

SET PERFORMANCE EXPECTATIONS

Clarity is kindness. The expectations of some roles are clearly defined—for a salesperson, numbers and metrics dictate your performance—however, for many roles, success or failure in the eyes of a manager is less clearly defined. It's up to you as a coach to articulate expectations and set up a review process by which Gen Z can measure their performance. As we'll discuss in later chapters, Gen Z is used to constant feedback and attention based on the performance of their social media content, and they expect some sort of scoreboard at work. You'll want to lay some ground rules starting on day two.

- Let your new hire know how frequently reviews will be conducted and how often you'll touch base (weekly/biweekly/monthly) to discuss projects and review goals.
- Show them the framework for the review up front. What metrics are involved? How will success be measured?
- Try a creative idea. Together, build a "success statement" that you mutually agree to within the first week. Each time you meet for coaching, review this statement and see if you're still focused on the goal together.
- Ask the Z'r what they think about the review process. Is the feedback often enough? Do they prefer formal reviews or just casual conversation?

LABEL THEIR FEARS

This is likely the first full-time job for the Gen Z'rs on your team. It's early in their career, at least, and they may not know what to expect from the workplace. By allaying the fears that your Gen Z hire might have, you help build trust from the start and minimize any misunderstandings that may arise. On the flip side, you may find your Gen Z'r has a misconception of the workplace after watching *The Office*! As odd as that sounds, Gen Z religiously follows *The Office*, influenced by celebrities like singer Billie Eilish, who swears the show is her therapy and even has episodes memorized.[41] Either way, you're bound to run into some possibly devastatingly funny misconceptions and fears that Gen Z has about work life. Of course, there are legitimate fears you may want to address (read your audience!) on the first day with your Z'r.

MINOR CONCERNS	COMMON CONCERNS	GEN Z'R FEARS
What counts as "office casual"? Can I wear a beanie and Crocs? Am I going to misstep somehow and create a bad impression?	Did my education actually prepare me for my job? Am I going to get fired because I don't have some technical expertise they assume I do?	How will the company respond if I'm running a side hustle? (See Chapter 6 on this topic.)
Which will my manager value more: the time I physically spend at work or the projects/tasks I complete?	What if I don't appear intelligent and I'm not taken seriously?	Can I feel safe at work? How does my company handle sexual harassment claims? Will they believe me if something happens? What about the security of the building?
Is there a cultural expectation that I work outside of normal business hours?	If I have a question, who do I turn to? Especially if it's a "stupid" question . . .	How will my manager and this company support/respect my mental health priorities? What about stress management?

At your lunch date, take the time to say, "Other new folks I've managed at work here have wanted me to guide them in knowing what to expect, so I want to be that listening ally for you. If you're concerned about things like 'Does our team expect me to work outside of business hours?' let's address those right now. We'll learn along the way as we get used to each other's working styles." If you take the initiative to put one fear on the table, they might bring up others they have, and you'll start off on the right foot. By labeling your Gen Z'rs' fears up front, you're demonstrating that you know what it's like to be in their shoes and that you have empathy for their situation. This is powerful.

CO-CREATE A 90-DAY PLAN

Within the first week on the job, it would behoove you and your Z'r to co-create a 90-day plan. There is a plethora of external resources on how to execute an effective one, so we won't dive into specifics here. What I will touch on are the elements you should include in the plan to make it successful for a Gen Z'r. Many 90-day plans focus only on metrics, but to fully engage your Gen Z'r you'll want to not only include tasks and skills they need to learn but also integrate ways to build relationships with other employees and organically create organizational buy-in.

- **Let us build our own plan:** While most managers have employees co-create a plan, take note of Gen Z's driven, do-it-yourself (DIY) nature, and let us draw up our first iteration of what our goals and ideas would be. Then meet with us to make changes and finalize the plan.

- **Include mentoring:** Mentoring is important in helping Gen Z connect the dots between their university experience and the workplace, and many large companies have senior-level employees mentor young talent. For example, IMC Trading in Chicago pairs new hires with a senior-level employee for an apprenticeship of sorts, where the mentor helps their mentee problem-solve in areas in which school didn't train them. Anytime they have a question, that senior mentor is a point person and trainer. Companies embracing mentorship will go far with Gen Z. However, to play into Gen Z's independent, driven nature and help us not only learn the ropes but also buy into the company's purpose (and find our own purpose), consider expanding your mentorship program. Here's what a successful mentoring cycle might look like for Gen Z:

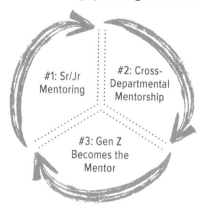

Let's walk through these steps. Start the 90-day plan with senior/junior mentorship. This senior-level leader and mentor might be you, but better yet it's an experienced peer who can help your new hire walk the ropes. At 45–60 days (depending on your company's function and training cycle), expand your new hire's perspective by giving them cross-departmental exposure and mentorship. Pair them with someone from another division that impacts the one they serve and help build cross-departmental empathy, or at least cross-functional understanding. Even better than the technical understanding your Z'r will gain is the network they will develop across the company, which will serve them well in their role.

Depending on the complexity of the work your Gen Z'r will be completing, or the role they've been hired for, as well as their personality, at 90–120 days your Z'r may be ready to "learn by instructing" and mentor someone new coming into the company. Help them become a co-mentor. As we all know, teaching is frequently the best way to learn, and while your Z'r shouldn't be fully responsible for mentoring a newcomer (they are still learning the ropes themselves!), they may add immense value as a co-mentor or someone who helps bridge the gap for the new hire. Some of the responsibilities of the co-mentor might include (1) scheduling a company-paid solo coffee with a new hire at the end of their first week and answering seemingly "stupid" questions that the newcomer may not be comfortable asking their boss, (2) learning to instruct parts of new-hire orientation (if your orientation is formal), and/or (3) serving on committees that are involved with cross-departmental initiatives like health and wellness, safety, etc. As long as your Z'r knows why they are receiving and giving mentorship, you have a powerful opportunity to engage them in the first three to four months in multiple facets of the company, and even have them begin embodying and training others on your culture early on. This is a powerful retention tool.

- **Help us network:** What's going to keep a Z'r engaged the longest at your company? It's not the gimmicks, swag, or free food, although those are fun. More so than millennials, Gen Z craves human interaction and authentic community.[42] So if you want to keep us at your firm, help us construct a spiderweb of meaningful relationships. You need to give your Gen Z'r an outside lens if your company is multidepartmental or even geographically diverse. In the first 90 days, facilitate meetings between your Z'r (whether over Zoom or in person) two times per month with employees at different levels serving in varying roles in the company. If your Z'r can say, "I've got a friend at work," not just on their inner team but also in other regions or departments, you are much more likely to create buy-in and less likely to lose them in the crucial first three months.

- **Know our story:** As my friend Mark Hecht would say: "The best coaches continually nurture interest in human stories—it is not the job of those we lead necessarily to be interesting people, but it is our daily commitment to be interested in each of them." Mark, the internationally bestselling author of *Revealing the Invisible: Coaching the People You Lead to Discover, Learn, and Grow*, helps coaches bring out the best in their staff. "People like working for real people," he continued, "and the more they know your story, the more they know that you have experienced success, joy, failure, and disappointment, just as they have." These points of connection are crucial to build with your Z'r staff from week one.

By the time your new hire's first week on the job is completed, they should feel energized and excited to be on your team but also healthily challenged to improve themselves and learn. Like an overture to a musical, this week sets the tone—whether invigorating and thrilling or tinged with carelessness and monotony—for both the Z'r and the leader, and you are the first violinist.

Like an overture to a musical, this week sets the tone—whether invigorating and thrilling or tinged with carelessness and monotony—for both the Z'r and the leader, and you are the first violinist.

SIMPLE STEPS YOU CAN TAKE:

Do you have a new hire starting at your firm? Test out these first-week practices and check the box once you've accomplished each task. (Remember: Refer to the appropriate chapter for specific examples of how to engage in these conversations.)

WEEK 1 CHECKLIST:
- ☐ Set expectations up front
  - ○ Tenure
  - ○ Learning & Development/Growth Opportunities (i.e., Help them think about their long-term success at the company)
  - ○ Performance Expectations (i.e., How will reviews be conducted? How often? How is success measured?)
- ☐ Introduce candidate to colleagues (i.e., Help them feel connected from the start, introduce them to others in the building they won't directly work with as well!)
- ☐ Label their fears—Truly understand what concerns they are entering the workplace with
  - ○ Discuss minor, normal, and major concerns they might have
  - ○ Ask the candidate if they have questions or any concerns they need to address—no question is stupid!
- ☐ Co-create a 90-day plan
  - ○ Walk through the 90-day plan process
  - ○ Have the candidate create their own plan
  - ○ Review the plan, tweak, and add thoughts
- ☐ Agree on a plan for success and set times to review
  - ○ Discuss mentorship opportunities (i.e., Are they interested in learning about a certain area of the company? Have they been assigned a mentor? Would they like to be a mentor themselves at some point?)

 Visit hannahgwilliams.com/downloads to access printable versions of exercises.

> "AN INTENTIONAL AND CARING MENTOR MAKES ALL THE DIFFERENCE IN HELPING GEN Z TRANSITION TO THE WORKPLACE."

CHAPTER 17
BRIDGE THE COLLEGE-TO-WORKPLACE GAP

THE TRADITIONALIST
KABIR PATEL (19 YEARS OLD)

Kabir Patel stares at the massive concrete building in front of him. To any onlooker, it would seem he's overwhelmed by the size, the height, or perhaps the buzz of activity. But in Kabir's head, it's actually what this building symbolizes. As a new junior project manager at Dynamic, Inc., in Dayton, Ohio, newly graduated from North Carolina State University, he's filled with excited anticipation on his first day—but more so, nerves. He believes his education has prepared him for any number of technical challenges, but what if he doesn't fit the team? What if he's asked to give presentations? Feigning confidence, he struts forward and opens the heavy entry door . . .

To prepare for new recruits like Kabir, the HR team at Dynamic has been brainstorming how to address the soft skills many students lack, just like most HR teams around the world.[43] There is a plethora of resources that employers can take advantage of to solve these challenges—some companies have chosen to invest in specialized training programs for young talent, as we'll discuss in later chapters, or partner with colleges to fill the skill gap. However, some of the larger questions that many leaders are asking seem to be: "Why does my new hire have to be told exactly what to do?" and the inevitable "Why do some college graduates think they know everything and aren't willing to adapt to the ways we've always done things?" In this chapter, I want to take a moment to dissect the pathway of today's student from college to the workplace, and I hope this will help build empathy on both sides.

THE SKILLS GAP GETTING LARGER?

It's no secret that the pace of change is widening the soft-skills gap. In fact, a report by Wiley revealed that the skills gap increased 12% from 2018 to 2019 according to the 600 HR executives surveyed.[44] To understand how organizations are helping leaders build the bridge from college to the workplace, from the perspective of a well-respected leader, I interviewed Ann Ashley, former vice president of talent and organizational development for The Biltmore Company. During my time at Biltmore, Ann founded and led Biltmore's corporate internship program, a highly selective program for high-potential young leaders. Over her 36-year tenure at the company, this program built a successful talent pipeline for innovation and leadership for Biltmore in all areas of the company, from marketing to horticulture operations. Recently, she founded the consulting firm Laurel Branch Perspectives, where she coaches executives and high-potential young people. From her Montreat, North Carolina, home, with glorious views sweeping the background of the Zoom meeting, she shared her heart for students with me.

ANN ASHLEY
Former VP of Talent and Organizational Development, The Biltmore Company

"In your work over the years with students, what have you found to be the greatest disconnects between the college experience and the workplace?" I posed to Ann, laughing a little as I recollected the most interesting Biltmore stories. "And what skills are students lacking that workplaces expect them to have? I'm sure you've come across quite a few..."

"With a student, when they must shift gears from someone who is learning and mastering content to being someone who is having to execute and live it, there are always challenges," Ann responded gently. I recalled how patient Ann had been when I first arrived at Biltmore with unrealistic expectations and overzealous confidence. "It's one thing to sit in a classroom and master a topic—whether it's finance, business, or accounting—but when you actually have to use it, and function on a team full of people who are also masters of that topic, you almost have to 'get your sea legs.'" I laughed, remembering the time I waltzed out of my inventory management class while interning in her division, and quickly thought I could reorganize the inventory ordering system for the office. I was devastated when my manager told me the system was overly complicated, but she appreciated the initiative—I had tried to implement protocols for a large warehouse in a 20-person office. Ann continued, "I don't see this just as a generation-specific challenge. The key is really mastering yourself. If you've mastered the content of the classroom, or later in life have mastered the 'content' of that new work situation, you have to figure it out and ask questions; and as humans, we aren't naturally good at asking questions. The gap can sometimes be that an individual is simply not equipped to take a deeper look at themselves, at the workplace, and continue to learn."

"That resonates with me deeply," I shared with Ann. "It was challenging for me to shift gears from having to prove myself in college to humbling myself in order to learn from the experts at work. Do you think the way students are taught to 'build our own résumé' all throughout high school and college in order to land the best scholarships, get accepted to the best colleges, etc., has dampened our ability to ask good questions? And how does that impact the workplace?"

Ann nodded in agreement, recalling the rigorous competition her students face, and responded, "I think you're really on the right trail with that. What every part of school teaches us, especially if that young person was very successful in school, is to build up their reputation of success and accolades. Suddenly they must shift gears and be humble again." Thinking back to my early days at Biltmore, I tried to remember how I had overcome that challenge. I believe the most impactful element was that my team allowed me to take Biltmore Leadership Training very early on. In these courses, mid-level managers were given leadership books to read and were taught principles of servant leadership. When I witnessed that even professionals 15 or 30 years into their career maintained an attitude of humility, I couldn't help but admire them and seek to emulate them. Ann continued, "Maintaining curiosity throughout our careers is a valuable part of our success. So how do students find the comfort to be curious? It all comes down to the role of a mentor. This mentor should be someone the young person feels comfortable talking to and asking questions of." This echoed my experience. My formal and informal mentors modeled behavior that I then chose to practice.

"What questions should the students be asking?" Ann responded, "One of the things a manager will always be looking for is someone who is able, through their expertise and own insight, to find meaningful work. No one wants someone they have to manage all day long. Because of school, students often bring with them an expectation of getting an assignment. They are used to receiving an assignment and delivering the product, and of course, they're also drilled into seeing answers in black-or-white, right-or-wrong contexts with little room for gray area or interpretation."

I sighed, agreeing with the deficiencies of the education system and lamenting that I've had to design career models around education and video games because schools don't teach initiative well. "Sometimes you'll have an 'assignment with a product as the end result' in the workplace, but more often than not, the end goal is vaguer. In any situation, it's critical for the student to come back to the manager and ask clarifying questions; or when they've completed the assignment and the manager isn't available to further the discussion, the student is empowered to find meaningful work that contributes to the organization. It's a conundrum."

"How can a manager help coach a student to think on their own?" I posited to Ann.

"Well, to ensure success, it's critical for the mentor to ask clarifying questions, such as 'What do you need from me to use your hours wisely?'" she responded. "Every young person takes a different approach to achieve the same goal. Encouragement is key to success from the manager's perspective. It's so easy to forget the encouragement piece. There should be a commitment from the manager in the early days to be available and answer questions, check in frequently until you know they've got it."

"I hear you. So, in other words, the manager needs to help the students answer their own questions and help them through the hurdles rather than taking over the work?" I posited. "And I love the piece about encouragement. As Z'rs, we're pessimistic on a statistically significant level and tend to doubt ourselves. The more our manager can encourage us, the better," I shared. "Let's move to another topic. You have your certification in neuroscience and its application to the workplace. How can leaders leverage neuroscience when engaging and mentoring young talent?"

Ann smiled as she began to speak about one of her favorite topics. "The idea of neuroscience is for a leader to become a master of drawing out the best thinking from a person. And the way they do that is by creating moments of insight through questioning. So, in the example of our intern who we are mentoring, we say, "Here's the end product and what I want you to achieve; now go think about that and tell me how you plan to get there." Before you set them free, you continue to have a little more conversation with them—ask what the pathway to get there might look like and have them think aloud in your presence. Through questioning, you can help them get to the place where they have that 'aha' moment and they are almost leaping from their chair to go get started.

"Here's another example to illustrate that these moments of insight can happen randomly," Ann continued. "As a leader, make an intentional point to stop by and check in on a project, and just ask your young person, 'Are there any barriers that have popped up that you weren't expecting?' Then the follow-up question: 'What are three ways that occur to you of how that challenge could be solved?' Contrast that approach with the typical human response when something goes wrong, which is usually to step in and solve the problem—or worse, become unduly frustrated with the employee, creating distrust and often confusion. Mentoring moments can happen in small bites and are usually more effective when they do. What is happening neurologically when you create these moments of insight is this: The brain is lazy and wants to push things into habit naturally. Our brains don't want to think of new things, so having a moment of insight is like having a spotlight go off in your brain that illuminates a new pathway or way of thinking. Have you ever had that happen?"

> **GEN Z MUSINGS**
> *Well, last time I made a mistake, my manager just fixed everything for me. Next time, I'll just let her do it herself. I'm obviously not skilled enough to handle it and she'd do it a whole lot better without me.*

I nodded. "Of course, countless times. And in fact, I usually find that those moments are activated by a friend, mentor, or leader—they don't typically occur when I'm sitting alone and thinking, which I imagine is what you want to highlight there. The leader has a major role to play in the activation of those thought processes."

"Absolutely, yes," Ann replied. "Then the leader needs to shift roles into being the encourager and accountability partner; in other words, the 'wind in their wings' to keep them moving toward the new destination. Otherwise, habit is going to kick in. The brain weighs 2 pounds but uses 20% of your energy—it is an exhaustible resource. It's normal to fall back on habits and bias, and they are similar because they are both unconscious."

Thinking about those biases that are so hard to overcome, I was curious about Ann's perspective from a neuroscience point of view. "That brings up an interesting question," I said. "When mentoring a young person, how can a leader avoid unconscious bias, particularly if they are trying to lead a cultural change in this direction?" I could sense the passion in Ann's voice as she shared, "First of all, it's important to build a team that is diverse in thought and experience. Most leaders agree that getting other perspectives is a good thing, but many companies fail to put processes in place that ensure leaders are consciously overcoming those biases, even perceived ones. One solution is to build in checkpoints for the biases your company wants to avoid. For example, say your company is struggling to value and acknowledge the insights that a young person brings to the table, and as a result, you've had unwanted turnover for people under age 30 before their six-month anniversary. One of those processes you could build in might be this: Have each of your managers hold a standing coffee meeting every Wednesday morning at 10 a.m. with their new hires. In advance, let the new hires know that the purpose of the meeting is to seek and hear insights from them, and in every meeting let them know you expect to hear updates on everything going on in their division. Once they've shared what could be changed or improved, you can give feedback such as, "Gosh, thank you. We've never looked at it that way! Those insights are exactly what we're looking for." By doing so, you are carving out intentional time in your week to show young people not only how greatly their opinions are respected but also that their ideas have the possibility of creating change in the workplace. Then measure how effective this listening is on your turnover."

Culture is the honest result of the actions taken by a group of people, so these simple and consistent actions can build powerful engagement throughout your organization.

—Ann Ashley

I couldn't help but smile, agreeing that listening goes a long way in any conversation, particularly with young people who don't expect to be heard. Ann concluded our conversation with some powerful wisdom: "Culture is the honest result of the actions taken by a group of people, so these simple and consistent actions can build powerful engagement throughout your organization."

I hope Ann's insight demonstrated that no matter the role you play in your organization, you can have a major impact on helping bridge the skills a student may lack as they enter the workplace through building moments of insight, asking great questions, and helping that student become curious and regain their humility, without diminishing their insights and the incredible perspective of fresh eyes. However, despite the wonderful fresh perspective Gen Z'rs bring, we also have some detrimental blind spots our leaders must help us overcome, some of which Ann highlighted. Let's look at an example.

LOOK OUT FOR GEN Z BLIND SPOTS!

Take Kabir, our Traditionalist. While he has a fresh perspective, he attended a traditional school and followed a traditional path, so he also brings natural stumbling blocks to the workplace. Some of these are:

- Habitually conducting life in the form of assignments. For every assignment there's a deadline. By every deadline I'm supposed to produce a product.
- If the product I produce is high quality, it warrants a good grade. If not, I'll do poorly. There are hardly middle-ground consequences. Everything's about the letter and there's not much room for creativity.
- Life is competitive. It's all about performing better than everyone else. Sometimes this is great and sometimes it becomes overwhelming and takes a toll on friendships.
- Once the project is complete, the work is done.

I encourage any leaders reading this to recognize that the largest stumbling block for Gen Z is their own habits. These have been ingrained in us by the education system for 22 years and, while there's room to change and adapt, it may not be easy to instantly overcome these blind spots. Have patience with us, but also take some intentional action. Let's dive into steps you can take.

SHAPE GEN Z'S TRANSITION TO THE WORKPLACE

If your company has resources, broad-scale training and development opportunities are one way to help Gen Z transition to the workplace. However, as a leader of Gen Z'rs, please know you are instrumental in shaping this transition on your own, one young person at a time. There are hundreds of ways organizations are trying to address the skills gap, so my focus for this visual is to help you practically assist your employees in making some of the mental transition from an academic lifestyle to the world of work. In Figure 1 is a visual aid to help you mentor your Gen Z'r through this transition—I've seen managers print this model and put it on their wall as a reminder of how to connect with their new talent each day:

The DAMN Model

DEMONSTRATE	ASK (Don't TELL)	MENTOR	NOTICE
Show grace and demonstrate humility. I am a lifelong learner and don't have everything figured out either!	I am a sounding board. Ask my colleagues: "How would you solve this?" or "What's one pathway to getting the result?" Don't give them the answer.	I must understand my employees' skill gaps and needs. I am an advocate for resources on their behalf. I help them self-assess their challenges and find productive and helpful solutions.	My #1 role is to encourage my staff! Send them words of encouragement. Next time I get up for a snack/coffee, stop for 10 seconds to encourage one of my employees.

Figure 1

DEMONSTRATE: As a leader, you must be a lifelong learner first. Your Gen Z'rs may come to the workplace thinking that their "education" is over when really it's just beginning! If you can emulate learning for them, they will learn through you. Also, as Ann Ashley articulated, the education and interviewing process often teaches us to be conceited and arrogant. If you demonstrate that humility is crucial to success at work, you can teach your Z'r that it's okay not to know the answer to every question.

ASK, Don't TELL: Review the questions Ann Ashley suggests asking your employees—help them overcome the block the education system creates by teaching Gen Z to think critically and find their own answers.

MENTOR: It's up to you to know the technical skill gaps your employees have and advocate for company resources. Whether it's through the Big 5, DISC, StrengthsFinder, or other self-assessment methods, you can also help them discover who they are, where their strengths lie, and how to leverage them on a daily basis.

NOTICE: Remember, Gen Z has grown up with a practical, realistic view of the world. We crave genuine encouragement. As our manager, you can help us transition from the often-brutal world of education into a supportive environment where our efforts are noticed and we are held accountable for work well done.

In future chapters, we'll discuss resources your team can use to develop soft skills that Gen Z often lacks, but also take a look at the simple steps you can take to build a solid foundation before moving forward.

SIMPLE STEPS YOU CAN TAKE:

- **Discuss your Z'r's education experience:** The young person you hired truly may not have considered how different the workplace is from school. If you are struggling to help a Gen Z'r develop the initiative to complete a project without hand-holding, have a conversation with them about their school experience. You'll want to bring this out in the open, perhaps asking questions such as "When you were in school, was there ever a project where you had full creative control?" and "What would it look like if you had the ability to get to the end result of this project any way you wanted, rather than just the way we've always done it or the way we taught you?" Then allow that Gen Z'r to describe their method of success and "unbox" them from what they've learned in school.

- **Build processes to overcome unconscious bias:** Think about an unconscious bias you (or your organization's culture) may have toward young people—whether it's the idea that they need tenure before their opinion is considered or that they don't deserve a seat at the leadership table—and build in a process, with the goal of creating a habit that combats this bias.

- **Create moments of insight:** This week, make a conscious effort to help your employees find three "moments of insight" through great conversation and questioning. These items can seem small, but if you can continue this practice, they'll have immense impact on your culture in the long run—other leaders may begin emulating your behavior as well!

 Visit hannahgwilliams.com/downloads to access printable versions of exercises.

> **IF YOU WANT TO RETAIN GEN Z TALENT, RECOGNIZE OUR RISK AVERSION AND NEED FOR AUTONOMY.**

CHAPTER 18
RECOGNIZE OUR RISK AVERSION

Think back to your middle-school lunchroom. Imagine sitting at the table with your PB&J (or insert favorite lunch here) engaging in lively banter with your classmates. But this lunchroom is very different from the one you grew up with. You see, in this room, every few minutes you glance furtively toward the swinging door almost expecting someone to barge in with a lethal weapon. You already lost friends in a shooting just a few days ago in a nearby school. Imagine, just weeks later, you stumbled into sudden lockdown for a pandemic. You're 12, you're just getting comfortable in your own shoes, and suddenly you can't see your friends anymore except through a screen. You lose the personal touch and, at times, it's difficult to remember what being with other kids was like. Worse, your grandmother who had recently gone into hospice care passed away and you weren't even allowed to be by her bedside because of visitation restrictions. Months pass, your parents have lost their jobs, and the constant arguing puts them on the brink of divorce. On top of this, you can't focus or learn online easily—your parents can't help, as they're too busy trying to make ends meet. What three words would you use to describe your 12-year-old self if you experienced this? I'd probably say anxious, confused, and frightened.

For many Gen Z'rs, this was the norm. It's no wonder our generation struggles with risk aversion. With tumultuous instability in our childhood, this has curated a generation seeking some sense of stability in our workplaces and we are willing to commit for the opportunity. You see, we are the first generation since Traditionalists who are actively searching for long, stable careers in healthy workplaces, and if you offer this, you will have our loyalty. Now, at this point you might be confused. How can a generation want stability, while simultaneously wanting to be entrepreneurs—one of the most unstable of roles—and at the same time, be continually seeking new experiences for fear of missing out? I get it. It's confusing. Let me attempt to explain how these pieces fit together and how you can tap into our risk aversion to build a high-quality workforce for years to come.

BACK TO THE NARCISSTORY

Let's shift some thinking around a bit. Remember the conversation we initially had about a NarcisStory? Let's dive into that a little bit more. Essentially, for Gen Z, everything in our life revolves around our personal NarcisStory:

What would you say is at the "center of your essence" as a leader from another generation? Is it your work? Is it your family? It may be odd to step into Gen Z's shoes and think about work as just one element of forming one's NarcisStory, rather than the center from which all things flow. However, for Gen Z, our work is a powerful component of fulfilling that personal brand—so it's no less important; it's simply not the focal point. It's part of a greater whole. So to return to our earlier question: How do risk aversion, entreprenuership, and FOMO all fit together? Let's take a look at Figure 1 for a visualization of how this works.

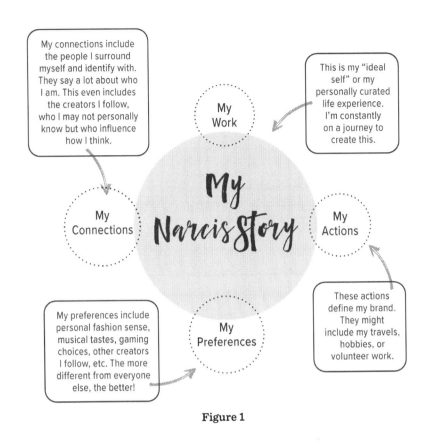

Figure 1

In essence, a desire for stability, a love for entreprenuership (or simply the reputation of a personal brand), and our FOMO are all wrapped up in our intense desire to live meaningfully.

Think about it this way: If I desire stability, what happens if I get laid off from my job? Where do I turn? Well, as young graduates found in the aftermath of COVID-19, finding a job without a preexisting network or online brand reputation was extraordinarily difficult. Unemployment for young Gen Z'rs spiked from 8.4% to 24.4% from 2019 to 2020 during the course of the pandemic,[45] and many career gurus urged job seekers of all generations to focus on building their LinkedIn profiles to stand out from the herd of job applicants. Anyone who was ahead of the curve and had already built up their personal brand was positioned for success when the pandemic threw everyone awry. You see, many Gen Z'rs may not consciously realize they are doing it, but in their self-compelled urges to "be different" they are inadvertently giving themselves an insurance policy should they ever lose their job. See Figure 2 for how the NarcisStory helps Gen Z hedge against risk. Whether entreprenuership or their job at your company, a Gen Z'r's work is simply a tool to living a meaningful life—that may be the work itself, but it can also simply be the way they supply the needed funds to travel the world or engage in hobbies they enjoy. In essence, a desire for stability, a love for entreprenuership (or simply the reputation of a personal brand), and our FOMO are all wrapped up in our intense desire to live meaningfully.

> **GEN Z MUSINGS**
> *What's my greatest fear? Well, oblivion. Irrelevance. I don't want my life to have been meaningless.*

IF GEN Z WANTS STABILITY AND IS RISK AVERSE, WHY AM I LOSING YOUNG TALENT?

If you are struggling with losing young talent, it's important to identify where that crucial turnover point is. Are you losing your talent within one month of hire? Six months? Two years? Once you've identified the crucial turnover point and the underlying root causes, put structures in place to reengage your Gen Z talent at that point. As an example, a very successful health care firm I've had the pleasure of working with for many years had a problem three years ago—they experienced more than 100% turnover in a single year. I interviewed Dr. Brad Butler, CEO, to understand how he remedied this challenge. Brad is a good friend, client, and partner of mine, and is one of the leading voices in innovative chiropractic care, author of the #1 Amazon best seller *The Blueprint for Back Pain Relief*, and a pioneer of the patient-centric office movement. "What's your story, and how does it shape the way you run your employee

DR. BRAD BUTLER
CEO, Oakland Spine & Physical Therapy
Best-Selling Author

engagement efforts at Oakland Spine and Physical Therapy?" I posed to Brad as he settled in, having just left another phone call with the team putting together the company's new employee wellness center.

"I started my company here in Oakland, New Jersey, to help as many people as I can," Brad shared. "I knew I wanted to be a chiropractor at 13 years old, after thinking, 'Wow, there's no needles and I can help people!' I struck out on my own after school and then quickly realized I didn't know how to run a business. Pain can be a great motivator. Heading into my more successful years after stumbling through, I came back to what I was in business to do: Help people. But at the time, 'helping people' meant helping patients, and I put little time into my employees." I smiled, remembering the early conversations he and I had, focused on patient experience. Eventually, we became friends and started discussing employee challenges that weighed on his mind.

"What prompted you to shift a bit of brain energy toward the employee experience?" I posited. He chuckled and responded, "Eventually, I got so tired of thinking I was investing in people without truly investing in them. We had over 100% turnover just a few years ago. We might have been giving out T-shirts, but what were we doing to actually recognize them? It wasn't long before I realized that the pain of not fixing my staff engagement challenges was more than the investment to fix it. We couldn't continue the way we were with high turnover and poor communication."

"So, it sounds like both business challenges and your conscience pushed you over the edge," I responded, knowing how kind and caring Brad is at heart. "Yes, precisely. But we didn't make changes overnight. We started small and slow. We began with one person, and now there are two people fully dedicated to celebrating and crafting the culture we want. My advice to other leaders is to recognize that engagement strategy is important, but it doesn't mean you have to dive in headfirst. Start small! Almost every business knows the value of their target customer—even cancer centers place a value on each person undergoing treatment with them and know the profit each individual brings, as terrible as that sounds—this exists in every industry. The truth is, we must have barometers for success. If I've got a high turnover rate, it means I'm not delivering value to the employees I have a responsibility to care for."

I am impressed with the steps Oakland Spine & Physical Therapy has taken toward employee engagement, particularly the investment of two staff people fully dedicated to culture development when the company has fewer than 100 employees in total between three locations.

Brad continued, "I took the conversation you and I had a couple of years ago, Hannah, about how to find our crucial turnover point at Oakland Spine. I wondered, 'Why are people leaving? We have beautiful facilities, great pay, and highly skilled doctors.' I didn't get it. Significant turnover was happening at the three- to five-month mark. You see, we had healthy turnover at one month after hire (employees would self-select out) and after five years; however, we needed to stop the bleeding in the first six months. What did we find?

"Well, our onboarding process wasn't great. We left it up to working managers to do the initial training and they were overwhelmed with both training and serving clients. We found an exceptional solution to this: The first day, our new hires are trained in a separate facility by two great members of our culture crew who are focused on them and invested in their success. Basically, the whole first week is an 'immersion week' where they are inducted into our values and the experience of being with our company. Only at that point do we slowly integrate them into the technical aspects of the job."

"I love that," I responded. "There is so much noise up front when you start a new position, especially if it's your first job! Focusing on helping the new hire feel at home is crucial."

"Exactly," Brad agreed. "When you're new, just the color of the walls, the lighting, the sounds, the radio, 25 faces you're supposed to be working with, 100 new patients each day you have to remember the names of, and the new phone system can be so overwhelming. How can you blame someone for bowing out of that environment? Our employees didn't have the chance to bond with our purpose. It was just a job. In the absence of good communication, the human brain creates stories like 'you don't care' or 'you didn't give me attention.' As a CEO, my first reaction was 'No, you're wrong! Look at all these manuals we gave you to help you succeed!' But actually, those new employees were right. We didn't truly connect with them deeply, and that's where I see the change come from.

"So I would posit the question to any leader reading this book: If you know what the average client's value is, what's your average staff member's value?"

I love the way Brad posed these questions. If you want to retain Gen Z talent, recognize our risk aversion and need for autonomy. Then identify your crucial turnover point and build an experience that resonates with us in terms of our personal brand. If you can get us over the hump of your crucial turnover point, we are bound to give you many hardworking years of 110% effort.

SIMPLE STEPS YOU CAN TAKE:

It's time to do some soul-searching. What is your crucial turnover point? If you're a business owner, think on the company level. If you're a leader/manager of a department, consider just your department. If you don't have the exact numbers below, that's okay*—just approximate them and be honest with yourself, then see if you can brainstorm some reasons:

Your Annual Turnover Rate (company-wide or department—approximating is fine)	
Industry Average Turnover Rate	
Age Range with Highest Turnover* (e.g., Under 25, 26–40, 41–55, 56+)	
Where in the employee life cycle do you experience the highest turnover (e.g., first month, 3–6 months, 6–12 months, after the first year, etc.)?	
Do you see any correlations between age and turnover point? If so, list them at right.	
List a few reasons why these correlations might exist:	

*You may not have this data and that's okay! If you don't, use this as a sign that you should be collecting demographic research in your exit interviews, employee engagement surveys, etc. You can use a gut feeling for the exercise if you're honest with yourself.

Which ideas from this book could you deploy to address the crucial turnover point? List a few creative thoughts:

1. _____
_____
_____
_____

2. _____
_____
_____
_____

3. _____
_____
_____
_____

 Visit hannahgwilliams.com/downloads to access printable versions of exercises.

"MORE THAN HALF OF GEN Z WOULD CONSIDER STAYING AT A COMPANY 3-5 YEARS IF THE CULTURE ALIGNS WITH THEIR VALUES AND THEY ENJOY THE PEOPLE THEY WORK WITH."

CHAPTER 19
RETAIN US THROUGH EMPOWERMENT

One of the most common frustrations I hear from founders and executives is "$!&# those millennials! They think they can waltz in their first week of work and expect to be promoted to vice president the next month." While I believe millennials get a bad rap (many are very hardworking, in fact!), I think boomers and Gen X will be in for a pleasant surprise at the attitude toward hard work that Gen Z is bringing to the workplace. As we've discussed in former chapters, research is showing that Gen Z is more pragmatic and less idealistic than their millennial predecessors. We are also the first generation since boomers who would prefer the stability of long tenure rather than the short job spurts for which millennials are known.

LONGER TENURE?

Guess how long Gen Z wants to stay at your company? According to the recent recruiting study from Yello, more than half of Gen Z expects to stay at an employer 3-5 years if the culture aligns with their values and they enjoy the people they work with.[46] Compare that with millennials, of whom, data shows, already 25% have worked five jobs by age 35 (averaging tenure of 2.6 years).[47] Why is this, you may ask? As we've discussed, Gen Z is risk averse. While we don't have the loyalty our grandparents had to a singular company with a pension plan, we have seen COVID-19 ruin our family's finances or even damage our own job prospects. Many of my friends completed their undergraduate degrees only to get denied for $7-per-hour grocery-stocking positions in 2020–2021, so to the majority of Gen Z'rs, the stability of a health care plan, steady compensation, and opportunity for learning and growth is appealing. While we have yet to capture significant data on how well Gen Z sticks with initial tenure projections, the current findings indicate that if companies focus on building cultures in which leadership empowers and empathizes with its people, Gen Z will discover their fit, will grow, and will offer value to the company for years.

To the majority of Gen Z'rs, the stability of a health care plan, steady compensation, and opportunity for learning and growth is appealing.

RETAIN US THROUGH EMPOWERMENT

There are specific ways to empower my generation to do their best work and I will be the first to say these suggestions aren't unique; they speak to the humanity in all of us. I'll dive deeper into some of these in subsequent chapters on coaching and mentoring:

- **Set clear expectations and guidelines.** As we discussed in chapter 16, Gen Z requires clear expectations and measurement when working with a group in order to ensure everyone is pulling their weight. Similarly, we expect to be given clear guidelines when accomplishing a task. The key word here is *guidelines*. You will empower a bright and driven Gen Z'r most when they have autonomy in the execution but guidelines to keep them on track.

- **Help us craft our own role.** Gen Z is used to customizing their own journey, as we've discussed. This translates to our roles—whether they be project based or career based—and we want to be an active and empowered part in shaping our future.
- **Get out of the way.** One of the best leaders I've ever had the pleasure of working under said, "My people do the best work when I get out of their way." Then he embodied that statement.
- **Focus on the "why," not the "how," and let us develop the "how" based on the "why."** Jon Tesser, the self-proclaimed "Career Whisperer," has grown a community of over 140,000 professionals on LinkedIn. As a Gen Xer, and the vice president of research and insight for NYC & Company, Jon has dedicated his life to helping the next generation succeed and has spoken with thousands of young professionals, for whom he offers "career whispering" services to help them figure out the next steps in their professional journey. On a rainy Wednesday afternoon, Jon and I met over Zoom and shared our mutual passion for cutting down inauthenticity on social media. Despite this being our first conversation, Jon's candor was refreshing as he passionately shared his perspective on how managers must shift to get the best work out of Gen Z, including satisfying Z'rs' need to understand the "why."

"Gen Z likes to be challenged to discover their own problems and solutions," Jon urged. "Just say, 'Here's the problem, here's why it's a problem, now go solve it.'" As a Z'r myself, I echo Jon's sentiment entirely—all too often, young people are spoon-fed information or not given the leeway to prove themselves. "You have to make young people feel like they have a voice, even if those contributions are small at first. If you as a manager do not help and guide young people to show off their uniqueness, you're effectively putting them into a box," he continued. "Quickly, you'll lose their engagement and respect."

Jon bluntly shared with me, "It's easy for older generations to take Gen Z's need to understand the 'why' behind every decision and their need for individuality as a lack of respect for authority. I get it. It's easy to assume the young person lacks obedience or respect, when really all they are seeking is equal partnership. Do they deserve it? In my mind, they are human beings deserving of respect, and while they have many areas for growth, they have a very different way of looking at life than we did in our generation. You see, respect looks different for them. Rather than 'respect for elders,' there is 'mutual respect' or 'partnership.'" (See Figure 1 for the contrast.)

LEADERSHIP KINKS

OLDER GENERATION	YOUNGER GENERATION
Assumes Gen Z lacks respect for authority	Believes we are all humans—don't we deserve equal respect?
Thinks young people lack obedience	Thinks everyone has equally valid ideas from different points of view. We should learn from each other.
Wants younger people to "do" things	Wants to understand "why" we do things so we can accomplish them to the best of our ability
Wants Partnership + To See Their Company Succeed	Wants Partnership + To See Their Company Succeed

Figure 1

What's most interesting is that, despite these differences, both generations are looking for one thing: success. They want the business to succeed, and they want individual success. Additionally, both generations can agree that partnership and teamwork are necessary to accomplish success. Now the question is: What steps is each generation willing to take to empower the other to succeed?

Now the question is: What steps is each generation willing to take to empower the other to succeed?

In Figure 2 there's a simple checklist for each generation.

> **STEPS OLDER GENERATIONS MUST TAKE TO EMPOWER GEN Z:**
> - Coach leaders and managers to "get out of the way" and do so yourself!
> - Celebrate the fresh eyes of Gen Z! Instead of tamping down their enthusiasm for work, see if you can gain innovative ideas from them before they are discouraged by bureaucracy, policies, or a slow pace of change.
> - Even though Gen Z hates to be micromanaged, we crave guidance. Empower us by teaching us what you've learned over the years and we'll be grateful for it.
> - Communicate "why" more frequently than you ever thought necessary.
> - Help us make mistakes.
> - Set clear expectations and guidelines.
> - Relearn how to be curious from your Gen Z colleagues!

Figure 2

This is not a one-sided problem. Gen Z must also step up the game and be willing to hear the perspective of older generations in the workforce. In Figure 3 there are some areas where we can grow.

> **STEPS GEN Z AND MILLENNIALS MUST TAKE TO EMPOWER AND RESPECT OLDER GENERATIONS:**
> - Listen with humility. The wealth of knowledge older generations can impart to Gen Z is immense!
> - Understand that the wisdom and experience that older generations have gives them a right to make the final calls and decisions in most scenarios.
> - Be teachable and coachable.
> - Learn to be patient. Change takes time.
> - Gain life wisdom and lessons. "Stand on the shoulders of giants" instead of re-creating the success of past generations.

Figure 3

The more respect and empathy we have for one another, the better the world will be.

SIMPLE STEPS YOU CAN TAKE:

Try this exercise—it will empower your team to see the value each person can bring to the table, no matter their age and abilities.

1. Gather your team together and break them up into groups of five or six. You want to ensure each group represents people from different generations.

2. Give each person a sheet of paper. Ask them to write a challenge they're having at the top of the page—it could be a business problem they want to solve, a decision they're absolutely stuck on and can't figure out, a professional challenge with another team, or anything else they want to share.

3. Have the group pass their paper with the challenge to the left. Have that colleague read the challenge, then offer one suggestion for how to solve the problem or give a perspective they may not have considered.

4. Pass the paper four more times, until the person who wrote the challenge has received their paper back.

5. Now that person has five perspectives they can read to help them conquer the problem!

6. Debrief with the group. Do they feel helped? Encouraged? Are they surprised by the wisdom each person could offer?

This exercise is an easy way to remove generational differences and highlight that, no matter one's age, each person has a unique perspective to offer and can help their friends and colleagues.

 Visit hannahgwilliams.com/downloads to access printable versions of exercises.

"I THINK GEN XERS WILL FIND GEN Z STRANGELY RELATABLE IN TERMS OF THEIR EQUALLY DRIVEN AND INDEPENDENT NATURE."

CHAPTER 20
FOCUS ON INDIVIDUAL EFFORT

I'll never forget my first time at an awards ceremony acknowledging "firms of the year" in the professional services industry. It was held as a black-tie dinner in the grandiose event center of a Vegas resort. Women wore dresses from Rent the Runway for the occasion and men donned their finest suits. The cocktail hour was filled with pleasant conversation, photo ops on a beautiful red carpet, and delicious hors d'oeuvres, all set to the sultry mood of a local jazz band. You know the typical extravaganza. Once dinnertime arrived, we were ushered into the main ballroom and dinner service began, along with the typical greetings and "thanks for attending" by the host. Then the award ceremony commenced. Approximately 100 firms were represented at this event from all over the country and, rather than being invitation-only, this conference was open to any leaders wanting to learn from industry experts. My presumption going into this event was that a few awards—perhaps "Best Firm to Work For" and "Best Client Experience"—would be received by a select few firms. Wow, was I wrong. A lengthy two hours later, firms continued walking across the stage to receive their unique award, and I felt myself nodding off to sleep—mind you, there was no keynote to break up the monotony—and placards such as "Runner-Up for Most Improved Website" were being given out. By the conclusion, nearly every single firm in the room had received an award, and frankly I couldn't believe what I had witnessed. How can any firm stand out if each one is recognized? What is there to aspire to? Essentially, the value of these awards had been reduced to that of a participation trophy.

IS EVERYONE A WINNER?

The mentality that "everyone is a winner" was one that many millennials were raised with, and when they entered the workforce, companies that wanted to retain them did their best to embrace it—whether through recognition programs or social media shout-outs. While many of these things were much-needed changes, please know that these same strategies may not work for Gen Z. On the whole, Gen Z is far more pessimistic than any generation since 1960, according to Jean Twenge, professor of psychology at San Diego State University and the author of *iGen: Why Today's Super-Connected Kids Are Growing Up Less Rebellious, More Tolerant, Less Happy—and Completely Unprepared for Adulthood*.[48] Why? According to Jean Twenge, it has much to do with how we were raised. You see, while our Gen X parents desired to create happy lives for their children, one reason for the dramatic drop in hopefulness between millennials and Generation Z may be the different generations that reared them. As Jean Twenge says, "Boomer parents brought up millennials telling them, 'You can be whatever you want to be, you're special,' and they believed it. And so, that had some benefits. Generation Z received 'you're special' messages from their Generation X parents, too. Indeed, more than any prior generation of American parents, Generation X set out deliberately to raise happy kids. But there was also a shift in parenting from encouragement to fear. As parents' anxiety about the world rose, they seem to have passed the feeling down."

As a Z'r myself, I can testify that this is indeed the way I was raised. My parents taught me from an early age that I would have to put in intense effort to achieve my goals, and that while the world is at my fingertips, I must expect hardship. I was taught that nothing in life comes easily, and I witnessed this parenting style among my friends as well.

PESSIMISM

What is Gen Z's natural response to this rearing? *Honest pessimism.* On one hand, this pessimism has created a depressed generation (between 2005 and 2017 rates of major depression increased 52% in adolescents 12 to 17, and 63% in young adults 18 to 25[49]), but on the other hand, young adults are using their pessimism about life to fuel honest, radical change toward a better life. It's driven us to ask better questions, challenge antiquated practices, and ask ourselves, "What's something I, personally, can do to make a difference in the world?" More than this, our perception can be (even if it's flawed) that other generations working together has only made the world worse or left us with a mess to clean up. When you couple this thinking with pessimism, our NarcisStories, and our entrepreneurial drive, what do you end up with? A very DIY and individually empowered generation.

INDIVIDUALISM OVER GROUP MENTALITY

This DIY mindset is going to create the largest rub between millennials and Gen Z'rs at work. You see, Gen Z would prefer to be handed a task, walk away, and get the job done, much like we would do if we were entrepreneurs running our own businesses. Millennials have shaped cultures to focus

> **GEN Z MUSINGS**
> *This would be SO much faster if I just did it myself. Seriously, cut out the meetings and all that. I can knock this out in a couple of hours.*

on group effort, where at least "two heads are better than one" when it comes to decision-making. As millennials begin to supervise Gen Z'rs, this will be certain to cause frustration at first, just as boomers were first taken aback when Gen X brought their solo work mindset into the workplace. As the saying goes, history tends to repeat itself. In this case, history is repeating itself within a mere two generations, and I think Gen Xers will find Gen Z strangely relatable in terms of their equally driven and independent nature.

COACHING GEN Z THROUGH INDIVIDUALISM

Because of these potential clashes, leaders should be prepared to have honest conversations with Gen Z, and focus coaching on a few specific areas:

- **Create healthy group project teams:** The collaborative approach millennials brought to the workplace can spur creativity and innovation when managed healthily—of course, studies have shown that unhealthy collaborations where "everyone has a voice" can devolve into groupthink, no matter which generations are involved. That being said, there are countless situations where group collaboration rather than individual work is vital to a project's success, or at least helpful. Gen Z will need to be coached to see the value in these efforts, and there are ways you as a leader can help. When Gen Z is part of a group project, (1) leaders should be clear about the expectations for each employee involved and what metrics or tasks should be completed by the next meeting, (2) each employee who completes their responsibilities on time and with quality should be recognized for that effort, and (3) an

> **GEN Z MUSINGS**
> *Okaaay...I guess I can see the value of having input from Jan and Isaac on this before I just jump straight in. They know a whole lot more than I do about branding.*

employee who falls behind should openly share with the group the reasons for that (as we know, often these situations are outside of work). However, if the reason is simply lack of effort or general laziness, Gen Z needs to see their leader taking steps to coach that employee or remove them from the team. You see, both Gen Z and millennials experienced group projects in school, in which one person usually carried an unequal load compared to the rest of the group. If a Gen Z employee finds themselves carrying the brunt of the load on a group project, they will become disenchanted with collaboration and likely retreat into their independent habits again.

- **Lean in to independent working style:** While Gen Z should learn how to successfully function on a team, Gen Z'rs' independent working style can benefit a company greatly. One of the most empowering things you can do for your young talent is give them a daunting task—perhaps it's a problem the company is trying to solve—then ask them to return to you within a certain number of weeks with their plan on how they'd solve the problem. You might be surprised what they produce. A good friend of mine, Melinda, is the regional vice president of an East Coast bank, and each year they hire two or three high-potential interns to learn the business and determine if their firm is a good fit for them. Last year, COVID-19 hit right as the new interns were getting on board, and Melinda was frantically trying to pull together projects her interns could conduct remotely while everyone was working from home. We met for lunch and I gave her the simple idea of asking her intern to solve a key problem their bank was facing—how to onboard young talent in an engaging way—and giving her liberty to do with the project as she would. To her surprise, her intern, Madeleine, returned in three weeks with a fully researched plan, including interviews with executives across the bank and some of her college peers, of a five-step process for how to better onboard young talent and solve some of the turnover problems they were facing. Long story short, Madeleine's plan was taken to corporate HR and elements are being incorporated into the firm's strategy. Sometimes a challenge is all your Gen Z'r employee needs to feel engaged and heard, and to produce the best work they possibly can by exercising their independence.

- **Help Gen Z learn to delegate:** As Gen Z'rs take on management roles, they may have trouble *delegating*. Given our mentality to "get 'er done," we may be frustrated by the seeming lack of efficiency groups and teams offer. There is a need and opportunity for our management to coach us into leadership roles by instructing us in how to delegate responsibilities and lead our teams, rather than assuming individual effort is the one and only way to accomplish a task.

SIMPLE STEPS YOU CAN TAKE:

Exercise #1: Understand Gen Z's working style

I encourage you to take whichever of the three aforementioned areas of coaching your Gen Z'rs (whether interns or employees) struggle with the most. Are they having difficulty engaging with teams or group projects? Are they struggling to delegate if they're in charge of others? Are they feeling stuck in a box and not empowered to run with a project? Pick one of those Gen Z'rs and ask them a couple of questions:

- What was your experience like with group projects in college?
- How do you think they impacted the way you work?
- In your opinion, what is the purpose of a meeting? How do you suggest we make team meetings more effective?

Asking these questions will help you ascertain whether your Gen Z'r prefers independence or not and how you can help them succeed in your workplace.

Exercise #2: Practice the "P3" exercise

Gen Z will "go rogue" naturally—we've got Google and YouTube to help us fill in the learning gaps, and we have short attention spans! The result? We will check out of meetings if they aren't purposeful. Try this exercise to help (and trust me—everyone will thank you, not just Gen Z):

Practice the "P3" before sending a meeting invitation.* When creating the invitation and determining the attendees, ask yourself: What's the Purpose, Process, and Payoff of this meeting?

- Purpose: Why are we meeting? Include a brief description in the invitation.
- Process: How will we reach our goals during the meeting?

- Payoff: What will every person in attendance leave the meeting with? And based on this, who should truly be at the meeting?

Practice this each time you send a meeting invitation—I've made it a daily practice. It helps me not only build respect with other leaders but also think through who should truly be involved in the meeting and can add value! In turn, it saves time for my whole team. By walking through this simple exercise, your meetings will be more purposeful, and Gen Z will begin to learn that meetings have a reason—they don't just impede workflow.

I can't take credit for this exercise. In the early days of my career, a consultant came to The Biltmore Company for a workshop and made this suggestion. It radically transformed the way we managed time as a team after implementing it!

 Visit hannahgwilliams.com/downloads to access printable versions of exercises.

> **GEN Z PREFERS TO FOCUS ON OUR STRENGTHS TO MAXIMIZE EFFICIENCY, WHILE OUTSOURCING OUR WEAKNESSES.**

CHAPTER 21
UNDERSTAND THE SHARED ECONOMY

While independent work is important to Gen Z, we've also grown up in an economy where increasing efficiency and convenience while reducing costs is vital to any company trying to get ahead. Just as we've never known a world without the internet, we were also young when Uber quickly disrupted the transportation market, and companies like Visible offered ways to save on our phone bills by "sharing" phone service and data.[50] Essentially, we are used to a world where consumer goods and services are shared or borrowed rather than purchased. Are you a photographer? Just go to borrowlenses.com to rent top-of-the-line lenses and cameras instead of buying them.[51] Don't want to pay for that wedding reception dress you'll wear only once? Just head over to Rent the Runway to get an outfit for the occasion at a fraction of the price. As a musician, I've seen these effects very personally in the streaming world, where my generation would intensely prefer to customize our Spotify and Apple Music playlists rather than purchase an entire album. Because we have grown up in a world where the economy is increasingly shared, we naturally bring this mentality to the workplace and it can manifest itself in many different ways.

THE SHARED ECONOMY CAN CREATE CLASHES

THE BABY MILLIONAIRE
RODRIGO GOMEZ (15 YEARS OLD)

Imagine "The Baby Millionaire," Rodrigo Gomez, walking into your office on a Wednesday morning. He started at your firm only a month ago, after deciding to opt out of college and start working at your tech start-up. Just last Monday, you had asked him to put together a client presentation complete with a Gantt chart, project data, and updates from project managers to present at the following week's leadership meeting. Considering the breadth of the updates and significant data visualization required, you anticipated it wouldn't be complete until at least Friday and are surprised when he emails you the completed file several days in advance. You ask Rodrigo how he managed to pull it off, and his response is, "I'm much more skilled on the data analysis side, so instead of spending hours on the graphics portion, I sent it over to someone on Fivrr and paid them $30 to take care of it, just like I always did with my streaming company." Depending on your past experience with a Gen Z'r, either your jaw might drop or you might wave this off as perfectly normal. You see, as Gen Z'rs, we are intensely (sometimes to a fault) focused on maximizing efficiency and effort—it's in our

> **GEN Z MUSINGS**
>
> *Why should I EVER have to learn to write proposals if Mel can do them better than I can? I shouldn't have to focus so hard on my weaknesses.... If only they'd let me show them a better way to use our different talents, we'd be able to help clients more efficiently.*

> blood—so it doesn't seem reasonable to us that we should waste time on areas in which we aren't as skilled or efficient; we'd prefer to leverage our strengths and hand off the work to someone else. This is starkly contradictory to the way many companies have thought for years, where certain tasks were considered a "rite of passage" to the next rank within an organization. Gen Z is disrupting this.

HELP GUIDE US IN LEVERAGING THE SHARED ECONOMY

Of course, this mentality is not without its faults and it can be taken to an extreme that can end negatively for a firm. For example, in the previous instance, if Rodrigo had not understood the fuller picture, had paid out of pocket for the Fivrr job, and, as a result, misrepresented the company by not following branding guidelines, this could reflect poorly on the team. There is a coaching opportunity for leaders to take advantage of Gen Z's perspective on how to increase efficiency while also reining in their independent nature and helping them see the bigger picture.

GAIN A BROADER PERSPECTIVE OF THE TALENT MARKET

Despite the possible pitfalls, Gen Z's focus on efficiency, economy, and convenience can bring great value to your organization's profit and productivity. Employers should take a broader view of the talent market in the first place and, based on research by Deloitte and McKinsey, companies should stay abreast of the future of work, which will require a careful re-analysis of the talent continuum to maintain relevance within the market. With 35% of the US workforce in supplemental, temporary, project, or contract-based work, it's evident the market is changing. Unsurprisingly, the freelance workforce is increasing nearly three times as rapidly as traditional positions. In 2019, the freelance market grew by 8.1% compared to 2.6% for all other jobs.[52] and during the COVID-19 pandemic, when the labor market turned upside down, freelance workers increased by 22% compared to the previous year.[53] In other words, the gig economy Gen Z grew up within is forcing the labor market to adjust, and not only are we along for the ride, but also we expect companies to adapt and accommodate our ever-changing work styles.

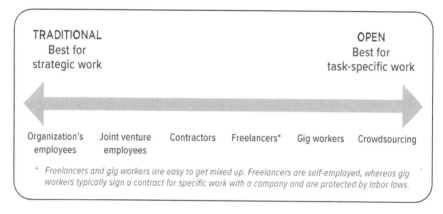

Figure 1

THE MODERN TALENT CONTINUUM

In the modern talent continuum, companies must begin to shift the functions of roles to freelancers, gig workers, and even crowdsourcing like never before. That being said, there are caveats to this model.

Disclaimer: While I strongly urge businesses to consider the breadth of the talent continuum (which ranges from traditional employees all the way to project-based crowdsourcing), there are numerous downsides to the rapid adoption of independent contractor positions in lieu of traditional hires. The full extent of the harm has yet to be discovered as companies embracing this model (DoorDash, Lyft, etc.) are heavily funded by seed capital. Gen Z is taking note (and many have felt the impact) of the problems with gig work, including insufficient pay, lack of benefits, and poor protection from discrimination and harassment. I strongly suggest companies analyze their goals and find talent models that support workers and also make financial sense, while considering ways to maintain a "gig economy" mindset without necessarily converting an entire labor force into an unsustainable black hole. Let's take a small step toward this in our exercise.

SIMPLE STEPS YOU CAN TAKE:

Take a look at Figure 1, and analyze the continuum for your business. What percentage of each type of labor is used in your company? Write your answers in Figure 2.

EMPLOYEE TYPE	% OF STAFF
Full-time/part-time staff (with benefits)	
Joint venture employees	
Independent contractors	
Freelancers	
Gig workers	
Crowdsourced workers	

Figure 2

Now, consider either the department you manage, your team, or (if you're a business owner) the company at large. List five tasks you believe could be shifted into one of the other buckets. For example, perhaps you currently have approximately 85% full-time/part-time staff, 10% contractors, and 5% freelancers. Of the full-time staff, you've got five marketing team members, but based on your business needs you believe that you need some new creativity. Instead of employing five full-time marketing members, what if you could retain one full-time marketing director and one part-time assistant, but have three or four college-age student "gig workers" create your social media content and do copywriting and editing under your director's supervision? They would have new ideas, but the brand voice would be maintained if managed well by the director.

List tasks below that you believe could be shifted from their current status to a new type of labor:

Task 1: _____

_____

_____

Task 2: _____

_____

_____

Task 3: _____

_____

_____

Task 4: _____

_____

_____

Task 5: _____

_____

_____

Now write in the Current Placement chart where the tasks currently fall. Then write where they could be placed in the New Placement chart.

CURRENT PLACEMENT

Joint Venture Employees	
Crowdsourced	
Full-time	
Freelancers	
Gig workers	
Contractors	

NEW PLACEMENT W/NEW TALENT CONTINUUM

Joint Venture Employees	
Crowdsourced	
Full-time	
Freelancers	
Gig workers	
Contractors	

Now pick one of those tasks that makes the most sense and bring it up in your next meeting. See if you can shift the labor around to benefit your company financially and respond to the market labor shortages.

 Visit hannahgwilliams.com/downloads to access printable versions of exercises.

"TO TRULY REACH GEN Z, WE NEED TO BE SOUGHT AFTER, IN PERSON, WITH INTENTIONAL TIME DEVOTED TO THE CONVERSATION."

CHAPTER 22
ENGAGE US FACE-TO-FACE

A few weeks ago, I walked in on a high school study session. It was a rather odd scene—pillows and old beanbags thrown everywhere and the scent of stale Doritos. While the smell was familiar and the scenery was reminiscent of my college days, the entire aura was off. Rather than a group of students lounging with a couple of books strewn about and laptops open with whiteboards in hand to jot down the next complex math problem, all that the students had on their desks was laptops. That was it. Two of the students were plugged in with AirPods, clearly occupied on a Zoom call, while the others scrolled through multiple hundred-page textbooks on their phones and laptops, squinting at the tiny text. You could feel the exhaustion in the room. Not from the studying itself, but from the endless Zoom calls. One student finally slammed his laptop shut and exclaimed, "How am I supposed to learn when I'm not in the same room as my professor and these textbooks are so hard to 'flip' through on my laptop I can't even think?"

Despite our reliance on tech, we don't love digital communication.

In this "Zoomer" age, where Gen Z is forcibly tied to our phones, we crave anything but technological devices. Don't get me wrong—we are a generation that claims to learn more from TikTok than we did in high school,[54] and, especially during COVID-19 lockdowns in 2020, 70% of Gen Z'rs increased their podcast consumption, while 79% watched shows they never would have during other circumstances, according to JUV Consulting's recent Gen Z report—meaning we are completely tech reliant.[55] However, you'll recall from Chapter 5 that despite our reliance on tech, we don't love digital communication, and this is important to understand when we discuss Gen Z's communication styles in the workplace. According to a live poll conducted during a presentation by millennial and Gen Z expert Ryan Jenkins, 72% of Gen Z workers prefer face-to-face communication at work, while only 11% prefer texts and 9% prefer email.[56]

CONNECTION AND POP CULTURE

In response to Gen Z's cravings for authentic connection over technological dependence, Instagram added the feature "ask to be added to the livestream" within Instagram stories so that we have the chance to personally connect with our favorite celebrities. Especially during the COVID-19 lockdowns, the #togetherathome hashtag attempted to bring American households together with celebrity performances that were more intimate than typical shows. Similarly, thought leaders have felt the pressure lately to appear more authentic and "normal" to their audiences to appeal to Gen Z and find ways to make themselves more easily accessible to their followers. "These [Gen Z] professionals likely seek connectedness and context because they thrive on genuine relationships, especially with authority figures," Bruce Tulgan, founder of RainmakerThinking, shared.[57] What does more face-to-face communication look like in practical terms for a Gen Z'r? Honestly, we have yet to see, as young people enter the workplace. With COVID-19 and the shift to remote working as the norm, digital communication is an imperative for any successful business, making face-to-face interactions all the more special and out of the norm for anyone—not just a Z'r. There are a few reasons in-person communication stands out for Gen Z.

IT BREAKS THROUGH THE MULTITASKING NOISE

It's not atypical on any given evening for a Gen Z'r to send a direct message (DM) to a friend on Instagram while simultaneously listening to music on their AirPods, watching a newly released YouTube video, browsing on their laptop with 20+ open tabs, responding to work emails, and interacting on a subreddit. We're talking serious distractions—and yet to us, this is normal. When our manager sends a text or email, it's just adding to the noise. To truly reach Gen Z, we need to be sought after, in person, with intentional time devoted to the conversation. The time a manager gives to take us out to coffee or get to know us through a Zoom meeting is more meaningful because of the chaos we are accustomed to. As a side note, managers, please know that despite the efficiency and progress that can come from our innate ability to multitask, there are a number of downsides in not only communication but also the quality of work we are capable of producing because of multitasking. Gen Z struggles to naturally focus on deep work. As our manager, you'll need to encourage us to find dedicated time to minimize distractions and produce the work we are fully capable of.

THE OLD-FASHIONED LETTER?

Because of the noise at work that surrounds us, imagine the delight of this experience: Instead of receiving praise for a job well done in front of co-workers at the morning team meeting, we received a handwritten letter at our home address one day after work. We could experience the delight of opening it around our family and/or friends and creating a memorable experience. Even if that day at work had been a grueling one, we would arrive home to a delightful surprise. A handwritten letter can be powerful for your Gen Z'r (especially when delivered at the right time—and if it includes a gift card, even better!) to show them you put intention into not only the contents but also the experience of opening it! Sometimes just changing the method of communication is an important way to connect with Gen Z.

In the next chapter, we'll talk about ways to connect with Gen Z's communication needs through meaningful feedback, which is a crucial part of retaining us.

SIMPLE STEPS YOU CAN TAKE:

Since high-touch interaction and face-to-face communication are so important to your Gen Z'r, here are some personalized ways you can interject meaningful face time into your Gen Z's work life to motivate and inspire them:

- **Arrange a lunch for your Z'r with a senior leader.** (Of course, make sure the leader pays and can accurately pronounce their name.) Before the lunch, help your Z'r brainstorm questions they can ask.

- **Volunteer opportunities.** Involve the team in a day of volunteer work with a meaningful organization. You'll want to have your Z'rs vote on the organization beforehand, and of course make sure the day is paid.

- **Film a TikTok together—and if it goes viral, give the employees a paid day off!** You can even put this in the TikTok video ("Our boss says if this goes viral, we get a day off!"). Your recruiting team can use the content on their channels too—it's a double win.

> **GEN Z MUSINGS**
> We had an awesome day today. Even if my manager, Bill, doesn't understand TikTok, he let us come up with our own way to create a fun video that the recruiting team can use. And I got to know my team better filming it.

- **$50 office redecorating bonus and shopping day.** Give the team $50 each to spend on improving their cubicle/office space, then send them on a shopping spree together! They'll enjoy the connection-building time and also get to improve their space.

- **Foodie tour.** Remember, Z'rs are the most ethnically diverse generation to date, and they'll appreciate a team outing where food is at the center. Have the team try something unique! Hit up a Korean corn dog dive or head over to the local El Salvadoran joint for pupusas, or maybe even try the Japanese supermarket for some mochi.

Try one of these ideas with your Gen Z'rs this week and see how it goes!

 Visit hannahgwilliams.com/downloads to access printable versions of exercises.

> 60% OF GEN Z MEMBERS PREFER MULTIPLE CHECK-INS WITH THEIR MANAGER DURING THE WEEK.

CHAPTER 23
SUPPORT US WITH DIRECT FEEDBACK

In every major sport there is a scoreboard. Why? Everyone knows the answer. We want to know which team is winning. Great books and strategies like *The 4 Disciplines of Execution* by Chris McChesney, Sean Covey, and Jim Huling[58] talk about the importance of a scoreboard in creating high-performing teams. Frequently, researchers will use this analogy to demonstrate that "just like a scoreboard in a game, social media has taught young people how they measure up to their peers and has shaped the way they want to receive feedback." While this is true, we need to go a little deeper—a little less black and white.

As Gen Z'rs, we have scoreboards all around us—how many "likes" we receive on our social media, how well we score on tests, and rubrics assessing our "performance potential"—but the results are much more vague. As an illustration, look at how the contestant journey on *America's Next Top Model* has changed over the years (if you haven't watched the show, no shame). When the show aired in 2003 it was simple: The judges assigned points to performance and everyone went on their merry way. Nowadays, it's not so simple. Contestants aren't just winning or losing each round based on a judge's opinion; they are rated (1) on their performance (how well they responded and connected with live audiences during live shoots for a "likability" score), (2) by the judges, and (3) by social media scores based only on the pictures they took that week. In other words, it's no longer enough to take great photos; it's also about a contestant's likability as a person. Technology has added a layer of complexity to "scoreboards" and it's not as easy to assess how one is measuring up.

Leaders must be explicitly clear in communicating and do it frequently.

Why do I bring this up? Simply put, social media has wired the Gen Z brain to do two things: (1) Instantly know how our photos/videos are performing based on the engagement, and (2) simultaneously fear that despite our best efforts, we are always at risk of doing something "wrong," which naturally creates mental downward spirals.

> **GEN Z MUSINGS**
> *I've never doubted myself so much. It's not like I've really told anyone, but I hit "down spirals" really easily. I turn on Driver's License so I can cry a bit.*

Because our brains are wired this way, leaders must be explicitly clear in communicating and do it frequently and be overtly intentional about praising us for work well done. Jason Dorsey and his team at The Center for Generational Kinetics found that 60% of Gen Z members prefer multiple check-ins with the boss during the week, and 40% of those workers prefer that those check-ins happen at least daily.[59] If these check-ins and interactions don't happen regularly, a Gen Z worker is likely to think they've done something wrong. This may sound daunting to any other generation, or even worse, extremely time-consuming. So let's break down what feedback should look like.

GIVE ATTENTION OFTEN—ATTENTION IS OUR NORMAL "STATE OF BEING"

A check-in for Gen Z can be simply an acknowledgment that we exist. Sometimes all we need is for our manager to stop in, say "good morning," and ask how we are. A servant-hearted gesture from a leader can make all the difference as well. One of my former bosses would ask me each time he went to refill his tea or coffee if I needed anything from the break room—which happened to be quite a bit of walking distance away—and this made a massive difference in showing me he cared. Also, if you want to ask our opinion on a lighthearted topic, you can bet we'll be happy to give it, and these interactions create wonderful connections. Here are some brief check-in questions you can ask your Z'rs this week:

- What's something you'd love to smash with a hammer if you wouldn't get in trouble for it and why?
- What has been one of the most memorable compliments you've ever received?
- If you had the power to re-create yourself, what are three things you would NOT change?
- What was the biggest highlight in your life in the last six months?
- Which one's better? A Ferris wheel or a roller coaster?
- If you won a million bucks today, what would you do with it?

In other words, acknowledge we exist and ask our opinions, even on unimportant topics. This not only builds a great relationship but also shows your young hire that you will listen to and respect their opinions on small things, thereby building a bridge to respect their voice on larger company decisions in the future.

BE DIRECT

A few days before I wrote this sentence, BuzzFeed came out with an unusual article titled "Gen Z'rs Are Sharing How They'll Parent Differently Than Their Boomer Parents and It's Eye-Opening."[60] Among the multifarious answers, one response indicated that Gen Z'rs will "tell my child when a pet dies"—or in other words, stop pretending that death doesn't exist and that it's something to be hidden. Also, Gen Z'rs are not afraid to stop addiction cycles in their family, and a growing population is choosing not to drink alcohol because of the problems that have arisen from their own upbringing around parents who drink. Each of these choices points to a single truth: Gen Z isn't afraid to be blunt. Whether a pet dies or a friend needs some tough truth about their addiction habits, Gen Z will be the first to point out the problem and not sugarcoat the truth. Because we aren't afraid to be blunt, we expect our managers to treat us the same way.

If you need to bring up a challenge with a Gen Z'r, please don't sugarcoat it. Give the feedback directly, then provide encouragement. Here's an example: Let's say your Gen Z employee fails to complete their part of a team project on time and you need to confront them. First of all, recognize that if you hired an independent Gen Z'r, they are likely going to know that they failed you and the team and already be self-correcting in their own head—we are naturally self-deprecating because of social media. When you confront them, here's what you should say:

> *Hey, Minaro, you probably already know why we're having this conversation, but I wanted to directly speak with you because I respect you, and don't want you to blow this mistake out of proportion because it isn't a big deal. Last week when you didn't complete your portion of our team project on time, I know you realize that it wasn't a positive experience for the team, but what you may not realize is the impact that missing deadlines has on other departments. You see, when our team doesn't complete (INSERT PROJECT) on time, it impacts (INSERT DIVISION) and they fall behind on (INSERT TASK/GOAL), which causes (INSERT*

RESULT). That being said, this is the first time it's happened, so I wanted to give you a greater glimpse of how our work affects other divisions. This time, all it did was cause a slight delay in (INSERT TASK) and you shouldn't be worried! I know you're probably concerned that this impacts my opinion of you, but I want you to know I'm not upset. I fully support you, and if you ever need help meeting a deadline or you're struggling with something, I am here to help. Is there anything I can do to help make sure we meet the next deadline? Also, you're doing a fantastic job getting integrated here with the team—I've noticed you taking initiative and getting to know your co-workers. Relationships on our team are very important to me and I'm glad you're spending time on them!

Notice a few things about this dialogue. First of all, the encouragement is at the end. Gen Z doesn't want sugarcoating up front, but that doesn't mean we don't need encouragement! Stick it at the end and you'll leave the conversation on a positive note. Second, acknowledge that the Gen Z'r might already know why you're having to confront them. We aren't clueless and we can see through the BS easily, having been conditioned by the bluntness that comes from social media feedback. By simply stating "you probably already know why we need to talk," you're acknowledging them as adults. Third, by stating "I don't want you to blow this out of proportion," you are empathizing with Gen Z's tendency to focus on mistakes more than successes (again, cultured by the negative impacts of social media) and helping them see the bigger picture. By reminding your Z'r they are doing great and that mistakes happen, you can help encourage positive mistake-making. Overall, be blunt and direct, but be clear in your intent.

GIVE SPECIFIC EXAMPLES

If you want your encouragement and praise to make a difference in how we work, make your feedback specific. Just as with millennials, don't think it's enough to say to a Gen Z'r, "Good work today!"—instead, go a little deeper. For example, say, "Claire, this morning when you shared your personal journey with our potential client, I admired how vulnerable you got with them. I could sense that their own story was similar to yours and it made our call stand out among the other vendors they were speaking with, which may mean we'll be able to onboard them. Thank you for your candor and keep up the good work!"

Notice in this feedback you included several important elements:

- Time—your feedback was timely and you remembered that the action had occurred that morning, showing your Z'r you paid attention.
- Specificity—A Z'r would have absolutely no question about what they did well in this case. They are going to go home and tell their friends/family/spouses about that compliment you gave!
- Impact—You shared how the action taken by the employee would impact the company and encouraged that they do it more often.

BUILD PURPOSEFUL TIMES OF CONNECTIONS

While a quick stop by our office and sporadic and specific feedback make us feel valued, scheduling times for deep conversation that is not focused on getting to know our preferences or correcting our behavior is also important. Schedule times, preferably weekly, to check in with your Z'r on how work is going. This doesn't have to be long—30 minutes at most—but it will pay dividends. In future chapters, we'll dive into the questions you can be asking during these conversations. Gen Z'rs are humans just like everyone else, with a keen desire to be heard. Social media has amplified our need for attention and feedback, but with some clear guidelines and direction, feedback will not just help with retention but will build intense loyalty from us too.

SIMPLE STEPS YOU CAN TAKE:

Before your next meeting or lunch with your Gen Z employee, have them fill out the rubric in Figure 1 so you can have an honest conversation about feedback. When you talk with them, you'll want to understand why they selected the answers they did so you can provide them with the most meaningful feedback possible.

Want to take this a step further? Have each of your Z'rs fill out this rubric, then laminate them and hang them in your office. Whenever you need a reminder of how Rodrigo prefers to be acknowledged or how Denisha wants you to address conflict with her, you've got the answers right in front of you.

WHAT ARE YOUR FAVORITE WAYS TO RECEIVE ACKNOWLEDGMENT?

1. In person, in private
2. In front of co-workers
3. At home with my family
4. E-card is fine
5. Something else (tell me below!)

IF WE HAVE CONFLICT (OR THERE'S TEAM CONFLICT), HOW WOULD YOU PREFER I BRING IT UP WITH YOU? LET ME KNOW WHICH OF THESE SCENARIOS RESONATE(S) WITH YOU.

- Just tell me straight up. Don't sugarcoat it.
- I'm prone to think "worst case" scenario, so encourage me in what I'm doing well before giving me constructive criticism.
- Make sure it's done in person.
- I'd prefer that you email me with the feedback first, so I have time to ponder it before we talk about it in person.

Give me some other thoughts of how I can best address conflict:

WHAT ARE YOUR "HOT BUTTONS"?

HOW OFTEN DO YOU LIKE TO BE RECOGNIZED FOR A JOB WELL DONE?

1. It's easy to doubt my ability. Anytime you see me do something worth acknowledging, I want to hear it, even if it's every single day!
2. A couple of times per week is plenty. As long as my ideas are heard, that is acknowledgment enough.
3. A few times per month is just fine. If I'm constantly acknowledged, it doesn't feel genuine.

Let me know other thoughts you have:

HOW OFTEN DO YOU WANT TO HEAR CHALLENGING, CONSTRUCTIVE CRITICISM SO YOU CAN LEARN AND GROW?

Figure 1

 Visit hannahgwilliams.com/downloads to access printable versions of exercises.

> **RESEARCH INDICATES THAT OUR GENERATION IS DRIVING A DEMAND FOR PAY TRANSPARENCY MORE SO THAN ANY GENERATION BEFORE US.**

CHAPTER 24
RETHINK COMPENSATION PACKAGES

Lately, I've been taking ballroom dancing lessons with high schoolers. It's a fascinating experience—not just the dancing; the high schoolers themselves are intriguing—and I've realized that with all the time I spend working alongside other generations, it's easy to forget what it was like to be a freshman, attempting to impress friends and sarcastically dissing celebrities. The first night of ballroom, the line was out the door with young students, guys and gals alike, eagerly awaiting their opportunity to sign in. Something quickly caught my attention. I began chatting with the kids in line—most of whom I had never met—and many exclaimed they had saved up their own money to take this class. I was shocked. First of all, their choice of dancing lesson was intriguing, but perhaps ballroom was making a comeback! But the fact they had worked odd jobs or chosen to defer other activities so they could pay for instruction, rather than their parents forcing them to learn how to dance and covering the cost, was surprising (and most surprising was the number of them who accurately wrote a check in line!). I was reminded of my great-grandparents' stories of working odd summer jobs to scrape together money to buy gadgets. You see, while most millennials got a (often unsound) bad rap for being the generation where everything was handed to them, Gen Z was taught by their parents to work hard and diligently for the rewards one expects in life.

Gen Z exhibits a heightened appreciation for the value of money and we frequently seek our own education (often online!) to feel confident about how we manage it. A study conducted by Raddon Research Insights found that 35% of Gen Z had attended a financial education seminar, while only 12% of millennials had.[61] Shocking, right? Gen Z has only been alive since 1996 and yet our generation consumes more financial education than the preceding one as a collective. That being said, 84% of us still rely on our parents for financial information, although this should come as no surprise given most of us are college age or younger.

With financial education more accessible than ever, our generation is poised to become the most financially progressive and literate in history, with a strong focus on investing from an early age. It's no surprise to Traditionalists that with the easy access to education, there is also a large spread of false information online, and parents are teaching their children to be wary. So as a result, Gen Z has been cautiously stepping into the digital realm and a surprising 34% still prefer in-person banking rather than using online investment tools; they are actually distrustful of online tools.[62] And while Gen Z is fascinated by trading and investing—51% say their risk tolerance during the COVID-19 pandemic had increased[63]—Robinhood's decisions in 2020 to restrict trading of specific stocks spurred outrage from young and old alike, and quickly taught our generation that gamified trading without thorough education can be dangerous.

The democratization of trading and financial education, along with tools like LinkedIn's "compare your salary to others in your field" feature, has begun to commoditize compensation, and Gen Z expects transparency in pay models just like every other piece of information we can easily access. Along with the circumstances of our upbringing, this change will drastically impact the compensation packages Gen Z is enthralled with, how pay transparency is conducted in the workplace, and how we view salary negotiations.

PAY TRANSPARENCY

A good friend of mine exuberantly told me, "If I ever work for a company where I hear the phrase from a manager or HR 'you're not supposed to be discussing your compensation with other employees,' I'll turn in my notice that day." While not every Gen Z'r feels this way, overall, research indicates that our generation is driving a demand for pay transparency more so than any generation before us. You see, given the knowledge and resources we have access to at a very early age, we can't understand why a company would keep from us how our pay compares to others or what we have to specifically accomplish to reach our growth goals.

Gen Z will learn to forgive mistakes that are common to humans as we grow, yet it defies a deep part of our character to allow inauthenticity to fester.

Gen Z will learn to forgive mistakes that are common to humans as we grow, yet it defies a deep part of our character to allow inauthenticity to fester. This leaks into all areas of the workplace, including compensation. On the flip side, think of how excitedly riled up young people become at a Drake concert (or pick the concert when you were a teenager!), and realize how little it takes to make us enthusiastic about something we love. You can build loyalty with us by making some small changes to compensation models. If our generation understands the salary ranges of our position and how to reach the next pay level, we will immediately trust you more. Frankly, we aren't the only generation demanding greater pay transparency, but perhaps unlike other generations it will quickly become a reason we'll leave the workplace rather than fighting to stay. Implementing full pay transparency in your organization helps in many ways:

- **It takes away the guessing game for everyone.** Simply knowing the CEO's salary shows their employees company priorities—whether the salary is high (and something to aspire to for Z'rs who appreciate higher pay!) or lower to indicate a selfless cause, simply knowing how executives are paid builds trust and loyalty. I won't pretend to know which pay model is ideal for your organization, as each is different; however, any company should strongly consider how pay is perceived across the firm, what the cost is of not building greater transparency into the scales, and what small changes can be made.
- **Salary negotiations begin to fade away.** Instead, salary discussions are embedded in forward-thinking career growth plans for all employees. Employees have a clear path forward and understand the salary that will accompany it, and if the pay models no longer work with our financial situation, we will self-select out.

PAY OVER MOST BENEFITS

Just as this generation is taking back control over knowledge of our pay, we also want more control over our salary itself. Think about it this way: Generation Z is leading a trend of minimalism in our daily lives, which means most of us think less is more—and thriftiness, ingenuity, and a fervor for saving money are key characteristics. When I launched a small YouTube music channel for fun during COVID-19, my husband and I were too cheap to purchase a real light box for filming; rather, he took a cardboard milk box, purchased a rotating multi-bulb device from Amazon for $7.99, and used zip ties to secure everything in place. The best part? You never would have known the difference in the video quality. Trust me, we aren't all as cheap and thrifty as he is, but the principle remains: Gen Z is "decluttering" our homes and we'd also prefer to declutter our benefits packages. Instead, a higher salary is the most important factor in hiring us.

COMPENSATION PACKAGES

Given all these facts, you'll find what a Gen Z compensation package should look like, listed in order of importance, in Figure 1. You'll notice that compared to the millennial version in Figure 2, salary is in the "critical" section rather the "important" category. Also take note that health care benefits are nearly as important as salary to Z'rs, this being because the youngest generation is least likely to be capable of weathering the storm if a large ER bill came up. The fear caused by COVID-19 strongly influenced this.[64]

Gen Z Compensation Packages

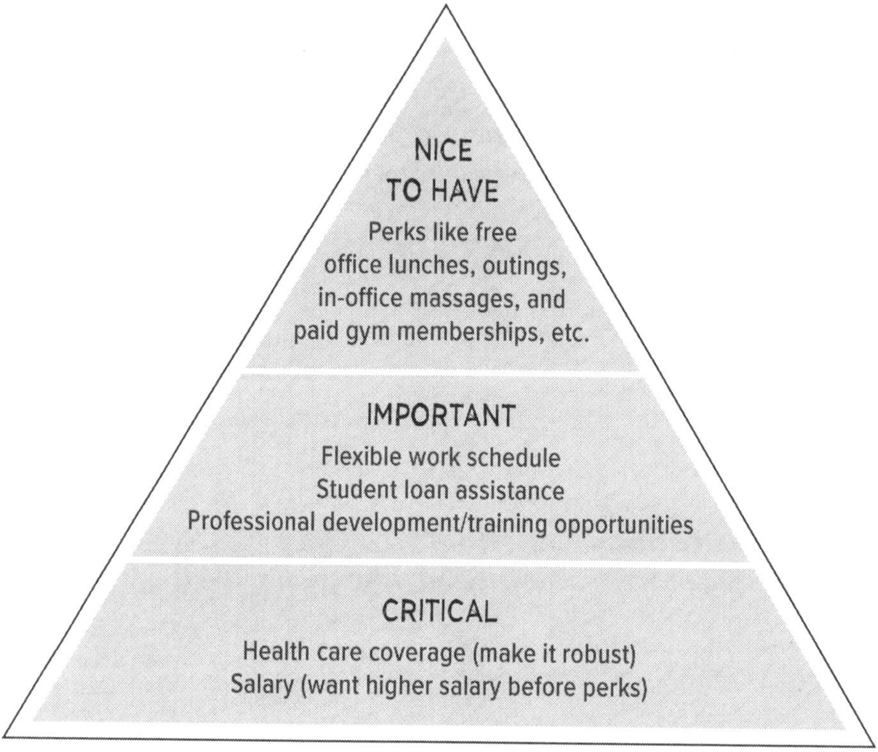

NICE TO HAVE
Perks like free office lunches, outings, in-office massages, and paid gym memberships, etc.

IMPORTANT
Flexible work schedule
Student loan assistance
Professional development/training opportunities

CRITICAL
Health care coverage (make it robust)
Salary (want higher salary before perks)

Figure 1

Millennial Compensation Packages

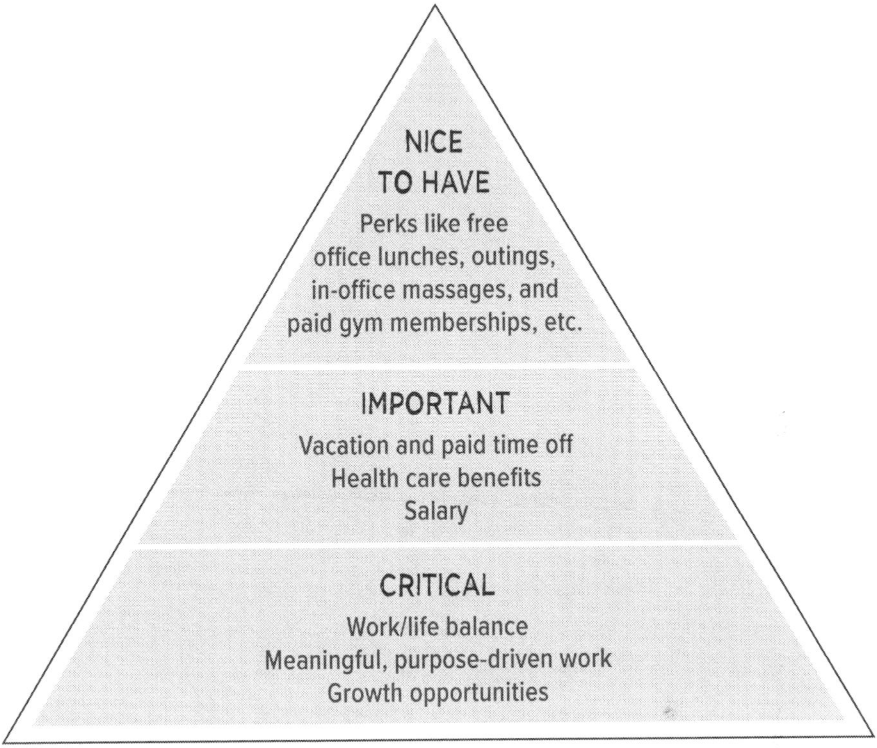

NICE TO HAVE
Perks like free office lunches, outings, in-office massages, and paid gym memberships, etc.

IMPORTANT
Vacation and paid time off
Health care benefits
Salary

CRITICAL
Work/life balance
Meaningful, purpose-driven work
Growth opportunities

Figure 2

If your company has resources to put into perks and benefits that Gen Z will gravitate toward, you should consider things like:

- **Financial planning/payment assistance:** Gen Z is extremely forward-thinking about our finances, with less than 23% of us believing Social Security benefits will exist when we retire, according to a 2021 study from Northwestern Mutual,[65] and any financial education you can provide us will be used. Additionally, student loan payoff assistance and/or programs to help us purchase a car, first home, real estate investment, etc., are highly attractive.

- **Mentorship and/or groups:** Coaching, counseling, and therapy are at the top of Gen Z's personal needs list, both in professional and personal spheres. Some Z'rs may opt for masterminds to help with professional growth while others may need personal therapy. They're probably paying for it themselves anyway!

- **Lifestyle benefits/lifestyle spending account:** Essentially the HSA for Gen Z, this is a company-sponsored, customized spending account with a monetary limit, and it is highly appealing to Gen Z. For example, we could be offered $1,500 a year to use toward discretionary activities such as online wellness classes, pet insurance, or home exercise equipment. But the company spends only what the employee does.

- **Charitable-giving stipends:** Set up small funds that employees can use to donate to their favorite causes.

Besides meaningful benefits that speak to the core of who we are, we need to have a brief conversation about the importance of personalization when it comes to benefits, so please step into the shoes of our Quintessential "Intrapreneur," Claire Beezley, for a moment.

PERSONALIZATION WITH BENEFITS

THE QUINTESSENTIAL "INTRAPRENEUR"
CLAIRE BEEZLEY (24 YEARS OLD)

Claire, the Quintessential "Intrapreneur," is happy with her job, and overall, the company offers great benefits, at least on a broad spectrum. But she can't help thinking from time to time, "Wouldn't it be nice if I could actually select which benefits I want?" You see, one of the benefits her employer offers is discounts on local restaurants; however, she's vegan and the majority of the discount partners don't serve plant-based options, so she finds herself rarely using the discount card. Also, she's 23 and her parents are still paying for her health insurance until she turns 28. Because she doesn't need it, she hasn't enrolled in her company's health plan (which they offer for free to employees). Even though health care is one of the more expensive benefits to the company, Claire didn't receive alternative benefits despite not taking advantage of the program. Also, her employer is wonderfully forward-thinking and offers student loan assistance to their staff; however, in Claire's case, her parents saved for her education and have already paid it off. While being debt free is wonderful for Claire, she can't help wondering why, even though her colleagues are getting thousands of dollars of student loan and health care benefits, her salary isn't benefiting because she's opted out of those programs.

> **GEN Z MUSINGS**
> *If I can't use this benefit, why isn't there a different option?*

RETHINK COMPENSATION PACKAGES

> *Employers* are often focused on providing the best benefits, not necessarily the most individually useful ones.

This is a common challenge the majority of employees face because employers are often focused on providing the best benefits, not necessarily the most individually useful ones. In the Simple Steps section, let's talk about how we can begin to remedy this situation.

SIMPLE STEPS YOU CAN TAKE:

All in all, I hope it's clear that while we are a financially astute, "saver" generation, Gen Z'rs view both salary and our compensation packages the same DIY way we see the rest of our lives. We are prepared to take control of our lives, finances, and beliefs, and we expect your benefits to align with those. Here's how you can personalize your benefits package to make sense for Gen Z:

THE "CHOOSE YOUR JOURNEY" BENEFITS PACKAGE

1. Pull up a list of your benefits as they are currently offered so you can see them throughout this exercise.

2. Decide which benefits are mandatory for employees. (For example, if you want to encourage healthy breaks from work, one week of vacation may be mandatory for your staff.)

3. Assign tiers to your benefits based on cost to the company.

4. Rework your benefits as a "menu," with options to increase salary by a certain percentage if an employee opts out of a particular benefit.

To illustrate what I mean, here's an example of a benefits menu:

CHOOSE YOUR BENEFITS JOURNEY

We want to offer you this menu of benefits so you can select which are most important to you, your family, and your lifestyle! Within each of the tiers, you can choose to opt in to ALL the benefits or you can opt out of the benefit in exchange for a salary increase.

There are certain benefits we require for all employees to ensure health, wellness, professional growth, and rest.

- 1 week of vacation annually
- Professional development and in-house training opportunities to help you grow. Your manager will help you select and participate in these.

TIER 1 BENEFITS

HEALTH INSURANCE:
- High-deductible (free for all employees, additional for family members)
- Low-deductible ($20 per month for employees, additional for family members)
- Opt out of coverage: Are you on a spouse's or parent's plan? Opt out and receive $200/month toward your salary.

PAID TIME OFF:
- 3 weeks of vacation time
- 80 hours of health/family leave
- 8 flexible holidays (so you can take the holidays most meaningful to you!)
  » I opt to exchange _____ days of vacation for % of salary increase

TIER 2 BENEFITS

Education: Let's talk about and decide which of the following programs works best. We offer one of these opportunities to each employee, with opportunities for additional help after your first year with the company.

Choose one:
- $200/month student loan payoff program to help you pay off debt
- $100–$500/month tuition reimbursement to take classes alongside work (these don't have to be through a school; they can be online training programs, financial courses, self-development, etc.)

Employer matching programs (we recommend opting in to all these programs):
- 401(k) match of 3% (see handbook for details)
- HSA—employer contribution of $100/month
- ESA—employer contribution of $50/month
- Company-sponsored first homebuyers program

TIER 3 BENEFITS

CHOOSE 3 OF EACH CATEGORY

PERKS:
- Gym membership
- Therapy sessions
- Season passes to local attraction
- Monthly massage package
- Local restaurant discount card

LIFE NECESSITIES:
- Commuter benefits
- Daycare reimbursement
- Dry cleaning
- Clothing stipend

OR opt out of all benefits for a ___% increase in salary

You'll see that the benefits/perks in this example are arranged where someone can make the benefits work for their life situation. Of course, each company's resources and situation are different. I encourage you to take a look at your own benefits and assign tiers to them based on company expense, then determine how much flexibility you can offer your employees. It may be only one step in the right direction at first, and that's okay!

Section IV

ENGAGE

I'm embarrassed to say I've started more projects than I've ever completed. This hadn't always been the case; in fact, until I graduated from high school, everyone around me saw nothing but a high-speed train that never slowed down, always completing challenges and tasks. If I was supposed to graduate from college by 18, I would. If I had committed to a month-long mission trip to Central America, I would not only go, I'd help other team members raise their funding too. But I distinctly remember a point in my life when that changed. I was 18. I had graduated from online college after a grueling few years with what felt like an unstoppable mind and ever-flowing energy. At the time, I couldn't even count the number of teachers, peers, and mentors who half-jokingly pushed me toward the path of a political office. Never allowing myself to relax, I can count maybe five movies I watched the entire four years I spent in school between the ages of 14 and 18, and while dear friends asked me to slow down a bit and enjoy life, I remember pushing them away, mostly because my definition of success at the time was shaped only by perfection and a so-called "omission" of failure. Looking back, I'm disgusted at how easy it was for me to push away the most important aspects of my life—close and meaningful relationships, serving others, and even experiencing joy—to bow down to the idol of productivity.

It wasn't until I moved from my parents' home at 18 that I discovered the escape of Netflix. Starting with *Sherlock*, then continuing to *Downton Abbey*, *Breaking Bad*, and *The Crown*, I soon became hooked. It became all too easy to come home from a full day of work, flip on the TV, and escape from reality. My friends encouraged me to relax, insisting that watching Netflix was a good and normal habit. Unfortunately for me, I'm drawn to extremes. Just as easily as I had lived 18 years barely touching TV (and having never watched the entirety of a show) and devoting every bit of energy to school, I thrust every bit of after-work energy into bingeing my favorite shows. Slowly, my half-completed music album floated to the wayside. My family/friend interactions dropped to maybe once per month. The Amazon business I tried to start absolutely flopped once it launched. I dragged myself into isolation. My half-finished projects lay all around me, and even though I still talked to people about all the grand visions I had set out to achieve, I backed those visions with little or no action.

One day, a close mentor of mine sought me out for a coffee date. During our very honest conversation, she asked me a probing (and at the time, unwelcome) question: "What would you have to give up in order to achieve the dream you pretend you have?" This question struck me powerfully, deeply. She saw how often since graduating from high school I had spoken about my dream of running a consulting business and writing a book. While I thought I was on the right track, to everyone else it seemed like I was pretending. From an outsider's perspective, how could my actions be perceived any other way? I was all talk.

Stricken by her honesty, I went home and began writing a list. What would I actually have to give up? The first few items on the list were easy to identify—I had to rein in my Netflix bingeing habits and I had to replace some of that time with realistic steps toward my goals. But the problems preventing my success were deeper than that . . . far deeper. I had to work on giving up my idol of productivity. I had to give up the shrine I'd built to perfectionism and learn to handle my tendency toward extremes—in practical terms, this meant building in intentional time for relaxation, Netflix, and escape without feeling guilty. Going even deeper, I had to give up my reliance on isolation and welcome back the people in my life who brought joy, encouragement, and ultimately fulfillment and a reason to succeed. In all honesty, I had to reconstruct my reasons for living a meaningful life.

That one question my mentor asked me, and then held me accountable to, not only has made me a better version of myself but also is the reason you are reading these words in the first place. Her words are the reason I've completed one project that has put me on a journey to impact people around the globe. It was also the gut-check I needed to bring healthy habits back into my life that have saved the essence of who I am and, while I'll always battle my natural tendencies, her guidance brought me back to a balance that is sustainable.

I share my personal journey with you because I want you to see how powerful a mentor has been in my life. An ordinary person can ask simple questions that can change the trajectory of how someone lives and shape how they see themselves. I'm sure each of you reading this has experienced a mentor in your life who impacted you much the same way. As you read this section on motivating, engaging, and leading Gen Z talent, know that your everyday, seemingly small interactions are equally as important as—if not more important than—the actions your company takes on a global level to meaningfully impact the next generation in your workforce. You hold the power to change someone's life, for better or for worse, and through this section I'll share how you can be a force for good in propelling Generation Z to places even they never believed possible.

> "IF YOU WANT TO SERVE THE NEXT GENERATION, YOU NEED TO MAINTAIN AN OPEN HEART AND AN OPEN MIND."

CHAPTER 25
BECOME A MENTOR

It's safe to say that our first stop in this journey should be a conversation about how to healthily approach organizational mentorship, and who would know better about this topic than Mark Miller, vice president of high-performance leadership for Chick-fil-A corporate. It goes without saying that Chick-fil-A's growth is one of the most compelling success stories of the 21st century, and Mark began working with the company 40 years ago. At the time of our interview, he'd authored nine books and counting, with more than 1 million copies in print in 25 languages, focused on building developing high-performance leadership, teams, and organizations. After meeting Mark at an annual leadership conference held conveniently near my hometown in Black Mountain, North Carolina, I asked him to share his thoughts on how leaders can effectively guide and mentor Gen Z talent and help them become the most courageous, best versions of themselves. Here is Mark's advice and the framework we developed to help leaders focus their efforts on mentees and approach mentorship effectively:

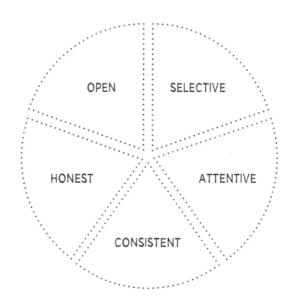

MARK MILLER
VP, High-Performance Leadership
Chick-fil-A

In Mark's words:

Be selective. This may seem counterintuitive. Wouldn't a leader want everyone on their team to learn and grow? Absolutely! However, a leader cannot personally mentor everyone in their organization. I encourage leaders to identify a few young people with potential (preferably future leaders) and overinvest in their growth and development. If you have more of these individuals than you can invest in personally, invite other trusted senior leaders to do the same. For everyone else, you should have more traditional learning and development opportunities provided by your company.

Be attentive. Pay attention to what your mentee wants to learn. I typically ask young people to send me the questions they want to address before every meeting. I don't want to invest time answering questions they are not asking. Also, asking them to prepare the questions does several things: One, it forces them to prepare in advance. If the questions don't arrive 48 hours before the meeting, you should cancel it. They obviously are not ready. Two, you learn a lot about someone by the questions they ask.

Be consistent. Mentoring is best done over time. Although it can be helpful to a mentee to have a single session with a senior leader, multiple sessions are preferred. This allows a relationship to form, content themes to emerge, and trust to be built. The right frequency is debatable—context, workload, objectives, and personal preference are all relevant factors. I like monthly sessions. This pacing allows some processing and application time for ideas discussed during sessions. Regardless of the timing, I suggest prescheduling the meetings as opposed to random events scheduled when you can get to it.

Be honest. If the mentee asks hard questions, you need to be prepared to answer them (maintaining appropriate boundaries of course). If you have feedback for your mentee, don't pull any punches—tell them the whole truth. It is most often the last 10% of the truth where the value is. As an example, if you are asked to critique a presentation given by the mentee, and it was good, you could just say it was good. However, if the mentee wasn't dressed appropriately and his appearance detracted from the message, you need to tell him. That's the last 10%!

> **GEN Z MUSINGS**
> *A lot of times I feel like I'm walking on glass at work. I just wish there was someone I could be really honest with... just someone I could rant to.*

Be open. If you want to serve the next generation, you need to maintain an open heart and an open mind. Your role is not to make them conform to your standards and your worldview and to adopt your methods. Your objective is to help them be successful. Be prepared to have different views on some issues. Be open to their challenges. Be open to their perspective. Be open to what you can learn from them. In my experience, I learn as much from young, emerging leaders as they learn from me. This would not be possible if I was not open to the possibility.

Mark's approach to highly selective mentoring is helpful for any generation, but let me draw attention to a few aspects that are crucial for Gen Z. First, for your own sanity, asking the Gen Z'r to prepare for a meeting (or canceling if they don't) shows our often-distracted generation that we must think deeply before using your time. Z'rs are so used to the idea of "receiving someone's time" (usually through virtual learning groups or social media live sessions) that we honestly may not realize the mental strain it puts on a leader when they take time away to mentor us. Of course, your Z'r will learn over time, but you must stake out your boundaries. Set requirements around what your mentee must send you before you'll take the meeting because, as odd as it may sound, it may not be intuitive for your mentee to prepare. Secondly, honesty is crucial for Gen Z. Because we are hyper-pessimistic as a generation and seek out challenges, if your feedback misses the "last 10%," as Mark put it, we may not take you seriously. And finally, your level of openness will make or break trust with your mentee.

Let me repeat that. The level of openness you show your mentee will make or break their trust in you.

The level of openness you show your mentee will make or break their trust in you.

VIRTUAL MENTORING AND TRAINING

Speaking of mentoring, with the broad-sweeping move toward online and flexible workspaces, mentoring and training online is inevitable, especially in the aftermath of COVID-19. But with the newest generation, companies may not realize they've gone too far in automating their online learning and mentoring. You see, Gen Z, who has grown up learning skills from YouTube and TikTok, is quite accustomed to the e-learning space, but studies are showing that Gen Z students are tired of squinting at e-textbooks and relying solely on the internet for learning. In fact, in a 2020 study conducted by Dell Technologies, 75% of Gen Z indicated they would prefer to learn from peers on the job rather than through technology.[66]

Because face-to-face connection is so important to Gen Z, maintaining personal touch will be key. Here are some ways to use the amazing benefits online meetings can provide while continuing to maintain creative and high levels of personalization for our generation:

- **Leverage virtual conferencing tools:** Online services such as MURAL[67] can get your team's creative juices flowing. Instead of just a coffee date, you can now mentor/train your Z'r by drawing on a blank online workspace. Make it fun by building a visual board together of your mentoring journey, including pictures, ideas, sketches, etc.

- **Engage mentoring software:** Tools like Mentoring Complete can be wonderful assets to broad-scale teams looking to connect team members across geographies in pairs. Engage with technology to make the mentorship experience more formalized and complete, and Gen Z will thank you.

- **Have a virtual "study party":** While Gen Z prefers independent work, there are lonely times when working from home. One fun way to break up the pace is to re-create a college "study" experience online! Have two to three people jump on a Zoom call together to work independently in the presence of others. Kids might be popping in and out of the room and that's fine! The point is that mentorship doesn't have to be formal—just being in other people's presence can make a difference. Turn on some music and do some deep work together.

Bringing authentic, real connection to virtual meetings doesn't have to be challenging; it just takes some creativity. Of course, for any mentor, it's important to be frank, candid, and vulnerable, whatever the communication medium. As we've discussed in previous chapters, you should expect a frankness from Z'rs that's not typical of other generations. Mentorship is sure to be fun and effective! Let's take Mark's advice and do a bit of self-reflection in this end-of-chapter exercise.

SIMPLE STEPS YOU CAN TAKE:

- **Select a mentee:** If you are not yet mentoring anyone from the next generation, consider selecting one high-potential individual in your company, community, or local school system. The goal? To learn from one another.

- **Download the Gen Z Mentorship Toolkit:** I've developed a toolkit you can use to help you and your Gen Z mentee connect deeper and learn from one another. Download it at hannahgwilliams.com/downloads.

- **State your boundaries:** If you are finding that too often your mentees take your time for granted or don't prepare adequately for conversations, teach them a life lesson and take Mark's advice: Cancel the meeting if they haven't sent you questions and/or conversation topics 48 hours prior. Of course, if current mentees have become used to lazy meetings, you may need to reframe the purpose for them.

 Visit hannahgwilliams.com/downloads to access printable versions of exercises.

"PART OF LEADING GENERATION Z IS LETTING US LEAD YOU."

CHAPTER 26
BE OPEN TO OUR INEXPERIENCE

My good friend and partner, Steven Keith, warned me about "blue goo." "Essentially," Steven shared, "when I consulted IBM years ago, staff talked about the 'blue goo' that began to stick to employees as time progressed. It was their way of saying, 'If you've been around too long, you start to become blinded.' If there was too much blue goo, it was time to bring in fresh eyes." As an organization, it may be tempting to value young people's talent contingent on their willingness to "pay their dues" and work there a few years before giving cultural advice. However, the most successful organizations actually begin taking advice from the youngest members of their staff as soon as they arrive. And get this: It's usually the company's competitive advantage.

Why is this? Simply put, the youngest generation's inexperience brings innovation and insight that is frequently lost through years in the workplace. I interviewed Steven to understand how his clients are leveraging Client & Employee Experience design to tap into the youngest generation's gifts. His firm, CX Pilots, is an unconventional boutique management consultancy that has worked with hundreds of brands, from Ford to RSM to Google, and the massive, culture-shifting Client & Employee Experience initiatives they undertake impact departments across the organization in a united effort to change for the better. Our conversation went something like this:

> **STEVEN KEITH**
> Founder, CX Pilots

HANNAH: Gen Z'rs are natural change agents—we've lived through the fastest-changing world of any generation, technologically and socioeconomically. How can organizations leverage Gen Z's fresh perspective as they shift to "continuous evolution" rather than "change and pause, change again and pause"?

STEVEN: When I speak to your generation, I'm amazed by the grit and drive I see—really, you have unrivaled determination that isn't evident amongst other generations. And here's the thing: When organizations don't harness these skills at the very beginning, they're missing their greatest change agents. At CX Pilots, when we work on major client experience (CX) initiatives with firms, one of the first elements is to design governance, which is essentially the force that prevents backsliding. It's the tool that will consistently disallow the firm to slip back into status quo. And what is governance? Well, it's a group of cross-functional people who come together to move forward an initiative. Of course, human instinct is to revert back to what's always been done, so to make sure the CX initiatives stick, we have to have people from all across the organization championing the movement.

How does Gen Z's skill set come into play? When engaging in a major initiative, we specifically select employees and leaders on a horizontal and vertical plane that includes a wealth of Gen Z folks, middle management, all the way to the C-suite. What may be surprising is, time after time, it's the youngest generation involved who bring the most positive contributions! They are also the most hawkish and will not stand for others not pulling their weight or not "walking the talk." We make an intentional effort to involve the newest generation—despite their inexperience—because their "bright eyes" and questions point us in directions we never thought of going.

HANNAH: So true. As a Z'r, I've seen incredible examples of this openness to a young person's thoughts. In fact, a CEO I formerly worked under made it a point to visit every single new-hire orientation to tell his staff how valuable their fresh eyes were. He gave an example of a time a student, fresh out of college, in her first week pointed out the profit the agriculture side of the business could make by converting the hundreds of gallons of canola oil used in the on-property restaurants into biodiesel for the tour buses. Instead of shutting her down, her management asked for a plan, and when she presented it, gave her a raise and put her in charge of the entire operation. That's just how the company operated. The result was immense employee loyalty.

STEVEN: Exactly. This is the type of innovation firms need to implement. One of my clients, a 2,000-person engineering firm, was having trouble hiring top Z'r talent, so what we've done is developed a pilot test where Z'rs are given an "experience by proxy" before being hired. Instead of taking the young candidates through the typical interview process, we actually have them sit in on live client meetings. Because they are involved in the actual construction of the client experience, we have them ask questions during the meeting, then ascertain their opinions of how it went afterward. Their fresh perspective of "why are things done this way" or "have you ever thought of X" adds value for our clients, it gives us insight into how well that employee understands the way our client experience is conducted, and it also gives the candidate a "day in the life" experience! This ultimately allows our firm to stand above the others they're considering.

Part of leading Generation Z is letting us lead you. What are some specific ways you can leverage Gen Z's natural "change agent" nature to promote innovation in your company?

- **Governance:** As Steven pointed out, bring Gen Z into your next major change initiative as a team member. Give that young person equal speaking rights and leadership ability. Of course, if they prove themselves week after week, give them greater responsibilities.

- **Innovation team lead:** If your company is one with various committees responsible for multifarious actions—we all know the safety committees, party-planning committees (no, not like *The Office!*), etc.—consider adding an innovation committee. And no, I'm not talking about the official R&D department. I'm talking about an innovation committee in HR! What about finance? How about operations? Rather than leaving innovation up to visionary leadership, what if you deployed a Z'r to put together a small team of forward-thinkers who met monthly to brainstorm innovative ideas for cost savings, efficiency increases, strategic movement, etc.?

  > **GEN Z MUSINGS**
  > *Dad, you won't believe it! I just started last month and my manager already asked me to lead the discussion on health and wellness at our next team meeting. He must really trust me.*

- **Research/professional development trip:** Could your Z'r be the one to travel abroad to find inspiration for that new product? Could they be responsible for interviewing the upcoming conference keynote speaker? Your Z'r might find this task easier than you do and might even enjoy it more, and they would find documenting the process on social media delightful.

PITFALLS FOR CHANGEMAKERS

Gen Z's enthusiasm for change and its ease is in our DNA; however, there are also challenges our leaders will need to help us work through. Often our quick response to change creates frustration with other generations in the workplace who understand that changes must be calculated and methodical and have intentional direction. Gen Z may tend to desire change "for the sake of change," without pausing to ask, "Why should we change?" or understanding the financial implications of doing so. We will lean on our leadership to communicate why change is or isn't necessary, or why the firm should go in one direction instead of another. Just as with anything, there should be wisdom brought to the table from both sides. However, as most organizations tend toward resisting change with more fervor than they do toward continual evolution, I strongly urge my readers to consider the value that your natural change agents can bring.

Instead of simple steps in this section, read the next chapter for exercises that will pertain to this topic and the one covered next.

> **BY ALLOWING A GEN Z'R TO TAKE OWNERSHIP OVER A PROJECT, YOU ARE GIVING THEM A VOICE AND STAKE IN THE DIRECTION OF YOUR COMPANY.**

CHAPTER 27
GIVE US A VOICE

Paige Borgman distinctly remembers the first few months at her first job after college. As a millennial entering an established PR firm, she was eager to learn and grow but also had ideas and fresh perspectives she knew the firm could find valuable. After a few weeks, though, it was clear that no matter how good the idea or how prepared she felt to handle the duties she was hired for, her manager was not going to trust her to make even small decisions. When it came to meeting with clients, she frequently heard phrases like "you're not ready to speak," and her manager made her bullet out what her conversations would be before they got on a phone with a client, as if making any slight error would ruin the firm's entire reputation. "You would think that at a PR firm, creativity would be encouraged—isn't that what they hired us for?" Paige expressed to me during our interview. "They wanted perfection and didn't know they were crushing creativity in doing so."

Now director of digital strategy at Reputation Partners, an agile and creative PR company, Paige is responsible for mentoring four Gen Z'rs at multiple organizations and she is committed to listening to and leading her young people with the care she wished she had received directly out of school. "I learned how not to manage by watching my first boss err so many times," Paige shared. Here are a few ways she encourages her Gen Z staff to use their voice:

1. Managing her team around deadlines, but always being sure to ask her direct report if the deadline makes sense for them rather than imposing deadlines on them.

2. Making sure that ownership of a project is always a two-way street. In other words, if a project has a deadline, making sure there's a reason for it and never allowing someone's hard effort to sit in her inbox for a week before she reviews it. This agreement ensures that there is mutual agreement between staff members on priorities and expectations, and that the boss doesn't need a project completed "just for the sake of it."

3. Placing intentional effort into listening to the ideas her staff bring her.

These ideas may seem so simple, but they take intentionality and time. Whether we like it or not, it's against human nature to take advice or correction from someone younger. But this approach is so very important in keeping talent engaged, learning, and passionate about their work. It's rarely the work that loses the charm; it's more often the dictator who hovers over that work who removes the charm, unaware of the possibility they are crushing.

TAKING SUGGESTIONS FROM SOMEONE YOUNGER?

On the other hand, it's easy to understand how difficult it is for any leader to listen to someone who hasn't "earned their right" to give suggestions. To better understand how to give Gen Z'rs a chance to gain a voice in the workplace, I spoke with Mark Bado, general manager of the Houston Country Club and former chair of the board of directors for the Club Management Association of America. Mark is a dear friend of mine and an incredible resource for anyone wanting to bring a touch of luxury hospitality into their workplace. Just a year prior to writing this chapter, Mark and I sat on the veranda of The Inn at Biltmore Estate sipping afternoon tea and snacking on raspberry scones, transported back to a more relaxed time. At the time of our interview, however, we "sat" in

Mark's office via Zoom, wishing we could have the conversation in person. Pictures of his adventures meeting Renée Fleming and eclectic golf pros graced his walls as we chatted.

> **MARK BADO**
> General Manager, Houston Country Club
> Former Chair of the Board, Club
> Management Association of America

"How do you empower young people at Houston Country Club to have a voice?" I asked Mark openly.

"First of all, many young people lack the confidence to warrant respect from others in the workplace, so it's our job as purposeful mentors to help them gain the respect of others," he began. "As an example, a young man our club recently hired had the guts to ask me, 'How do I gain a voice?' and I had a responsibility to be honest with him. Truthfully, he majorly lacked confidence and didn't know how to dress for a club environment. I gave him a couple of tips, such as coming to meetings prepared and dressing appropriately for the occasion, and I encouraged him to feel confident in himself. A few months later, he came back to me and was a completely transformed person. It just goes to show the power of giving someone a bit of your time, to be honest.

> *If a young leader* wants to gain a voice in the workplace, they need to seek out a mentor who will challenge them.

"Ultimately, the change was up to him and he had to put in the work (I couldn't do it for him), but you as a leader can be the catalyst for that young person's transformation. If a young leader wants to gain a voice in the workplace, they need to seek out a mentor who will challenge them in these areas:

- You need to find a workplace with people who care about you. I encourage young people not to chase logos; rather, chase people who care about them.

- No matter who you are, you've got to develop credibility. No one gives a s**t about your degrees and certifications, especially when you're right out of college. You have to build credibility with others in the workplace.

- At a new job, you'll be tested. You've got to be patient. There's going to be some grinding to get through it. You'll have to push through the learning of any new workplace and not give up immediately. Developing resiliency will go a long way in your career.

"Ultimately, pushing graduates to take ownership of the mountains they'll face, while also guiding them toward developing their credibility, will help them gain a voice in the workplace. It's a two-way street, not just companies bowing down to the whims of the new generation."

"I couldn't agree more," I responded. "In fact, in one of my earlier roles, I didn't take time to develop my credibility and just assumed leaders would give it to me. I ran up against obstacles with this approach and was quickly disenchanted with the culture. In reality, it was my problem. So, here's a question: Once a young person has a voice, how do you help them spring into action and build their credibility?"

"Young people's ideas can be powerful when they are guided," Mark answered. "Someone who's brand new to a company may not understand the overall vision of the brand and might make suggestions outside of the direction. So first of all, they need to watch and observe for a little while—but once they've earned that respect, it's time to truly look at their ideas and possibilities. For example, we have an incredible Gen Z'r who works in our clubhouse, Haley. She's been here over a year at this point but has certainly earned respect from her peers; I've put her through numerous challenges to build her resilience. This year we were faced with COVID-19, bringing a major hit to club revenue and hurting the majority of hospitality businesses significantly. Haley approached me with a few thoughts and ideas for the pool bar and how we could drive traffic and engagement for members, and rather than shutting her ideas down or immediately implementing them, I asked her for a plan. If she could put together a plan and present it to the executive team, we would consider her ideas. 'Until there's a plan in place, ideas are just daydreaming,' I shared with her. I will tell you, for a driven Gen Z'r, you are asking to be impressed when you give them ownership to run with a project that is their own idea. Within a week, she brought me a plan she and her manager had written together. It was fantastic. By the next day, we had taken her suggestions. They were so effective that we had more traffic and efficiency on our verandas from members than we had during the entirety of the former months during COVID-19. We were able to increase revenue, create greater efficiency, and increase member engagement. When everything during COVID-19 is about being relevant to members, a young person was the one who helped us with that. They have powerful ideas.

> **GEN Z MUSINGS**
> *Wow, that feels good. I've proven myself enough to where the GM isn't just listening to my suggestions. He's actually using them! And look at the difference I've made.*

You are asking to be impressed when you give a Gen Z'r ownership to run with a project that is their own idea.

"On the same note, you can apply this principle to raising your kids," he continued. "When my children were young, if they asked for a pet, I would have them write a few paragraphs as to why they wanted it. Basically, I put a brick wall in front of them. By their actions, they'd tell me how badly they wanted that pet, and I'd ask them, 'How meaningful is it to you? Is it important enough for time and effort?' I've found this approach is incredibly helpful with both my children and the young people I mentor to build courage, resilience, and intent in their actions."

I believe Mark's direction resonates with both Gen Z and older generations alike. Giving Gen Z a voice is inevitable at some point, but will you be the leader who can coach a Gen Z'r into how to respectfully and courageously gain their voice and command the respect of those in the workplace? And how soon are you willing to listen?

SIMPLE STEPS YOU CAN TAKE:

Intern project: Are you struggling to find projects for your intern or new hire to take on without direct guidance? Consider doing this: Ask them, "What is a change you think would enhance our company's efficiency, revenue, customer care, or hiring methods (or insert any challenge you're facing)?"

1. Give them a deadline.

2. Grant them free rein to speak with anyone in the firm and help them make any connections they need.

3. Ask them to put together a plan for how they would address that issue after collecting feedback from others in the firm.

If you give this project to a high-potential young person, you will be amazed at some of the results you will see. Have them present their project to you and a few select others and give them feedback. If the suggestions are promising (you might be surprised!), use that information or make some of the suggested changes. By allowing that Gen Z'r to take ownership over a project, you are giving them a voice and stake in the direction of your company—and they have skin in the game; their reputation is on the line.

Empower the Z'r to build a plan: Maybe you have a Z'r who's always bringing you ideas for changes. Instead of shutting their idea down, hand them the following template and have them complete it. Then, when they bring the idea back to you, it will be a well-researched idea that you can discuss effectively.

What is the idea?

What problem does it solve or benefit does it provide? (Think cost savings, employee happiness/well-being, increased profit, etc.)

How does the idea align with our team's/company's goals?

Who will be your "first follower"? (Think about the team you'd need to have involved to make your idea happen and what buy-in you'd need to earn.)

What's the cost of the project/idea?

How would you execute it? Walk through specific steps you plan to take.

 Visit hannahgwilliams.com/downloads to access printable versions of exercises.

> **IT'S IMPORTANT FOR US TO REMEMBER AS LEADERS THAT AT THE CORE, NO MATTER THE AGE OF THE YOUNG PERSON WE MANAGE, WE ARE ALL HUMAN.**

CHAPTER 28
SUPPORT OUR MENTAL HEALTH

It's a fact: Gen Z is the most stressed out and anxious generation of the modern era. Let me show why this is the case in the words of my good friend and expert on mental health in the workplace, Suzanne Baker Brown. As a boomer on the cusp of the Gen X generation, Suzanne shared with me that she grew up in a small Protestant town—most of the families were white, Christian, and knit together tightly. There was little to no diversity of race, religion, or culture, and roles were clearly defined. Growing up in this community, the boomer generation (kids at the time) was just beginning to question the traditional roles their parents took on, and despite this sense of entrepreneurship and curiosity, there was a straight road to walk. Traditionally, you attended church, went to school, and chose a career path in alignment with your parents' expectations. If you were a female, you were still breaking tradition if you pursued a career outside of homemaking, which was a major step in this generation. Fast-forward to Gen Z and the plethora of options for the path we choose no longer begins with our career choices—they also have to do with decisions that were once simple. My generation is starting to make life-altering choices at very young ages and, whether for good or bad, technology, science, and a redefining of traditional values have enabled young children to become entrepreneurs and even modify their gender. With all the choices my generation has at our fingertips, and the uncertainty in the world around us, we've lost some of the most important and necessary things in life—which ultimately begin at the bottom of Maslow's hierarchy of needs: safety, stability, and often purpose.

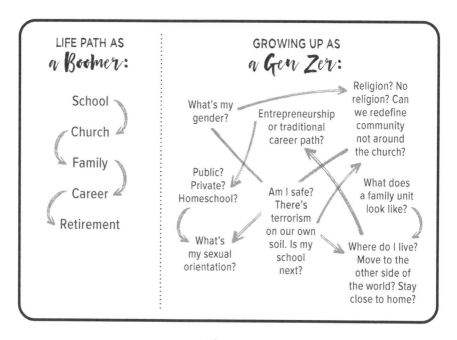

Figure 1

Ultimately, this chaos of decisions at a very early age (see Figure 1), compounded with economic and political instability, has created an anxious and mentally exhausted generation. According to a 2020 study by The Harris Poll, in their personal lives, Gen Z'rs say safety, money, and work are leading stressors. More than eight in 10 Gen Z'rs between the ages of 18 and 21 report money as a source of significant stress, with nearly as many saying the same about work. Nearly two in three Gen Z'rs ages 15 to 17 report that their families, not having enough money is a significant source of stress. For one-third of Gen Z'rs, personal debt and housing instability are a significant source of stress, while one-quarter cite hunger or getting enough to eat. Compared to 74% of adults overall, 91% of Gen Z'rs between ages 18 and 21 say they have experienced at least one physical or emotional symptom due to stress in the past month.[68] Much of this research was conducted during the height of the COVID-19 pandemic, which has shaped young people more than any other generation—many Gen Z'rs were trying to find jobs for the first time out of college. Any company should anticipate that, unless addressed, Gen Z's mental health concerns will take a toll on the overall well-being and productivity of the workplace.

> **GEN Z MUSINGS**
>
> *I literally don't know WTF I'm doing in life. All I can do is be honest that I don't know and make sure I'm taking care of myself and helping my friends so they don't give up because it's too hard.*

ADDRESSING MENTAL HEALTH CHALLENGES

So how do we address mental health and wellness in the workplace for young talent? To seek some practical solutions, I interviewed my friend Suzanne, who has consultanted on mental health and wellness who has consulted for companies such as Deloitte, Ernst & Young, Anderson, and Katten Munchin, and who was one of the thought leaders promoting work/life integration over work/life balance in early 2005. As a mentor and coach for high-potential young talent, she offered her thoughts that are refreshing and simple to implement.

SUZANNE BAKER BROWN
President, Leadership Investments Group

QUESTION: Why do you believe Gen Z is the most anxious generation of the modern era?

SUZANNE: During my years as an employee and consultant to several major professional services firms, I observed a shift in the way companies conducted business when leading firms began preaching "maximize shareholder value." In the past, businesses truly cared about the well-being of their employees, but there was a distinct shift toward productivity and efficiency rather than well-being in the '90s. While a shift is beginning toward awareness of mental health in the workplace, Gen Z has had to face trying crises during their young years that are nearly unprecedented. Not only this—the choices and options that are available to them at such young ages must create confusion and a lack of stability in their lives that carries into the workplace. I feel for them!

QUESTION: How can leaders support whole-life health for Gen Z'rs who are workaholics and help them create healthy habits?

SUZANNE: It's important for us to remember as leaders that at the core, no matter the age of the young person we manage, we are all human. We all have a need to be heard, valued, and appreciated. Generation Z is highly driven, which partially results in the desire to overachieve and exhaust themselves. Gen Z is stressed immensely with the strains of economic strife during their college years, the daunting number of choices that are available, and even the challenge of knowing how to distinguish truth from falsehoods with the proliferation of media influence in their young years. Here are some practical first steps you can take as a leader to encourage healthier habits in your young talent:

1. **Model relationship-driven leadership:** It's our responsibility as leaders to encourage relationship-focused paths for our young talent, not merely productivity and efficiency. I ask my team before each major meeting: "Does anyone have any extreme highs or lows to share before we get to business?" Of course, I've built safety and trust with my team where they are comfortable sharing this, but once you've built the groundwork, you can ask questions like this to demonstrate your investment in staff over whatever business matters may be on the table.

2. **Ask hard questions:** The divorce rate among American executives is exorbitantly high, pointing to a core problem that work takes a toll on the most important areas of life—health, relationships, and overall well-being—if not managed properly. As leaders, we should be speaking truth into the lives of our young talent that will carry them to success in future years as they take on their own leadership roles. For example, if you repeatedly see a recently married young man staying late at work every night, ask the tough question: "Is your wife expecting you? Shouldn't you be home?" Instill and model behavior that creates a healthy workplace for all.

3. **Create lightness and laughter:** Call out your employees' strengths whenever you can. The world is already so heavy. As a leader, I want to leave every interaction with an employee, family member, or friend with them feeling either a little lighter, a little more relieved, or like they've grown just a little, even if the conversation is hard. Our focus should always be to build others up rather than tear them down. Particularly when leading our young talent, we should be focused on identifying their strengths and helping them find their path. If Gen Z is seeking stability and something concrete in life to hold onto, you can provide that pillar of guidance and wisdom. Who knows, that time you spend with a young person may be the reason they find their true purpose in life.

I couldn't agree more with Suzanne's assessment. Mental health will continue being a challenge for Gen Z and there are many free ways individual leaders can address the challenge head-on without the intervention of company policy or company-paid yoga sessions. The core of the problem and the key resolution begins with dialogue, honesty, and leadership support.

SIMPLE STEPS YOU CAN TAKE:

For this section, I want to point you toward resources for helping your organization thrive by focusing on the whole person. Here are some resources I recommend you take a look at:

1. If you are a professional services firm, follow the HX Collective (Human Experience)—this group of thought leaders are experts on creating sustainable well-being in people-driven firms. Each person has dedicated their lives to helping professionals build relationships and meaningful connections to elevate human flourishing. Check it out at thehxcollective.com.

2. If you haven't already, bring in an employee assistance program (EAP), or even Marketplace Chaplains. According to numerous studies,[69] employees report that having a third party at work to share sensitive information with demonstrates that their employer cares about them. Having an EAP or chaplain (or both!) where employees can seek advice, counseling, or a helping hand can aid with personal hardship affecting their work. In turn, this helps their mental well-being.

3. Listen to the *Lawyers with Depression* podcast. The podcast was started by Dan Lukasik, a lawyer who struggled with depression and started a support group for others like him. Now his mission is helping other professionals bring mental health topics out into the open and support one another through the crises.

4. Encourage your Gen Z staff to join Sophie Beren's "The Conversationist," a platform where Gen Z can help each other deal peer-to-peer with all things Gen Z, including mental health and well-being.

Of course, adapting to mental health needs in the workplace will be continually evolving. Your young Gen Z'rs will have a lot to say on the subject if you ask them. The best thing you can do is be a listening ear and continually ask your staff what they need, while also being vulnerable with them yourself.

 Visit hannahgwilliams.com/downloads to access printable versions of exercises.

> **WHILE CREATING PSYCHOLOGICAL SAFETY FOR ANY EMPLOYEE OR TEAM IS IMPORTANT, LEADERS SHOULD EXPECT TO CREATE THIS QUICKLY FOR GENERATION Z OR THEY WON'T HESITATE TO LEAVE A COMPANY.**

CHAPTER 29
CREATE PSYCHOLOGICAL SAFETY

As we close our conversation about motivating, engaging, and leading Generation Z, it's vital we have a discussion about creating psychological safety so that Gen Z can thrive on our teams. For Gen Z, many of these conversations start with the influence of social media. Let's start there.

What types of social media posts make Gen Z cringe? Sometimes it's the "perfect parenting" photos. The "here's my new tattoo" or "here's what I had for lunch" posts are imposters too. How about the political bashing? These social media transgressions can be embarrassing and show people's true colors. As Gen Z'rs, we've watched our parents make these (often relationally damaging or even dangerous) mistakes on social media from a very young age. Generation Z uses social media with much more discernment and intention—for example, to promote their small business through a personal brand—than previous generations. In the workplace, we bring this reservedness and privacy that was less common for Gen X and millennials in particular.

THE CLASH OF MILLENNIALS AND GEN Z

Millennials and Gen Z are inevitably going to clash on this point, particularly if they are in a manager–direct report relationship. I remember a millennial boss of mine who "liked" his own Facebook posts to boost his social media engagement—perhaps he didn't realize everyone else could see that he was doing so. Beyond other challenges in the relationship that were rooted in generational differences, sometimes the simple choices he made undermined my trust in him as a leader, creating a sense of psychological distance rather than safety. While creating psychological safety for any employee or team is important, leaders should expect to create this quickly for Generation Z or they won't hesitate to leave a company.

THE FEARLESS ORGANIZATION

How can you as a leader create psychological safety for a young person? First of all, it starts with an honest assessment of where your team stands currently. In her book *The Fearless Organization,* Amy Edmondson talks about the key identifiers of psychological safety in a team. How many of the areas below would the individuals on your team say is true of your organization?

a. If you make a mistake on this team, it is rarely held against you.

b. Members of this team are able to bring up problems and tough issues.

c. People on this team rarely reject others for being different.

d. It is safe to take a risk.

e. It isn't difficult to ask other members for help.

f. No one would deliberately act in a way that undermines my efforts.

g. Working with members of this team, I feel my unique skills and talents are valued and utilized.

Edmondson says that if each member of your team could say that at least five of these areas are true, that's fantastic. You have a great start on creating a psychologically safe team. If only two to three of these items are true, you have some work to do. While all of these areas are extremely important for humans in general on high-functioning teams, one that will most affect Gen Z's psychological safety at work is a company's willingness to let us fail.

ENCOURAGING MISTAKES

As we've discussed, Generation Z's anxiety is worse than that of any other generation currently alive. Leaders will need to be aware of the battle that rages within many Gen Z'rs' heads. "Should I try?" "What if I fail?" Even though multitudes of leadership books preach the need to help teams fail smartly, Generation Z will struggle more with taking that next risky step than millennials did. To understand how leaders can give their young talent permission to fail, I spoke with Mike Kelly, former vice president of learning and development at Macys and now managing member of Right Path Enterprises, a consulting organization helping firms solve their crucial hiring challenges. Mike is a dear friend of mine, and although he calls Cincinnati home, he serves on the board of Mars Hill University, not far from my hometown of Asheville, North Carolina. As a Black business owner, Mike has had the privilege of counseling and speaking across the country about racial equality and servant leadership and has made a powerful impact on my personal life.

MIKE KELLY
Founder, Right Path Enterprises

We met on a particularly rainy day, smack in the middle of the COVID-19 pandemic, and hoped our Zoom connection wouldn't die. After exchanging thoughts on our various real estate endeavors, we jumped into a fruitful discussion on leadership. Given his varied background from operations to HR to executive leadership, I asked Mike, "How can leaders encourage their teams to fail?"

"That's a great question, Hannah. Sometimes leaders think that getting a team to succeed through failure is all about others, but I say that leaders need to work harder on themselves than their job. If a leader can personally examine their own motives and perspective, they'll realize that it's only human to shy away from failure—we've been taught to fear it our whole lives—so as [entrepreneur, author, and motivational speaker] Jim Rohn says, leaders must do the critical job of pushing themselves to ask hard questions of themselves first."

"So true," I responded. "I've seen leaders who fail to show their teams that making mistakes is important and it teaches them to be far too cautious. Of course, they have trouble innovating when they func- tion this way."

"Exactly," Mike continued. "People need permission to fail. I recall my first days leading a large nonprofit in Ohio where I had the challenge of reframing failure for an entire team of high-powered executives who

> **GEN Z MUSINGS**
> *They're actually telling me to make mistakes? This is literally the opposite of what I did in school.... Kinda reminds me of Ryan Trahan when he got all those weird looks selling candy to live off a penny for a week in Texas. Guess I need to learn how to make mistakes and get creative.*

were working together on a high-stakes project. I knew what the volunteer leaders were capable of and trusted them. I told them, 'I don't want you to be afraid to fail. In fact, if you fail doing something good, blame it on me. If someone wants to know what happened here, tell them it's Mike Kelly's fault.' It was as if the entire room exhaled. Being willing to go to bat for your people is crucial and putting your neck on the line when something goes awry is an incredible way to build trust and spur healthy failure."

People need permission to fail.

"That's incredibly powerful!" I exclaimed. "So often we fear failure because of the potential repercussions—that we'll lose our job, damage our reputation, or lose respect—but if our leaders give us permission to fail and place the blame on them, that's the highest form of encouragement and direction. The leader is not only saying, 'It's okay if you fail.' They're saying, 'I want you to experiment and fail healthily.'"

"Yes, this is a major mindset shift," Mike shared. "It's also crucial to ask yourself: How do I respond when someone on my team fails? Do I lose my cool? Do I worry about my own press clipping? Or do I do what I said I'd do and teach through failure? If I keep my word, I'll build trust with my team and create the psychological safety required to form true bonds between us. Any great leader of any generation will not only respond constructively when someone fails, they'll actually encourage their people to fail."

"So good. Do you recall a time when a leader responded favorably to failure versus one when they didn't? And how did that affect you as a leader and your team's morale?" I posited.

"Absolutely," he answered. "As a young professional, I distinctly recall a time when I was chosen for a North American high-potential performers program. I worked for a large manufacturing firm in upstate South Carolina. My group was tasked with creating a brand-new global forecasting system for North American production. We had an open line of communication with anyone in the company as we were gathering data, and the executive who sponsored me noticed something: I was coming to conclusions from the data I collected very quickly, but in the process, I was making mistakes that were harming the project's progress. Rather than kicking me off the team, he said, "Hey, Mike, you're going to be great in this organization—you already are—but I'm gonna give you some feedback on some things I've noticed." I took it and made some major shifts that turned out extremely positively for me. The fact that he embraced my mistakes and helped guide me was a crucial point in my engagement with the company.

"In another firm, I entered as a new leader in one of the most crucial areas of production for their manufacturing facility. They had a lot of troubles with leaders in the past. I came in with a new participatory leadership style and people got excited. As a result, we began to swiftly ramp up production and take many new risks. We produced thousands of units in record time—but there was a quality miss. In the excitement and success, we had produced hundreds of units that were defective. We didn't realize until the last inspection. After shutting down production, my boss came over. I told him what happened and he looked at me and said, 'Okay. I understand.' And went on about his business. He knew that I knew the mistake I had made. As a result of his wise response, my team went on to break production records night after night after night without quality issues."

"That's powerful," I responded. "The leaders obviously respected your abilities and recognized that failure was part of the learning process. They built room for failure into their projections!"

"Yes, exactly," Mike continued. "Contrarily, in my first manufacturing manager job out of college, I made a mistake. I was working a third-shift schedule as a new ground floor leader and something went wrong with production. The next morning, my boss came up to me yelling and screaming. To make matters worse, he hadn't done his research and didn't know exactly what mistake had been made. I let him finish yelling, then I said, 'You have five seconds to get out of my face or they'll be picking you up off the floor.' That was the wrong way to respond on both our parts, but as a young Black leader in the authoritarian management days with a white boss, I knew he had a challenge with me as a young leader. My team was performing well because I respected them, not yelled at them. The result? I spoke with upper management and took a position in a different area of the company under another leader. That one interaction broke any potential relationship I could have with that former boss."

Mike's advice is so important for any generation, not just young people. Embracing failure will resonate with Gen Z and will build the psychological safety crucial to a high-performing team.

SIMPLE STEPS YOU CAN TAKE:

Try this exercise: You know that awkward feeling when a group of executives pull together a team meeting and ask their direct reports, "What do you think we could do better?" The whole room feels that awkward, uncomfortable silence as young people (who do have plenty of thoughts, mind you) struggle to express them for fear of repercussions for saying the wrong thing. Try this multigenerational team exercise instead on your next company retreat, or even over Zoom.

1. Place 5–10 chairs in a circle (adjust for your team's size). Have your newest talent sit and have a brutally honest conversation about challenges they are facing. To make it easier, put hard questions on cards like "What would you do differently on this team?" "How can we better utilize the skills of our talent?" "Does leadership support me?"

2. After 5–10 minutes, add a couple of chairs and bring in one to two supervisors/managers. Continue the dialogue with them, with the managers listening and also adding their own points.

3. After 5–10 more minutes, bring in one director, followed by one VP. Continue the process until executives are in the room. Over time, you've built a psychologically safe environment where people find common ground and have trust with one another, so that by the time executives are in the room, they'll be able to hear the opinions of the people around them.

 Visit hannahgwilliams.com/downloads to access printable versions of exercises.

As we come to the end of this journey, I hope you'll see that engaging Gen Z does not take a "one size fits all" approach. Instead, individual leaders should find a personalized method that works for the particular Gen Z'rs they manage, and keep up with societal trends that may be impacting their staff's personal and mental well-being. As we can see, remaining in rhythm with a Gen Z'r to keep them engaged can, in many cases, be as simple as choosing not to discount how your Z'r is thinking, feeling, and acting. Instead, each person in the workplace being shown equal respect for our unique perspectives is invaluable for any age and any walk of life. Now we're at the end—where do we go from here?

WHERE DO WE GO FROM HERE?

Think back to your teenage years and your first introduction to the world's potential. Perhaps you watched, wide-eyed, as Marty McFly time traveled in *Back to the Future*. While working your summer fast-food job you dreamt about changing the world through tech innovation—maybe enabling your kids to one day live in a world that movies could only speculate about! Perhaps one of your relatives owned a small business buying and selling cars, and you were invigorated by the hustle you witnessed. Maybe as a middle schooler, you walked into a local grocery store and thought, "I wonder how this fresh produce makes it here from all over the world..." Whatever your experience was, now travel to the future with me.

You're a teenager with those same dreams and realizations, but this time you are born in 2005. By age 4, you can work an iPad better than your parents. By age 15, instead of watching your relatives buy and sell cars and wishing you could too, you simply start your own online business where you review cars, make thousands of dollars in ad revenue, and gain access to the most exclusive international car shows because of the reputation of your YouTube channel. You have connections in the car industry many dream of—and you're only 15! Instead of wondering how that fresh produce landed in the grocery store, you watch a couple of YouTube videos about the produce supply chain, then take an international internship where you visit those countries and learn firsthand how to ship the supplies. Everywhere you look, there is a new frontier, a new digital horizon, a cutting-edge social age—and you have the power to shape it using the technology in your hands.

If you were a teenager again living in this new age, what would you do with that power? How would you handle that responsibility? How would you shape your future? What would change about the way you did business?

You're not a teenager anymore, but now you have an even greater asset: The power to unlock the potential of the next generation and shape the future through them. You have the best of both worlds. At the tips of your fingers, you have access to millions of digital natives who understand the technological frontier, who have greater entrepreneurial spirit than any generation the world has ever seen, and who have a burning passion for shaping the future with zeal. You also have the wisdom to guide and mentor these young people to become the best versions of themselves.

Without you, Generation Z is lost to their own devices and inexperience. Without you, Gen Z is fated to make the same mistakes as generations before them. As the pace of change increases, Gen Z can succeed with a rapidity rarely seen in the past, but they will also fail faster and harder. Even though Gen Z'rs may not realize it right now, they are reliant on you to shape the future they desire. Gen Z'rs must stand on the shoulders of giants.

WHERE DOES THAT LEAVE YOU?

As I hope this book has shown you, no matter your role, you have the power to make an incredible difference in shaping the future of society. While some of you reading may be on fire to make broad-sweeping company changes immediately to attract, retain, and lead my generation, it's my hope that you feel empowered to do your part—no matter if you're a millennial manager who is mentoring Gen Z interns or the business owner of a successful firm with 100,000 employees. Who knows... the Gen Z'r you take under your wing could be the next Elon Musk. She could be the next Indra Nooyi. Maybe they won't be a celebrity but rather a young person who knows they have a reliable and wise mentor they can count on despite the chaos and uncertainty of the world they're living in, and this enables them to be the best human they can be. What a powerful reason to be alive!

This is only the beginning of the journey. As you and your company apply the simple steps in this book, you're bound to run into questions: How can we truly harness the NarcisStory and lean into Gen Z's way of thinking? How do we develop career pathways that make sense for our Z'rs and keep them growing and learning? What happens when millennials and Gen Z bump heads? The strategies in this book are a starting place, and as we step into the Future of Work it is the responsibility of every leader to foster an organizational mindset focused on continuous evolution rather than start-and-stop talent strategy. Don't just stop here! Follow thought leaders who are continually researching the changing talent market and shift your strategies accordingly. Try something new every month and test, experiment, change. This is the new world.

The most forward-thinking companies will begin saying things like:

"Let's hire high schoolers now so we can shape their skills, cultural identity, and loyalty to serve our company long term!"

Instead of...

"Well, I guess we have to hire those young people at some point, but we'd rather let someone else train them and knock some sense into them before they work for us..."

And:

"Let's put together a team of Gen Z'rs to spearhead our R&D so we can stay ahead of the curve, and so they can learn quickly!"

Instead of...

"Let's stick those new hires in coordinator roles and see what happens."

It's time for your business to get strategic and unlock the power of the next generation at work. It's time to use the bright eyes of Generation Z as a competitive advantage for your business. It's time to stop relying on formal schools to train your talent, and instead build programs where the best and brightest talent is created through skill-based training they could never acquire from school. If your business expects to be viable and successful in the next 15 years, you must start now. It's no longer enough to simply react to the talent market. You must position your business ahead of the curve and put strategies in place now to remain sustainable in the future.

So I pose these questions to you once more as a leader: What will you do with the power of the next generation? How will you handle this responsibility? How will you shape your children's future? What will change about the way you lead your business?

And most importantly, are you willing to step up and boldly lead Gen Z to change the world? The decision is yours to make.

ACKNOWLEDGMENTS

Through this process of writing a book, I've realized that the final creation has a little to do with me and a whole lot more to do with the stories the people in my life have shared with me that I'm simply given the honor of sharing. For their sake, I want to address directly each of the people who made this narrative possible.

This book would not have been written if my parents had not poured their entire lives into making me the woman I am today. I'm eternally grateful to you, Dad, for pushing me to see the world the way most people never do—not sucking up to wealth and fame but treating people as human beings. I'm indebted to you, Mom, for having never-faltering trust in my abilities and for giving me the most personalized education a child could ever ask for.

I'm speechless when I think about the support my husband, Michael, has given me every day. Michael, you know what you did.

When I was a fledgling 18-year-old, Chris Maslin and Anna Sullins, you did not see me for my age, but rather for my potential. I am humbled you took a chance on me and let me explore how far my wings could take me.

Deb Knupp, I'm forever indebted to you for your simple honesty. The first night we met in Durham, you compelled me to be proud of my young age and to use it to my advantage instead of hiding it. You're the reason I had the confidence to start this project in the first place.

To my incredible publishing consultant, Reed Bilbray, who has believed in my vision for a better future of work from the beginning, I thank you. I would have been lost through this process without your guidance.

This book is the result of many hours of careful thought. Thank you Alyssa, Anne, and Kim for the phenomenal editing, proofing, and design work you slaved over to take this project from helpful to beautiful.

Writing a narrative about my generation would not be impactful unless I had stood on the shoulders of giants. I'm deeply grateful to you, the millennial, Gen X, and boomer leaders who have shaped the direction of this project. Thank you to Ann Ashley, Mark Bado, Paige Borgman, Suzanne Baker Brown, Dr. Brad Butler, Keith Glover, Mark Hecht, Jonathan Javier, Steven Keith, Mike Kelly, Scott Ledford, Dave McAuley, Mark Miller, Maryam Salehijam, Elizabeth Solaru, and Jon Tesser for your undying commitment to my generation.

To my family. My sisters Sam, Katherine, Mimi, Becca, and Nina, and my brother, Cameron, thanks for being your authentic Gen-Z-Tik-Toking selves and reminding me every day why I've embarked on this project for our generation.

Finally, in true Gen Z fashion, thank you HubSpot for hosting thought-provoking events where ideas like this can be birthed! I'll forever consider Boston the birthplace of my business.

ENDNOTES

1. David Stillman and Jonah Stillman, *Gen Z @ Work* (New York, NY: Harper Business, 2017).
2. Amy Adkins, "Millennials: The Job-Hopping Generation," Gallup (Gallup, December 16, 2019), https://www.gallup.com/workplace/231587/millennials-job-hopping-generation.aspx#:~:text=Gallup%20estimates%20that%20millennial%20turnover,company%20one%20year%20from%20now.
3. Amanda Stansell, "The Next Generation of Talent: Where Gen Z Wants to Work," Glassdoor Economic Research (Glassdoor, February 20, 2019), https://www.glassdoor.com/research/gen-z-workers/.
4. "The Everything Guide to Generation Z." (Toronto: Vision Critical, March 17, 2016), https://cdn2.hubspot.net/hubfs/4976390/E-books/English%20e-books/The%20everything%20guide%20to%20gen%20z/the-everything-guide-to-gen-z.pdf.
5. *Helping a Subscriber Get His Dream Job!!*, YouTube (Yes Theory, 2020), https://www.youtube.com/watch?v=91uLBj8rAfA.
6. Oobah Butler, "I Made My Shed the Top-Rated Restaurant on TripAdvisor," VICE, December 6, 2017, https://www.vice.com/en_in/article/434gqw/i-made-my-shed-the-top-rated-restaurant-on-tripadvisor.
7. Richard Carufel, "Are Online Reviews Important to Gen Z? Not So Much, Survey Finds," Agility PR Solutions, January 28, 2020, https://www.agilitypr.com/pr-news/public-relations/are-online-reviews-important-to-gen-z-not-so-much-survey-finds/.
8. Karianne Gomez, Tiffany Mawhinney, and Kimberly Betts, "Welcome to Generation Z," Deloitte LLP (Network of Executive Women, n.d.), https://www2.deloitte.com/content/dam/Deloitte/us/Documents/consumer-business/welcome-to-gen-z.pdf.

9. "Philanthropy," Biltmore, June 25, 2021, https://www.biltmore.com/our-story/our-culture/philanthropy/.
10. Kim Parker and Ruth Igielnik, "On the Cusp of Adulthood and Facing an Uncertain Future: What We Know About Gen Z So Far," Pew Research Center (May 14, 2020), https://www.pewresearch.org/social-trends/2020/05/14/on-the-cusp-of-adulthood-and-facing-an-uncertain-future-what-we-know-about-gen-z-so-far-2/.
11. "Inclusion: The Deciding Factor," Intel, 2020, https://newsroom.intel.com/wp-content/uploads/sites/11/2020/08/intel-inclusion-diversity-report.pdf.
12. Lucius Couloute and Daniel Kopf, "Out of Prison & Out of Work: Unemployment among Formerly Incarcerated People," Prison Policy Initiative, July 2019, https://www.prisonpolicy.org/reports/outofwork.html.
13. "RightStep™ Empowers Future Leaders," Deloitte, accessed April 20, 2021, https://www2.deloitte.com/us/en/pages/about-deloitte/articles/corporate-citizenship-inspiring-future-leaders.html.
14. "The Mentoring Connector," MENTOR National, accessed June 29, 2021, https://www.mentoring.org/what-we-do/mentoring-connector/.
15. "Cornbread Hustle," LinkedIn, n.d., https://www.linkedin.com/company/cornbreadhustle/.
16. David Stillman and Jonah Stillman, *Gen Z @ Work* (New York, NY: Harper Business, 2017).
17. Dan Schawbel, "How Coronavirus Is Accelerating Remote Job Searching, Interviewing and Hiring," LinkedIn, July 6, 2020, https://www.linkedin.com/pulse/how-coronavirus-accelerating-remote-job-searching-hiring-dan-schawbel.
18. Clare McDonald, "Accenture to Use Virtual Reality for Inclusive Hiring Practices," ComputerWeekly.com, February 13, 2019, https://www.computerweekly.com/news/252457613/Accenture-to-use-virtual-reality-for-inclusive-hiring-practices#:~:text=Tech%20giant%20Accenture%20has%20started,its%20hiring%20process%20

less%20biased&text=Accenture%20will%20be%20using%20technologies,develop%20more%20inclusive%20hiring%20processes.

19. Bernhard Schroeder, "A Majority of Gen Z Aspires to Be Entrepreneurs and Perhaps Delay or Skip College. Why That Might Be a Good Idea," Forbes (*Forbes* Magazine, February 18, 2020), https://www.forbes.com/sites/bernhardschroeder/2020/02/18/a-majority-of-gen-z-aspires-to-be-entrepreneurs-and-perhaps-delay-or-skip-college-why-that-might-be-a-good-idea/#4739585e5a45.

20. "Four Definitions for the Intrapreneur," The Pinchot Perspective, October 30, 2017, https://www.pinchot.com/2017/10/four-definitions-for-the-intrapreneur.html.

21. Greg McKeown, *Essentialism: The Disciplined Pursuit of Less* (New York, NY: Crown Business, 2014).

22. "NARTS: The Association of Resale Professionals," NARTS, 2021, https://www.narts.org/i4a/pages/index.cfm?pageid=1.

23. "The End of a Controversial Era: Is the Open Office Dying?" Business News Daily, June 1, 2020, https://www.businessnewsdaily.com/10923-is-open-office-dead.html.

24. "Designing a Modern Workplace for Millennials and Generation Z," Office Principles, November 29, 2019, https://officeprinciples.com/designing-modern-workplace-millennials-generation-z/.

25. David Stillman and Jonah Stillman, "Move Over, Millennials; Generation Z Is Here," SHRM, April 11, 2017, https://www.shrm.org/resourcesandtools/hr-topics/behavioral-competencies/global-and-cultural-effectiveness/pages/move-over-millennials-generation-z-is-here.aspx.

26. Joanne Sammer, "Welcome, Generation Z: Here's Your Benefits Package," SHRM, July 6, 2018, https://www.shrm.org/resourcesandtools/hr-topics/benefits/pages/generation-z-benefits-package.aspx.

27. "The State of Gen Z," Jason Dorsey, accessed November 17, 2020, https://jasondorsey.com/our-research/state-of-gen-z/.

28. https://yello.co/blog/research-gen-zs-favorite-places-to-look-for-jobs/ (see the complete downloadable report)
29. https://makearpl.com/
30. Laura McGuire, "GENERATION Z: New Video CV App Launches for UK's Digital Natives," Real Business, June 11, 2020, https://realbusiness.co.uk/cv-app-gen-z/.
31. "Jobma," Jobma, accessed July 6, 2021, https://www.jobma.com/.
32. "SHRM Customized Talent Acquisition Benchmarking Report," SHRM, 2017, https://www.shrm.org/ResourcesAndTools/business-solutions/Documents/Talent-Acquisition-Report-All-Industries-All-FTEs.pdf.
33. Frances Dodds, "Gen Z Considers This Benefit More Important Than Salary," Entrepreneur, June 30, 2020, https://www.entrepreneur.com/article/352493.
34. "Cross-Functional Innovation," pymetrics, accessed July 6, 2021, https://www.pymetrics.ai/science.
35. "Average Cost-per-Hire for Companies Is $4,129, SHRM Survey Finds," SHRM, August 3, 2016, https://www.shrm.org/about-shrm/press-room/press-releases/pages/human-capital-benchmarking-report.aspx#:~:text=Sign%20In-,Average%20Cost%2Dper%2DHire%20for%20Companies,Is%20%244%2C129%2C%20SHRM%20Survey%20Finds&text=ALEXANDRIA%2C%20Va.,new%20Human%20Capital%20Benchmarking%20Report.
36. Zack Friedman, "Student Loan Debt Statistics in 2020: A Record $1.6 Trillion," Forbes (Forbes Magazine, February 3, 2020), https://www.forbes.com/sites/zackfriedman/2020/02/03/student-loan-debt-statistics/?sh=62419875281f.
37. "Young Americans & College Survey" (TD Ameritrade, August 2019), https://s2.q4cdn.com/437609071/files/doc_news/research/2019/young-americans-and-college-survey.pdf.
38. Paul Jankowski, "Gaming Is the Best Social Media Platform for Brands to Reach Gen-Z," Forbes (Forbes Magazine, June 1, 2020), https://www.forbes.com/sites/pauljankowski/2020/06/01/

gaming-is-the-best-social-media-platform-for-brands-to-reach-gen-z/?sh=79a386c37cfe.

39. "Starbucks College Achievement Plan," Starbucks Coffee Company, 2021, https://www.starbucks.com/careers/working-at-starbucks/education.
40. Jennie Mae Yang, "The Alliance—A Book Summary," Medium, June 30, 2017, https://medium.com/@jenniemaeyang/the-alliance-a-book-summary-6dc3659fda8f.
41. Sonia Saraiya, "Why Is Gen Z Obsessed with *The Office*?," Vanity Fair, April 26, 2019, https://www.vanityfair.com/hollywood/2019/04/billie-eilish-the-office-gen-z-netflix.
42. David Stillman and Jonah Stillman, *Gen Z @ Work* (New York, NY: Harper Business, 2017).
43. Ezequiel Minaya, "Companies Seek to Fill Skills Gap by Retraining Their Own Workers," The Wall Street Journal (Dow Jones & Company, March 8, 2019), https://www.wsj.com/articles/companies-seek-to-fill-skills-gap-by-retraining-their-own-workers-11552041000.
44. "Closing the Skills Gap 2019 Research Report," Wiley (Wiley Education Services, accessed December 17, 2020), https://edservices.wiley.com/closing-the-skills-gap-report-19/.
45. Martha Ross and Thomas Showalter, "Millions of Young Adults Are Out of School or Work. We Need an Education and Employment Promise," Brookings, December 18, 2020, https://www.brookings.edu/blog/the-avenue/2020/12/18/making-a-promise-to-americas-young-people/.
46. David Stillman and Jonah Stillman, *Gen Z @ Work* (New York, NY: Harper Business, 2017).
47. Sarah Landrum, "Millennials Aren't Afraid to Change Jobs, And Here's Why," Forbes (Forbes Magazine, November 10, 2017), https://www.forbes.com/sites/sarahlandrum/2017/11/10/millennials-arent-afraid-to-change-jobs-and-heres-why/?sh=242045a619a5.

48. Abigail Shrier, "To Be Young and Pessimistic in America," The Wall Street Journal (Dow Jones & Company, May 14, 2021), https://www.wsj.com/articles/to-be-young-and-pessimistic-in-america-11621019488?st=vqrt8h1udsycr27&reflink=article_email_share.
49. Ibid.
50. "The History of Uber," Uber Newsroom (Uber, 2021), https://www.uber.com/newsroom/history.
51. "Borrow Lenses," BorrowLenses.com, accessed July 6, 2021, https://www.borrowlenses.com/.
52. Jeff Schwartz et al., "What Is the Future of Work?" Deloitte Insights, April 1, 2019, https://www2.deloitte.com/us/en/insights/focus/technology-and-the-future-of-work/redefining-work-workforces-workplaces.html.
53. Lori Ioannou, "A Snapshot of the $1.2 Trillion Freelance Economy in the U.S. in the Age of COVID-19," CNBC (CNBC, September 15, 2020), https://www.cnbc.com/2020/09/15/a-snapshot-of-the-1point2-trillion-freelance-economy-in-the-us-in-2020.html.
54. Maria Coronado, "Could TikTok Be Teaching Us More than School?," Crusader News, February 18, 2021, https://crusadernews.com/19105/lifestyles/entertainment/could-tiktok-be-teaching-us-more-than-school/.
55. Ziad Ahmed, "Memes and Movements: 20 Trends that Defined Gen Z in 2020," JUV Consulting, accessed July 6, 2021, https://www.juv2020.com/.
56. Ryan Jenkins, "This Is How Generation Z Will Communicate at Work," Inc.com (Inc., November 8, 2017), https://www.inc.com/ryan-jenkins/72-percent-of-generation-z-want-this-communication-at-work.html.
57. Angela Campiere, "How Gen Z Communicates at Work," PCMA, February 14, 2019, https://www.pcma.org/how-generation-z-communicates-work/#:~:text=Generation%20Z%20has%20arrived%20%E2%80%94%20and%20it's%20causing%20shifts%20in%20the%20workplace.&text=According%20to%20a%20live%20poll,and%209%20percent%20prefer%20email.

58. "The 4 Disciplines of Execution," FranklinCovey, accessed June 29, 2021, https://www.franklincovey.com/the-4-disciplines/.
59. "State of Gen Z 2018: Surprising New Research on Gen Z as Employees and Consumers," The Center for Generational Kinetics, accessed April 15, 2020, https://genhq.com/generation-z-research-2018/.
60. Ryan Schocket, "Gen Z'ers Are Sharing How They'll Parent Differently than Their Boomer Parents and It's Eye-Opening," BuzzFeed (BuzzFeed, February 14, 2021), https://www.buzzfeed.com/ryanschocket2/gen-z-parent-different-than-boomer-parents.
61. "Generation Z: The Kids Are All Right," Raddon (Raddon Research Insights, 2017), https://www.raddon.com/sites/default/files/genz-executive-summary.pdf.
62. Ibid.
63. Stuart Lane, "Millennials and Gen Z Lead Surge in Trading Interest, But at a Cost," Finance Monthly, November 24, 2020, https://www.finance-monthly.com/2020/11/millennials-and-gen-z-lead-surge-in-trading-interest-but-at-a-cost/.
64. Sherri Bockhorst, "How Might a Pandemic Change Gen Z's Approach to Benefits?" Employee Benefit News (Employee Benefits, November 20, 2020).
65. "Planning & Progress Study 2020," Northwestern Mutual, 2020, https://news.northwesternmutual.com/planning-and-progress-2020.
66. "Gen Z Is Here. Are You Ready?" Dell Technologies, accessed July 6, 2021, https://www.delltechnologies.com/en-us/perspectives/gen-z.htm.
67. "Mural," MURAL, accessed July 6, 2021, https://www.mural.co/.
68. "Today's Tense Political Climate Is Stressing Gen Z Out but They Are More Likely to Seek Mental Help," The Harris Poll, October 31, 2018, https://theharrispoll.com/annual-apa-harris-poll-survey-shows-gen-z-is-stressed-about-the-nation-but-least-likely-to-vote/.

69. David W. Miller, Faith Wambura Ngunjiri, and James D. Lorusso, "'The Suits Care about Us': Employee Perceptions of Workplace Chaplains," Journal of Management, Spirituality & Religion, July 26, 2018, https://www.iamsr.org/wp-content/uploads/2018/08/The-suits-care-about-us-employee-perceptions-of-workplace-chaplains.pdf..

RECOMMENDED RESOURCES

OTHER GEN Z INFLUENCERS YOU SHOULD BE FOLLOWING:

- **Sophie Beren**, host of POVz, the first Gen Z talk show, and founder of "The Conversationalist," a community of Gen Zr's who get together online to talk about life and work. Follow Sophie to hear Gen Z'rs point of view on key issues within politics, culture, and more. I've personally found Sophie's work to be incredibly enlightening, as younger and younger voices are influencing the political sphere.

- **Jimmy Slagle**, co-founder at Trend Z. Follow Jimmy to learn the latest ways to leverage TikTok to remain relevant to the next generation. Trend Z helps companies market their brands on TikTok, so if you want your advertising to stay relevant, hit him up!

- **Jessica Stollings-Holder**, president of ReGenerations. Follow Jessica for recent research and insights on Generation Z and how to coach management toward more cohesive and functional teams of multiple generations.

- **Gen Z Talks:** Follow Gen Z Talks on LinkedIn for interviews, podcasts, and video content showcasing how Gen Z lives and works. They even feature conversations between leaders and Z'rs!

- **Dylan Gambardella,** co-founder of Next Gen HQ. If you're looking for ways to help Gen Z employees learn key skills like creativity, confidence, and time management, Next Gen HQ could be a fantastic partner for you. They've worked with organizations like Target, Comcast, and American Express to help the next generation succeed at work.

OTHER BOOKS THAT HELP UNPACK GEN Z:

- **Jason Dorsey's** *Zconomy*—If you want to understand how Z'rs are changing the consumer and marketing game, pick up Jason Dorsey's recent book. Filled with research and insights, Jason unpacks the global impact Z'rs' spending and purchasing habits have and how companies can adapt.

- *Clash of the Generations* **by Valerie M. Grubb**—You're likely experiencing the challenge of managing five generations at work, and what an interesting kerfuffle you may find yourself in! Check out Valerie's book, which includes helpful case studies and helps leaders navigate through the complexities of managing five age groups.

- *The Millennial Whisperer*—Don't neglect leveling-up education on millennials as well. This book by Chris Tuff helps leaders understand how to harness the uniqueness millennials bring to the workplace and is equally important to understanding Z'rs!

ABOUT THE AUTHOR

Hannah Grady Williams was only 12 years old and in middle school when her dad took her to work at his start-up one day per week. Usually they would visit properties, collect rent, and file paperwork—but one afternoon was different. "Hey, Hannah, the phone is ringing. There's a guy on the other line with a house for sale and you're going to close the deal." Hannah took the phone and fumbled through the call, but sure enough, within weeks, they owned the property.

Before long, Hannah was devouring business books. She enrolled in college at age 14 and graduated with a degree in international business by 18. Her efforts to hone her skills during her school years resulted in numerous accolades, including North Carolina Public Speaker of the Year. Hannah was invited onto the board of the Honduras Fountain of

Life to provide a Gen Z perspective on Central American missions.

Over the last decade, Hannah has consulted Fortune 500 companies and boutique luxury brands and has had the pleasure of working with some of the best and brightest leaders across the globe, including Chick-fil-A franchises, Oakland Spine & Physical Therapy, and 9Round. Her young introduction to the world of real estate led her to continue investing as an adult. She still finds time to explore her diverse passions including cooking and enjoying cuisine in her hometown, the foodie city of Asheville, North Carolina; backpacking with her husband; and hosting jam sessions with her musician friends. If she had a magic wand, she'd take the world back to '50s-style fashion.

Now, with the help of her recently published book, *A Leader's Guide to Unlocking Gen Z*, Hannah is on a mission to help companies connect with her generation. In a time when the world is increasingly divided, Hannah has made it her mission to foster #RadicalEmpathy in the workplace—helping people of all generations gain a voice. Her work provides a bridge of connection between different generations and helps businesses positively engage Gen Z, the newest members of the workforce.

CONNECT WITH THE AUTHOR

You are not alone in the process of Attracting, Recruiting, Retaining, and Engaging (ARRE) Gen Z! Here's the thing: If you've read this book and are wondering "where do I start?" we heard you and have developed a plan just for you.

START HERE! GEN Z ARRE AUDIT + SCORE™

Take this audit, and we'll figure out exactly where your company should begin! Bring Hannah in to assess how well you Attract, Recruit, Retain, and Engage Gen Z. She'll mystery-shop your recruiting and online brand, conduct blind interviews with your staff, and review your employee handbook and policies. Then she'll give you a score! The output is an in-person (and written) report, *2 Critical Areas of Focus*, in which your company needs to make changes in order to become or remain relevant to Gen Z. Want more info? Email us: hannah@hannahgwilliams.com

OTHER RESOURCES:

SPEAKING

Bring the message of how Gen Z is transforming the Future of Work to your next company retreat, conference, or association meeting. Hannah conducts live audience polls and brings a story-filled keynote experience to every event! Check out speaking topics at hannahgwilliams.com/speaking.

TEAM WORKSHOPS

Hannah and her team at OVRTURE Consulting facilitate numerous workshops for teams of recruiters, executives, and mid-level managers. If you want to reduce Gen Z turnover and improve overall company retention, discover workshops that will help managers better lead Gen Z staff, communicate with them, and foster a culture that helps them remain engaged. Check out the workshop topics at hannahgwilliams.com/training.

BULK COPIES OF *A LEADER'S GUIDE TO UNLOCKING GEN Z*

Want your team to read this book and conduct the exercises together? You can purchase copies in bulk at hannahgwilliams.com/bookstore. These personalized packages even include coaching with Hannah!

CONNECT WITH HANNAH!

LinkedIn: Follow Hannah to receive 3 weekly tips on Gen Z talent: linkedin.com/in/hannah-williams-genzconsultant/
Website: hannahgwilliams.com (P.S. Don't forget to subscribe to the newsletter to receive exclusive content from Hannah!)
Blog: hannahgwilliams.com/blog
Twitter: @Hannah_OVRTURE
Email: hannah@hannahgwilliams.com

Please don't hesitate to reach out to us if we can help you in any way. Your success means a better future of work for everyone, and that's our shared passion. Let's build #RadicalEmpathy together at work!

Made in the USA
Columbia, SC
22 July 2024